THE ANTIQUE DRUMS OF WAR

THE ANTIQUE
DRUMS ·
OF WAR)

James H. McRandle

TEXAS A&M UNIVERSITY PRESS
College Station, Texas

LIBRARY OF CONGRESS CATALOGING-IN-
PUBLICATION DATA

McRANDLE, JAMES H., 1925–
    THE ANTIQUE DRUMS OF WAR / JAMES H.
McRANDLE.
        P.   CM. — (TEXAS A&M UNIVERSITY MIL-
ITARY HISTORY SERIES ; NO. 33)
    INCLUDES BIBLIOGRAPHICAL REFERENCES
AND INDEX.
    ISBN 0-89096-591-9
    I. WAR. 2. WAR AND SOCIETY. I. TITLE.
II. SERIES: TEXAS A&M UNIVERSITY MILI-
TARY HISTORY SERIES ; 33.
U21.2.M38   1994
355.02'09 — DC20   93-41325
                                    CIP

To all those who served with
A Company 342 Infantry

Contents

Illustrations

Preface

FOR HISTORIANS, whatever their field of concentration, it is very difficult to avoid the subject of warfare. Although not continuous in the nature of the activity as is economic activity, warfare impinges itself so mightily upon the lives of peoples when it does occur that it necessarily raises questions about the causes of particular wars, and the further question of why it should exist at all. My own introduction to these problems came from a childhood growing up between the two great conflicts, World Wars I and II, and service in the latter. My choice of history as a major in college was much influenced by these experiences; I learned to analyze such things as immediate and underlying causes of particular conflicts, the conduct of the campaigns, and the changes occasioned by the outcome of the various wars. However, it seemed to me that a very important aspect was left virtually untouched: the subject of the experience itself. If everyone agreed, as all right-minded persons should agree, that war is horrible and unprofitable, then it should have been obvious that it was in the interest of all to eliminate the practice. Equally obviously, this had not occurred. If explanations such as original sin or fundamental human nature were rejected, then one was still left with the question of why, given all of its disadvantages, war seemed so attractive to successive generations of humans.

It was in the reading of memoirs of soldiers from other ages, in my conversations with veterans, and in the comparison of my limited experience of combat with the experiences of these others, that I began to find patterns which had nothing to do with the causes of particular wars but were, rather, general characteristics of the phenomenon itself. It is an area now being explored by a considerable number of gifted students of the subject, such as John Keegan, Sue Mansfield, Richard Holmes, Eric Leed, Modris Eksteins, and Paul Fussell. I have benefited much from their work, though I tend to go off in a somewhat different direction, perhaps most particularly in my belief that the origins of warfare are to be found in the earliest history of mankind.

It is a simple truism that nobody accomplishes a scholarly task alone. Certainly I owe a heavy debt to the many authors whose works I have ransacked without, I hope, misusing them. In addition I feel much gratitude to those friends and colleagues who have lent me encouragement, criticism, and advice. I particularly wish to thank Durward Allen, David Cady, G. G. Hatheway, Robert Goldstein, Eric Klinghammer, Edward M. Levine, Peter Loewenberg, Ronald C. Newton, James P. Quirk, and Andrew Rolle, and Dale Wilson. Nor could this work have been done without the resources of the following libraries and the friendly assistance of their staffs: Purdue University, the University of Illinois, the University of California at Los Angeles, Western Washington University, and the Bellingham Public Library. The drawing in chapter 3 was done by Jill Hunt-Thompson.

I particularly wish to thank the Texas A&M Press. Without the constant support, advice, and careful attention to detail on the part of Noel R. Parsons and the editorial staff, this book could not, and should not, have been published. I, of course, take full responsibility for any errors of omission or commission in this work.

My special thanks to my wife, Dr. Carol C. McRandle, for taking time from her own academic pursuits to read and criticize the manuscript as it developed, and to our sons John and Paul, who showed remarkable forbearance with what must have often appeared to be a morbid fascination with a dismal subject.

THE ANTIQUE DRUMS OF WAR

1

The Living Museum

A NUMBER OF YEARS AGO, in a museum on the campus of the University of Michigan, I happened to read the translation of a scrap of papyrus—a letter written by a naval recruit to his mother. It was one of those instances which occur with fair frequency in the study of history where the thoughts of a person long dead strike a familiar note in the living mind. While his circumstances and his view of the world were far different from mine, the two thousand years that separated us were erased, for a few moments, as he wrote of rumors that his unit was moving out and of his feelings about being in the service. He did not write of war or the great things of the world of his day, yet one could sense that, with all of the differences in military practice and weaponry, there is a sameness about the life of the soldier that surmounts the passage of time and gives a unity to the experience which can be immediately recognized. Since then I have had the opportunity to read the memoirs and the scraps of letters of other soldiers from other times, and have seen again and again this unity of experience, of involvement in something other than the ordinary life. This sense of involvement is, perhaps, most immediately reflected in the small things: the care of weapons, the sharing of meals, the searching along unknown roads, the uneasy anticipation of battle. It is these things which mark the life of the soldier, not the great questions of the causes and effects of wars or the critique of generalship.

Yet the common experience of the soldier should not be overlooked simply because it provides no direct answers to the problem of the existence of war. I believe that the writer of the song "The Universal

Soldier" was correct in stating that the man in the ranks was ultimately the reason why Caesar and all of the other great captains of
history could carry out their dreams.[1] If we are ever to eliminate the
practice of warfare we must, among other things, grapple with this
question of why individuals are willing to participate in an activity
which seems to run so much against common human feelings and
even common sense. Why is it that, contrary to much current opinion, men seem in the past and even today to gain some kind of delight
in combat?[2]

The question of humanity's proclivity for making war must be
approached with both care and candor, for there is much disagreement on the subject. On the one hand we have the group which
maintains that men have always fought and that this is, in and of
itself, proof of humanity's innate drive for war. On the other are those
who argue that the vast majority of humans are peaceable and only
brought to war by the machinations of the malevolent few. Between
these extremes lie a bewildering number of variations on these themes.
Arguments that humans are instinctively warlike can be countered by
the demonstration that most people do not engage in combat, nor is
warfare a continuous activity.[3] The question of aggression as an instinctive drive in all animal species, a position raised to prominence
by the writings of Konrad Lorenz and a number of other ethologists,
has resulted in a very large number of counterarguments, some advanced with a curious ferocity. The alternative—that throughout the
hunting-gathering phase of humanity's existence (which comprises 99
percent of its history), humans were peaceable, only to be corrupted
by imperialistic civilization—sounds so much like the statement of
some twentieth-century Jean Jacques Rousseau tricked out with field
notes, that one is tempted to reject it out of hand. Certainly it seems
improbable that a convincing pacifistic argument can be made from
the evidence of a few nonwarlike tribes, such as the recently discovered (and even more recently discredited) Tasaday or the now extinct
Patagonians.

Since much of the present argument centers on the term "human
aggression" and questions raised by Lorenz's book *On Aggression*, it
might prove worth looking more closely at the term and the various
possible interpretations of its meaning. Aggression is defined as "the
act of commencing hostilities" or "hostile behavior." The adjective
"aggressive" however, is given a second definition of "assertive, bold,

enterprising." The Latin root *aggredi* (to approach with hostility) is derived from *ad* (toward) + *gradi* (to step) and, to delve even further, the Indo-European root is *gredh* (to walk).[4] Thus, while those who see all aggression as hostile in intent seem to be on solid ground so far as the current meaning of the term is concerned, there is also good etymological foundation for what I take to be Lorenz's meaning that aggressiveness is basically a propensity to seek out, to explore. In this latter sense, it is a quality which is absolutely necessary for the survival of an animal species, and only under special conditions does it emerge as hostile behavior. In this wide definition of the term, aggressiveness could include everything from berrypicking to strategic bombardment. Furthermore, one can argue that humans are aggressive without arguing that they are necessarily warlike.

Aggressiveness, the act of going out, involves, ultimately, the encounter with other organisms. These organisms may be of another species, in which case the reaction would be one of interest or disinterest, the interest depending on the question of whether the other organism is dangerous to oneself, a possible addition to the evening table, or simply the object of curiosity. The interest itself does not, in most cases, arouse hostility. The hunter, though perhaps irritated by the deerflies, does not hate the quarry. However, if the organism encountered is a member of one's own species, there appears a whole range of reactions not otherwise exhibited. The meeting of two males may well give rise to threat behavior, particularly if there has been no previous contact. Among social animals, those males belonging to the same group will probably have established a form of hierarchy which will only infrequently be challenged, though it may be regularly reinforced by almost imperceptible actions. Each animal species has its own repertoire of threatening and submissive behavior patterns that elicit appropriate reactions from others of its own kind. Curiously, behavior which arouses hostility between two males may give rise to sexual responses between a male and a female.

Hostile behavior between groups is also observable among a number of animal species. The social insects exhibit, perhaps, the widest range of such activity; they not only kill intruders but form groups to fend off invasion, and even develop specialized members to handle these defense activities. In some cases prisoners are taken and enslaved. Among mammals, Howler monkeys make daily demonstrations at the borders of their territories, apparently to warn off intruders. Male lions raid other prides, and rats will fight vicious battles in defense of their territories. The traditional observation that humanity is the only animal that kills its own kind has been demonstrated to be quite overstated. Even excluding the insect, it has been shown that lions, wolves, apes, and rats do the same, though pride of place in terms of sheer numbers killed still seems to be held by human beings. As observation of the animal world is intensified, it is to be expected that the examples of intraspecific killings will be extended significantly.

Among animals it has been observed that hostile behavior of both the individual and group varieties serves certain purposes. At the individual level, it provides a method for establishing rank between males and access to the females within the group. Between groups it insures that the space necessary for the several activities of the groups will be provided. This spacing can be established in terms of territory or time. Certain scarce but vital facilities, such as water holes, may be visited at various times during the day by groups of the same species, thus minimizing the necessity for fighting, though the scheduling was probably arrived at by some form of hostile action. Ethological studies indicate quite clearly that aggressive behavior works to secure social order, sexual preference, and economic well being. It must be noted that these desirable results are not attributable to aggressive behavior alone, for animals, scarcely less than human beings, are not simple mechanisms. Apparent altruism, caring responses, and sexuality play their important role in the achievement of a stable social order. What must be noted is that hostile behavior does not, in the long run, produce chaos in the animal world.[5]

Those who reject, either wholly or in part, the findings of the ethologists, often raise the objection that a human is such a complex being that no valid comparisons can be made between humans and animals, or that humans have evolved beyond the stage of instinctive response. It is most astonishing to find, a century after Darwin wrote, that the scholars, who accept quite readily the evidence of a physiological relationship between humanity and the rest of the animal world, are unwilling to accept the possibility of a behavioral relationship, particularly when that relationship is grounded in physiology. Admittedly, the term "instinct" was given a bad name when overenthusiastic adherents chose to discover instincts for the entire range of human activity. Inevitably such excesses brought a severe reaction. The nature versus nurture conflict served to point up the weaknesses in the old instinctive theories. Modern instinct theory emphasizes the fact that a learning component (often large) exists in the behavioral repertoire of many animals. Studies have given us examples of the female cheetah as schoolmarm, the chimpanzee discoverer of tools, the lazy bee, and the smart wasp. In the animal world, learning does alter behavior but does not eliminate instinctive responses. To be blunt, the same is true for human beings.

The human being is a veritable warehouse of artifacts of ancient design. A backbone inherited from the earliest chordates, lungs of amphibian origin, binocular vision, and a foot crafted for efficient bipedal locomotion are all evidence of this many-faceted building of the modern body. The list goes on: a brain housing very early elements along with much later developments, eye-hand coordination, and the capability for language. Add to this the instincts or drives of fear, hunger, sexuality and aggression—all very ancient, all very much a part of the makeup of modern humans. We carry these physical and behavioral characteristics with us, traits which extend our powers while at the same time placing limits, traits that make possible wonderful accomplishments and the foulest deeds. Like baggage received at some biological railway express office, we are only dimly aware of all the contents even as we are busily opening the various boxes.

The fact of individual aggressiveness among humans is scarcely in dispute. Acts of hostility, ranging from the verbal to the lethal, are to be observed in every society, though the degree of control of this hostility varies widely between them. Without doubt there is a large portion of learned responses to these hostile activities. In societies where little boys are encouraged to demonstrate manliness by fighting, they will fight. Psychological and physical trauma has great effect upon the attitudes of persons and looms large in the personal history of the very violent.[6] Yet there is a whole category of hostile actions, gestures, and facial and verbal expressions, which are apparently universal among human beings and which have their exact counterparts in the animal world as well. The grimace, the stance which enlarges the bodily appearance, the distance maintained between individuals, encroachment upon which is a signal of hostile intent, are all examples of hostile activity, which are, in all probability, not learned but innate. There are also gestures which carry hostile significance between males but which have sexual connotations between male and female. Such gestures are capable of great refinement so that many gradations of feeling can be expressed. There is also variation between human groups, as Hall has demonstrated in the case of the distances maintained between individuals, but the basic meaning is the same for all these groups.[7]

Just as basic as aggressiveness is the sense of fear, a sense of self-preservation which fundamentally does not have to be learned, and which does find its expression in a wide range of gestures common to all human society and having their counterparts in the animal world. Furthermore, the element of hostility is usually compounded with the sense of fear in what has sometimes been labeled the "fight-flight syndrome."

At the individual level then, good evidence of instinctive aggressive and fearful behavior exists. But does this carry over to the group level, so that one may speak of the "warlike instinct"? For a number of reasons this seems very doubtful. While it is true that similar emotions may affect a whole group of persons, as is the case of a crowd in panic, it would be rash to conclude that humanity has, as a group, an innate urge to kill. In fact, even at the individual level, it is difficult to demonstrate a "killer instinct." Men (and it is usually the male) do kill other persons, and almost invariably the killing is done with some instrument, since it is very difficult to kill with the bare hands. One may also suspect that humans hold a distinct horror for this type of killing. It is not unusual for the killer to deny intention or to lay the blame on the instrument. A variation of this response is to deny the humanity of the person killed. The cold-blooded killer presents another problem. There is no doubt, for instance, of the popularity of the "hit man" in recent movies and television, but it is the popularity of horrified fascination with the man who has turned himself into an instrument for the sole purpose of killing. He has, in a very real sense, become other than human.

In the case of killing by individuals, there is little evidence of the killer instinct. There are, however, no very strong prohibitions against killing. Among the great carnivores, whose jaws and claws form deadly weapons, a number of submissive expressions and gestures exist which serve to stop the act of killing and, thus, to reduce the deadliness of their intraspecific fighting. These "inhibitors" can be certain types of cries or actions, such as cringing or showing the cub's belly to the adult wolf, or simply the distinctive conformation of the immature face. All of these tend to reduce aggression if they do not guarantee absolute safety. Among human beings there is also a set of inhibitors, signals of submissiveness, which are only partially effective. It has been speculated that because humans evolved from a largely noncarnivorous animal, and thus an animal with no powerful ability to kill, the inhibitors against killing its own kind are not deeply grounded. Certainly, it is historically true that humanity has felt little compunction about killing those outside its own group. In fact, the definition of what is truly human has been traditionally most parochial in character. This provincialism, which finds other dialects peculiar and other customs distasteful, tends to picture other groups as dangerous, an assessment which was, sadly enough, often true. Thus, the inhibitory devices which were, and are, only partially effective within the immediate group, have even less impact on dealings with the outside.

But outsiders seldom impinged upon the group as individuals. They were most often encountered in groups of their own and, therefore, had to be dealt with on a group basis. Such meetings were not necessarily hostile, though often they proved to be. Therefore, it was mandatory that each group develop means by which potential dangers could be handled. Avoidance and flight were obvious but not always practical answers to such problems. In a world where the sites for hunting and gathering were not evenly distributed, these tactics could lead to a most marginal existence and even to extinction. If the consequences of avoidance were minimal, human groups would probably have chosen this course. If the stakes were higher, then fighting might well have been the method selected for dealing with the problem. It was a problem which could not be handled effectively at the individual level, since the person ranged against the group would have had little impact.

The solution struck upon was the institution of warfare. Hostility is an attribute of the individual, not the group. But groups are able to channel this hostility for ostensibly useful purposes through the institution of warfare. An analogy may be drawn between sexuality and the institution of marriage. The sexual instinct is not a group property but, unless properly guided, it can have devastating results for the group. Thus, every society has devised rules and rituals to handle this powerful force. Unbridled hostility towards other groups could be either ineffective or disastrous. Typically, therefore, societies generate the rules and rituals which mobilize individual aggressiveness for social purposes. Selection and training of warriors, establishment of the purposes and causes for fighting, and the manner in which the fighting shall be conducted all fall under the purview of the institution of warfare. The institution makes use of individual instinctive behavior patterns without itself being an instinctive activity. It marshals certain elements of group behavior for its own particular purposes and seizes and modifies for those purposes the tools of the culture. It owes its existence to individual human beings, but like the other great institutions of human society, it is carried over from generation to generation and provides form for human lives.

Like the family, the institution of warfare varies widely from society to society. Even this variation has its limits, however, as it is everywhere recognizable for what it is. It is a male group activity, though an important female role exists. It is dualistic; that is, war is always an affair between two contesting parties, with the rare exception where a higher authority interposes itself between two warring factions and finds itself battling with both of them (such seems to be the case for the British in Northern Ireland). It is noncontinuous: wars are separated by periods of peace (often of long duration) though the organizations charged with making war tend to remain in existence. There are two basic forms of warfare, the raid or ambush and the linear battle, either or both of which may be practiced by a particular society.[8] Linear battle, which in the historical period has been the more prevalent form, is almost completely a daytime activity. Raiding, on the other hand, tends to be nocturnal in character. Killing is not the necessary goal of war, but the possibility of being killed is omnipresent, even in the so-called ritual battles of primitive tribes.

The comparison of the warfare institution with that of the family suggests that it is a very ancient form of human organization. Yet it has already been noted that this is not accepted by many anthropologists and other students of human affairs. The case against the antiquity of warfare rests first on the presumed lack of evidence for the hunting-gathering period and, second, upon the assumption that wars are fought for presently understandable purposes, the principal one being economic. War is pictured by these students as a product of the period of agricultural development or even the result of the growth of towns and cities. With agriculture, and even more with city life, humans for the first time possessed property, which it was necessary to defend in place. The old tactic of avoidance could no longer be employed, since it was impossible to move the fields and buildings.

There are a number of reasons for doubting this late dating for the introduction of warfare. The first is simply the intuition that a practice so widespread in historical times must have had antecedents, and well-established ones, in the prehistoric past. A second and more substantial, albeit not uncontested, reason is to be found in the evidence of violence connected with the discovered remains of *Homo sapiens neanderthalensis, Homo erectus,* and, if one accepts Dart's hypothesis, Australopithecus.[9] Broken bones and scooped out skulls at Choukoutien and other sites seem to attest to the existence of cannibalism as early as the period of *Homo erectus.* There is a question whether these were victims of deadly assault or whether, having died of natural causes, they were then eaten. Certainly the eating of one's recently departed kith and kin is a practice which has been observed in recent times among some primitive groups; it has even been resorted to in crisis situations by persons who would normally hold the practice in abhorrence. Yet, what we know of cannibalism in recent times indicates that most often it involves persons who were not members of the group.[10]

While the early evidence of cannibalism cannot be conclusive, it is at least more indicative of a violent past than arcadian innocence. In its own way more compelling is the close relationship between the practice of hunting and that of war. There has been, until recent years, a traditionally close connection between the weapons of the hunt and those of battle. Hunting tactics, such as the surround or the ambush, have their parallels in military tactics; so much so in fact, that one might well argue that no major military tactic exists which does not have its counterpart in the traditional methods of hunting. It is not so much that warfare is a form of hunting, though that point can be made, as that the core of military practice would seem to rest on techniques devised prior to the appearance of agriculture.[11]

A variation of the argument that warfare has no long history is the contention that ritual warfare, though it may have been practiced for a very long time, is not true warfare. In terms of losses in a particular battle, in the numbers engaged, or in the pursuit of widely accepted military goals, the point may have some validity, just as there is reason for making the distinction between the warrior and the soldier. However, to the individual in combat, the difference is not very apparent. The emotions of the tribal warrior embarked upon a raid on a neighboring village may have much in common with the feelings of a soldier of a high civilization about to enter battle. Neither of these two will have any panoramic view of the battlefield once engaged; each will have to concern himself with what is immediately in front of him. It may be argued that there can be no comparison between the emotions and reactions of persons raised in two such very different value systems, but the similarities of battle at various times in history and the sameness of the recorded statements of the combatants would seem to contradict this assumption.

Since the purpose of this study is to concentrate upon aspects of the battle experience as a means of understanding the institution of warfare, no fundamental distinction will be made between primitive and civilized war. It further seems necessary, in order to understand the nature of combat, to include examples from types of conflict not often taken into consideration. John Keegan, in his book, *The Face of Battle*, concentrates his attention upon major battles and would deny the appellation "battle" to a large number of minor contests.[12] Yet, in certain ways, street gang fights and civil disturbances present some of the same circumstances as military conflict and point to the fact that militant attitudes are not the exclusive property of the military.

One may question whether a study that ignores what are viewed as the traditional "causes" of war can make any real contribution to the understanding of this phenomenon. In dealing with the question of war, the various academic disciplines have dwelt upon the immediate and underlying causes of particular wars, of the economic, political, social, and psychological causes of war in general, as well as the consequences of war either in the particular or the general case. This concentration on the causes and effects of war has left little time for the consideration of the wars or the very concept of war itself. Studies of battle have been viewed as either interesting (possibly) but not consequential, or as necessary for the further development of the art and science of war. Therefore, they are best left to the military or the military historian, or as a branch of scholarship better left unlearned because it could only produce disaster. We believe that when we analyze the causes and effects of war, we are studying what war is really about. But war is also about battle, and battle may be studied, not only from the viewpoint of the tactics involved and the effect upon the campaign as a whole, but also as experience. Seen in this fashion, the questions of generalship and statecraft fade into the background, and the perceptions of the individual soldier assume central significance. It is by approaching the question of war in this manner that we can come to grips with the problem that there is some kind of enjoyment in combat. When a man says, with the greatest sincerity, that he never felt more alive than when he was flying combat missions, or when an infantryman confesses that "in a way" he wishes that he had seen more combat, we must accept the possibility that they are telling the truth.[13] It is not necessary to assume that the persons making such statements are particularly bloodthirsty or morally obtuse. They are simply stating a fact that is, among other things, puzzling to them.

Such evidence from veterans of combat may be brushed aside with the explanation that it is only a form of old soldier braggadocio, or the expression of a longing for a time of comradeship and simple solutions. In fact, these sentiments, confessed hesitantly and usually only to fellow veterans, indicate the attractiveness of battle. To go one step further, one of the central causes of war is, paradoxically, battle itself. It is the common wisdom of our age that there is no glory in war. Any particle of enjoyment which might have been attached to the wearing of bright uniforms or the vision of the panorama of the battlefield has disappeared in the grim holocausts of the twentieth century. This is a reasonable observation, but the subject itself is not reasonable.

Johan Huizinga, in his seminal work, *Homo Ludens*, saw war (at least war in the past) as one of the sacred games marked by rituals and separated from the profane life of everyday affairs.[14] It is the contention of this study that war has never lost that quality, and that this is sensed not only by the high command but also by the men in the ranks. The rituals which will concern us are not, in the first instance, those which have been built by the various armies for the purpose of maintaining unit order and morale. The games are not those played by the members of the military establishment in order to gain promotion. These may, in fact, be considered subgames, subordinate rituals which grow from and reinforce the substructure of battle itself. The ritual of battle, as dealt with here, also entails the actual process of battle. What the reader will have to understand is that the utilitarian activities of war have their ritual aspect, and that what is understood as necessary from the point of view of the general planning the battle, or the historian writing a study of the war, is seen by the individual participant as a ritual action as well as being a matter of life and death. In fact, because the game is played for these high stakes, the ritual aspect is inescapable.

To speak of war as ritual or as a form of play would seem to imply that it is either purposeless or its own reason for being. Obviously this flies in the face of common understanding. We know, for example, that particular wars are begun for specific reasons, although the reasons may not be very good or acceptable ones. We know also that war has developed as a means of protecting and aggrandizing society. Yet, we also know that many people have acted as though they believe that war is the highest value in their lives. As recently as the Second World War, a team of U.S. Army psychologists questioning men in combat on the reasons why they were fighting got practically no answers indicating that the men were doing it in order to protect society or to achieve some political or moral ideal. Very few exhibited any real hatred for the enemy.[15] Nor does coercion seem to have played any large part in the individual's decision to fight. Units did not have to be forced into battle at gunpoint. The pressure seems to have been mainly that of concern for the opinion of the other members of the unit. Given the fact that most infantrymen were not volunteers, some coercion was obviously involved. But once the decision had been made for them, most men seem to have accepted it with something like equanimity. The picture of men being driven into battle like sheep to the slaughter does not accord well with what we know of the actions of units in the wars of this century, or at least of the units in those armies with relatively good morale.

We must be prepared to face the question whether, fundamentally, war is a purposeless activity or whether its purposes may lie deeper than we had ever imagined. It will be necessary to go well beyond the ritual and myth of warfare into the social, psychological, and even biological implications of battle. The conclusions reached must, in many cases, be tentative, but it is hoped that by focusing attention on that often neglected part of warfare, the experience of battle, our understanding of the subject will be furthered.

2

The Masked Ball

We knew it was the "cannon's opening roar."
The ball had opened and we should soon be dancing.
———John W. Haley, *The Rebel Yell and the Yankee Hurrah*

IN A TIME SO SEEMINGLY POOR IN RITUAL OBSERVANCES, some explanation is, perhaps, required as to why battle, one of the most serious of human endeavors, should be called "ritual." To some extent this poverty can be traced to the turning away from former beliefs so that many of the old rituals are but meagerly attended to; but it is also true that we fail to identify ritual where it exists and we confuse ritual observance with lack of seriousness. When we say that something has become mere ritual, we condemn it to the category of the unimportant, a simple waste of time. Since this is a position so commonly held, and since it is so wrongheaded, it would be well to review briefly what ritual is and where it can be seen in action.

There is scarcely a moment of the day when we are entirely free from ritual's influence, be it in the unvarying way in which we arise in the morning with our habits of washing and dress, the manner in which we greet our acquaintances, or the uses of mealtime. All are, to some degree, ritualistic; that is, they are patterned and habitual. As human beings we are, perhaps, bored and restless with the patterned and the platitudinous, but it must be admitted that this governs much of our daily life—and without it, life would be chaos. Thus, we shave in a particular fashion each morning and indulge in a few comfortable remarks to our companions on the bus and at our place of business so that things may function more smoothly. Deviation from this routine would cause comment from others and, perhaps, some wonderment in ourselves. The type of ritual behavior will change according to the circumstances: we act differently as a member of the household than

we would as an employee in a place of business, a member of a frater-
nal lodge, or with a group of strangers.

We scarcely note such minor rituals which carry us through the day
because they are so familiar and so useful. With major rituals we are
more aware of what they, in fact, are, since the utilitarian aspect is
supplanted to a greater degree by the purely formal character of the
function. This can be most clearly seen in religious rituals, particularly those which employ a rigid and often ancient liturgy. Here the
utilitarian is obviously subordinated to the formal. If the religious
celebration serves to bind the community together, this appears to
the believer simply as a side effect of attendance at the exposition of a
central mystery of existence. It is only by comparing the social results
of a large number of religious observances that we are able to define
clearly the utilitarian functions. For the person immersed in the religious community, the outstanding characteristics are the formal ones:
the special and sacred location, the specialized clothing of the cele-
brant and the congregation, the special set of actions typical of this
place and no other. Engulfed in the forms, the mind of the participant
is directed to the contemplation of statements about the nature of the
universe and the individual's place within it which are particular to
that religious group. Many of these statements are not enunciated but
are implicit in the forms themselves. Perceived in this fashion, the
truths are apodictic; they cannot be analyzed or contradicted without
rending the fabric of ritual and belief.

Ritual then is an organized collection of symbols and ceremonies
which give visible form to ideas. It is highly conservative in that it
cannot be lightly changed. This apparent unchanging nature is one of
its most comforting qualities. It is characterized by specific location
in time and space. These times and spaces are in themselves sacred in
that they cannot be invaded by ordinary activities. Everything about
ritual is marked by this special quality. The clothing, the language,
and the actions are not those used in daily intercourse. Within the
individual, the attendance at these rituals may arouse feelings of awe
and fear, though it has often been noted that little apparent carryover
to the daily life of the majority of believers occurs. Despite this failure
it cannot be said that ritual is without effect. It provides for the
periodic reaffirmation of belief and may provide the motivation for
important civil activities as varied as charitable acts and religious
war.[1]

Between the highly ritualized functions of the religious sphere and the minor rituals of everyday life lies a group of ritualized activities which also serve an obvious utilitarian function. An outstanding example of this class is the system of law and of the court. Highly ritualized in terms of location, time, action, and language, the dignity of the court is upheld and a sense of awe and fear is inspired in the community, thus enhancing the operation of the legal system within the society. Besides the courts of law, government, the stock exchange, and a wide variety of associations make use of ritual to enhance their powers. It is to this middle group of ritualized functions that the military belongs.

That military organizations employ rituals in order to enforce their discipline is plain to see and would not, therefore, be worth extended discussion. The point that must be established is that battle itself is a ritual, that the preparation for it, the combat itself, and the reactions to the results of the struggle are all parts of a ritual as well as being actions which lead to tangible results. It is the function of this ritual to both draw men into conflict and to hold them there contrary to reasonable expectation.

The method of selection of persons for military service varies quite widely from society to society. The first and perhaps most important restriction, which seems common to all societies, is that war is a male occupation. It is true that women have from time to time served as individuals in combat units, usually adopting a male disguise. Even the most famous of these female warriors, Joan of Arc, was severely criticized by her enemies for the "unnaturalness" of her dress, not to mention her occupation. It is true that there are ancient legends of female warriors and there have been a few instances of battalions of women serving in modern battles—women will be thrown into the fight when the need is dire. In addition, it is also true that women are drafted and accepted into the military, but usually a clear distinction is made between combat service and support service. The very important role that women play in the ritual of battle will be discussed in a later section.

A second set of restrictions concerns age. Generally speaking, children are not called upon to perform military duties, though the definition of "child" is an elastic one. The onset of puberty seems to mark the lower limit at which a boy can become a soldier, but again there are isolated instances where boys younger than this have served.[2]

However, in both modern and primitive societies, youths at or just past the age of puberty seem to be protected from involvement in the worst rigors of war except in the worst of circumstances. In many societies—one is tempted to say most societies—this does not preclude inculcating the young with the virtues of warfare. Military games and play with toy weapons are widespread phenomena which, if they do not develop the "killer instinct," certainly help to make war a seemingly desirable occupation.

There also exists a somewhat variable, but generally agreed upon, upper age limit for military duty. With the exception of higher command positions, which commonly require qualities other than physical prowess, the beginning of middle age can be said to mark the end of one's liability for service in war. The age classes 18 to 44, which bear the main responsibility for military duty in western society, are also the main age groups charged with this task in other societies. As has been noted, a certain elasticity is involved in selection, but on the whole the military duties and capabilities depend upon this one-third of the male population.

Within this group, liability is not universal. As a rule, the larger and more advanced the society, the smaller will be the percentage called upon to serve. In very small groups, such as hunting bands, the defense of the society may fall upon all men and many of the women and children as well. Under certain conditions of warfare, such as the cavalry conflicts of the middle ages, it was not feasible to arm more than a small minority of the population. Certainly, in modern industrial society, the demands of the weapons industries and other necessary occupations make universal military service unlikely. Among hunting-gathering peoples and groups which depend upon primitive garden agriculture, the concept that all adult males are warriors is most fully evident, but even here specialized military organizations can be noted.[3] At times these specialized groups will bear the whole burden of arms. Among the Haida of the Northwest coast of North America, a very few men, highly skilled and highly privileged, were responsible for defense and attack. On the other hand, among the Plains Indians, service was demanded of all able-bodied men. The same is true of the warlike Kurulu of New Guinea and the Yanomamoe of South America. With the Kurulu, any adult male who did not wish to serve (and there were some) was treated as a woman, his possessions and even his wife being subject to seizure by the warriors.[4]

Where military service is not universal, either the selected group may bear the entire burden of warfare, or it may be an elite group which forms the core of the army in wartime. Selection for this elite group has been based at times upon birth, the right to bear arms being given to only a highly privileged stratum of society. In other cases men have been chosen for their physical ability and daring. This daring may be, in some instances, of a suicidal nature, as was the practice with certain of the Plains Indian tribes. A few highly honored members staked themselves in place on the battlefield and promised to die rather than move from that position. As may be expected, they often kept that promise. Some armies have been composed of slaves, others of hired mercenaries, and still others, such as the European armies of the seventeenth and eighteenth centuries, of the least privileged members of the society, the unskilled laborers of town and countryside, officered by the most privileged members of that same society.

Despite these many variations, there is reason to believe that the basic form of military duty was that of universal service with unavoidable exceptions for reasons of health or age. In almost all primitive societies, all boys are treated as potential warriors, and service in war is accorded the highest honors. Even in advanced societies boys are taught that the bearing of arms is an honorable activity, though for a number of reasons many will not be called upon to do so. There does exist a basic difference, however, between primitive and modern societies in this matter. A boy growing up among the Plains Indians, the Kurulu, or the Yanomamoe learned not only to regard warfare as the highest expression of manhood, but also how to conduct himself in battle long before he was called upon to do so. His training for the profession of arms was part and parcel of his training to assume an adult role in society. The initiation ceremonies which marked the culmination of this training inducted him into manhood, marked him as a warrior capable of using his weapons effectively and able to conduct himself well and bravely on the battlefield. The young man growing up in modern society may have been trained to respect the military and to see war as necessary in some circumstances. He may even regard it as a glorious occupation, but it is quite likely that he has never handled a weapon, has never experienced anything approaching military discipline, has never been subjected to severe privation and pain for the purpose of hardening him to the military life, and he certainly has not been raised to believe that killing a stranger is a normal human activity. Yet, curiously enough, he can, within a few months, learn all these things and in the process become even more murderously efficient than his primitive brother.

It might be important here to distinguish between the terms "warrior" and "soldier." To be a warrior is to participate in a way of life which envelops the entire adult existence of a man. It is to live in a society which accepts war as an integral and praiseworthy part of living. In such a society, to be a warrior is only another way of saying that one is fully a man. Soldiering, on the other hand, is an occupation which is a lifetime profession for only a few. The majority of soldiers are such for a relatively brief period, after which they turn to other occupations. Within this time they may temporarily accept some of the attitudes of the warrior and remember them fondly at some later date. But soldiering is not, except for the professional, a way of life. The veteran may find himself changed and his attitudes toward life different as a result of his experiences. He may even feel himself separated in important ways from those who have not served, but he is no more a warrior than any of them, for modern society does not provide the support needed to sustain this way of life.

By whatever gate the young man enters upon the path of war, be it by conscription or the tribal life, he must be trained for martial duties. For the sons of the tribe, training begins at an early age, when it is made clear to them that the life of the adult male involves fighting. He is encouraged to be aggressive with his fellows and (very frequently) to adopt a superior attitude toward women. Obviously, this attitude toward women is not entirely restricted to primitive groups. For young boys the training will include the use of weapons and engagement in mock battles. This training is strongly reinforced by the evidence of its practical utility in those tribes engaging in frequent skirmishes with their neighbors. Since primitive warfare almost habitually neglects to consider women and children as noncombatants, he may, very early, be faced with the real dangers of the battlefield and its aftermath. In a world where strangers are considered enemies, where sex and age are not protections, the lone stranger is all too often marked for an early death.

While recent wars have seen a return to the habit of attacking civilian populations, the chances are still very good that the male child growing up in modern society will neither have had any personal experience with the realities of battle nor have had much, if any, training in the use of weapons. Thus, modern societies have adopted the practice of conducting a relatively short period of intensive training in the use of arms and military life. In this respect "modern" must be understood to include all urbanized societies. The training program outlined by Vegetius for the troops of the Roman Empire resembles, in most basic details, the training programs of twentieth-century armies. However, since Vegetius was used as the basic handbook for the development of European armies, this is, perhaps, scarcely surprising. In one major respect, this type of training differs from that given by primitive groups. The fathers of the boys have been replaced by father surrogates, the officers and, to an even greater extent, the sergeants. The tremendous respect with which these men are regarded is attested by the frequency with which they are described and remembered in soldiers' accounts of their experiences. Often this respect is mingled with fear and loathing, but only relatively seldom are they treated as buffoons.[5]

By concentrating the period of training, modern military forces tend to exaggerate certain features which have always been present. Most particularly this can be noted in the tendency to separate the recruit from his normal society. While the initiation period of the primitive groups involves a separation, it is usually not lengthy and is directed towards transforming the boy into a full adult member of the community, not simply to make him a warrior. The separation of the recruit involves not only the removal from family, but also from the company of women or, indeed, any society outside of the military unit. For some weeks or months he will find himself constantly under the attention of martial overseers. He will adopt a distinctive type of clothing, be taught to stand, walk, and speak in a distinctive fashion; even his hairstyle will undergo a change. Thus, he will be forced to assume a number of outward signs that he has undergone an inner transformation, and it is this inner change which makes the real difference. He must accept a discipline which is at odds with his previous training. The extent to which this discipline is necessary is a matter for conjecture. It is worth noting that the discipline of most armies has declined in ferocity over the past century, even as the discipline in the home has been relaxed. Less than one hundred years ago, men were still hung by the thumbs and spread-eagled on cannon wheels for relatively minor offenses, and execution was a much more common sentence than is presently the case.[6] Interestingly enough, this amelioration has not resulted in an increase in the desertion rates or in a lack of willingness to fight. One cannot, however, conclude that discipline can be entirely abandoned. It is still mandatory that men act at times in ways which are certainly contrary to their individual self-interests and often enough in ways which run counter to their deepest instincts for self-preservation. The soldier must be prepared to obey, without question, orders that are apparently (or even patently) nonsensical, or orders which are fatal. No system of discipline has ever been fully effective in achieving this type of acquiescence, but the fact that armies operate at all indicates that discipline does have its effect.

If discipline has its practical uses, it must be remembered that it serves also to give form to the military unit. It distinguishes the military from all other activities. There is, for instance, nothing practical about the German Army's goose step or the slow march of the British Army's Brigade of Guards, but they do place a distinctive mark upon these organizations. Nor does discipline have to be of this rigidly mechanical sort. The apparent casualness of the Israeli army, or the rolled-up shirtsleeves of the French "Paras," are not so much an aberration from high discipline and motivation as they are its distinctive trademark. The forms of discipline tend to be highly expressive. The freewheeling activity of the primitive battle formation, or that of the medieval knights, sacrificed military sophistication to allow for the expression of individual prowess. Both the Comanche and the chivalry of medieval Europe were, individually, highly disciplined fighters, though their organization was rudimentary. By contrast, the armies of the eighteenth century presented a picture of clockwork precision, another manifestation of that century's fascination with the machine. In the twentieth century, the form of the factory has influenced the style of discipline. The clothing of the soldier is more functional, even casual, and one encounters such self-descriptions as "wage earners of the battlefield."[7] The form of discipline varies, but it always serves the purpose of casting the individual in a role suitable for the enactment of the ritual of battle.

Training is the period when the neophyte learns the mysteries connected with the operation of and care for his weapons; the latter will form a large and continuing part of his activity in the military. Whether he is hardening the tip of his spear, feathering his arrows, sharpening the blade of his sword, or cleaning the chamber of his rifle, the warrior or the soldier spends a part of each day with an instrument that tends to take on magical qualities. The marine who is told to sleep with his rifle, the warrior who names his sword and sings songs to it are both endowing their weapons with a kind of personality. It will be the soldier's protection in battle; it will be, in fact, an extension of his "soldier" self. For a soldier to abandon his weapon has long been considered not only a serious military offense, but also a sign of lost honor. The injunction of Spartan mothers to their sons to "return with your shield or on it" has been echoed down through time. There is, of course, another tradition, less heroic certainly, but reflecting the concern of the soldier for his own life. The poet Archilochus states it most boldly:

> Some Thracian strutteth with my shield;
> For, being somewhat flurried,
> I left it in a wayside bush,
> When from the field I hurried,
> A right good targe, but I got off,
> The deuce may take the shield;
> I'll get another just as good
> When next I go afield.[8]

Throughout history there are numerous instances of this sort which indicate that there is always a fair readiness to leave the role of the soldier-warrior, if not permanently, then at least for the time being.

Drill in the use of weapons is also used to inculcate men with the willingness to kill. The Roman soldier learning to use his sword necessarily learned the weak points in the opponent's armor at which his thrust should be aimed. The Swiss pikeman learned the use of his weapon in warding off cavalry and dragging men from horseback with the billhook. The modern soldier is trained in the accurate firing of his rifle, but, since this a rather distant method of killing, he is also given training with the bayonet, a weapon that he will seldom if ever use. Philip Caputo tells of his group of officer candidates chanting, "Gung Ho! Gung Ho! Gung Ho! Pray for war!" as a part of a classroom exercise.[9] In some cases the use of the weapon can be learned fairly easily (such is the case with the modern rifle). In other cases a great deal of practice is necessary, thus placing a premium upon the long-term professional soldier. Whatever the weapon, the soldier, through repeated practice, learns how to kill, or at least how to threaten to kill, an opponent. It is doubtful that he learns to hate his opponent by this training; it is more likely that the result is the reduction of the enemy to the status of "target."

The soldier must also be trained in the techniques of handling himself on the battlefield. These skills include the seeking of cover, avoiding the blows of an opponent, dodging arrows and spears, and working with other soldiers as a unit. Essentially, what he is learning is not primarily to protect himself but how to accept danger and even death, for the longer he stays on the battlefield, the more likely it is that an enemy weapon will find its mark. The soldier must be trained to accept death as a possibly unavoidable consequence of battle. Yanomamoe warriors composed and practiced speeches to be given as they were dying, and the history and lore of battle is rich with the dying quotations of soldiers, both famous and unknown. Again, in character with the role for which the soldier is being prepared, these statements are almost uniformly heroic. "Go, stranger, and tell the Lacaedaemonians that we lie here in obedience to their command" makes a fine epitaph, but one is justified in wondering whether even a Spartan might not feel some misgivings about being selected for immortality in this manner.[10] Yet the evidence is clear that, with personal reservations or not, soldiers often play out the roles assigned to them—even to the dismal end.

Soldiers must be inured not only to the possibility of death, but also to pain and hardship. Marching has long been a favorite method of building this endurance, as well as for strengthening men physically. Loaded like pack mules, infantrymen for centuries have learned that it is possible to live with the pain of an overburdened and exhausted body marched for endless miles on lacerated feet, and, if necessary, to fight in such a condition. But marching is also a rhythmic exercise, like dancing. This is most clearly seen in the practice of close order drill.

Developed in order to carry out the precise battlefield maneuvers of eighteenth-century warfare, this form of drill is often regarded as a useless holdover maintained for the purpose of plaguing the life of the common soldier. Military leaders who support the continuation of the practice assert that it is very useful as a means of instilling discipline. Yet, it is possible to offer an alternative explanation. While close order drill can be the bane of the recruit, it can be a rather enjoyable exercise when carried out by disciplined men under the leadership of a skilled drill sergeant. It is, in fact, stimulating to find oneself the member of a group spread to the four corners of the drill field and then, at command, brought back together in correct time and order. The unit can experiment with elaborations such as the Queen Anne drill or chanting the cadence count. It can, in brief, show itself off. In this, close order drill is closely related to the dancing which was so much a part of the primitive preparation for battle. Like the dance it is a ritually fierce and joyful expression of membership in a warrior group. Like war dances, the steps must be done correctly with the brandishing of weapons and accompanied by ritual shouting. If it strains credulity too much to call this an invocation for success in battle, it is certainly a process which draws one ever further into the entire body of the battle ritual. Without doubt, the ancients considered such demonstrations of vast importance. Among the questions asked by the Bulgarian King Boris I of Pope Nicholas I, as Boris pondered the possibility of conversion to Christianity, was whether the Bulgarians would be allowed to retain their war songs and dances. The pope's negative answer may have contributed to Boris' decision to accept communion with the Orthodox rite.[11]

The focal point for the administration of discipline and the evocation of loyalty from the individual soldier is the unit of which he is a member. For the warrior of a hunter-gatherer group, this may be the particular companions who habitually hunt and fight together, or, if the society is small enough, it may be all of the warriors of that society. For the soldiers of a modern army, it will be one of the smaller subunits of that army. Very few soldiers will show much attachment to an organization as large as a field army. For, with its hundreds of thousands of members, such a large organization is essentially unknowable. He may feel a strong loyalty towards a famous general, but there can be little that is personal in this relationship. A sense of loyalty may be established towards some unit of intermediate size, such as the division whose patch he wears. But the real subject of his loyalty will be a unit of a size in which all or most of the members can be known and who share a common set of experiences. In recent times this has most often been the company (of about one hundred and fifty members), the platoon (forty members), or the squad (about ten members). Within these units the soldier will form his friendships and share his meals. It is with these men that he will enter combat. He will be known to the officers in these units, and he will form a rather accurate estimation of their abilities. In past centuries, when armies fought in closer formations than is the case today, this sense of belonging could extend to the battalion and regimental level. Even in these cases, however, we are seldom speaking of more than five hundred men. But here also, the strongest loyalties would be directed towards one's messmates, a group of probably not more than ten men.

These small groups, however, share not only food and danger. They are also the social units which can award or withhold esteem and, as such, are one of the most important factors that keep men fighting. Ideals like national honor, or justice, have little meaning to soldiers at those moments when they are in the presence of the enemy if, indeed, they ever bulk large in the thinking of most soldiers. Even the estimation of the people at home is of little import at these times. Here one may note a difference in the situation of the primitive warrior and the modern soldier. The former is often fighting very close to home territory, and his actions can be observed by the whole tribe (or at least its male members). He will have to live with his battlefield behavior for the rest of his life. The modern soldier knows that he will probably never again see most of his wartime companions. Yet, even though he realizes that this society is a transitory one, he places high value on the opinion of its members. For a short time at least, it is his home.

By the end of the training period, whether it has extended over the lifetime of the youth or been concentrated into a shorter period, the soldier-warrior is prepared to enter into the central actions of the ritual of battle. He has been prepared for his role with considerable care, and he has been provided with the implements necessary to the task. Many would argue that in the process he has also been dehumanized. Both his willingness to kill and his willingness to be killed have been promoted out of all normal proportions. Further, by entering the company of warriors, he has removed himself from ordinary society. Women are either largely or wholly excluded. In numbers of primitive groups, where it is unlikely that the separation will be of any great duration, the warriors are enjoined to practice sexual abstinence. The justification for this ban is that, presumably, contact with women will weaken the warrior both physically and spiritually. It should be noted, though, that the separation of the sexes is a practice common to many rituals that have nothing to do with fighting.

At some time prior to joining battle, there occur ceremonies which seem to fall under the general classification of dance. In primitive societies they are, in the strictest sense, dances. Tales from the American west describe the war dances of the Indians, in which both men and women participated. While industrial society does not foster the development of war dances, it does have marches which, as noted earlier, may be considered a type of dance. In the opening days of the First World War, men from the different countries marching to battle were showered with flowers from women along the route. Those early days of August, 1914, were generally marked by frenzied crowd activity. In other wars the last gala ball before the onset of the campaign featuring brightly dressed young hussars, dragoons, and guards, the young women clothed like flowers, possibly the emperor in attendance, are not only the stuff of romantic literature, but did actually take place. Some of these remembered occasions were of that fabled time the "prewar years," while others were on the eve of battle. At Waterloo, officers appeared on the field in the clothes worn the previous night at a ball in Brussels. Such a dance was the farewell occasion for the Army of the Potomac before plunging into the Wilderness. Or it may have been a high school prom, reeking of gardenias, an affair ineffably sweet but colored by the knowledge that the draft machinery was already processing the notices. The fevered gaiety of these last gatherings only serve to mark more clearly the passage from peace to war.

More clearly martial in its import is the unit review which has often preceded the departure for war. Since it is not often that large units are brought together for this type of formal parade, it tends to be a very impressive affair. This is true not only for the spectators, but, perhaps, even more so for those involved. To participate in the review of, let us say, a regiment with its supporting arms is to get a feeling of the power which has been brought together for the purpose of displaying that strength. To catch a glimpse out of the corner of one's eye of the line of men stretching far in either direction gives the individual soldier an immediate and visual awareness of the supports which have been gathered about him.

Akin to this is the habit of listing the names of units about to enter the battle. As with the review, the knowledge that one will be accompanied by famous fighters is comforting. Homer's "catalogue of ships" accomplishes this purpose and mentions the outstanding qualities of the fighters as well:

those of Styra—all
Who had young Elephanor for . . . commander,
Quick on their feet. . . . Troops enlisted hungering for body armor
Of enemies to pierce with ashen spears;
and Elephanor's black ships numbered forty.[12]

Three thousand years later, the men of the British Expeditionary Force took comfort in listing the names of famous regiments, Ox and Bucks, Black Watch, Royal Welch Fusiliers, Rifle Brigade, and, of course, the Guards, whose battalions were serving beside them in the trenches. Crazy Horse and his men watched with satisfaction the gathering of famous warriors from the many tribes as he prepared for the meeting at Little Big Horn. Even the antiwar demonstrators of the sixties felt this sense of strength, when they saw assembling the banners of the SDS, Progressive Labor, the Yippies, Women's Liberation, Gay Liberation, and the Panthers, together with all of the lesser regiments and splinter groups of "the movement."

Such demonstrations and clangor of names are but a fleeting instant in the onrushing progress of the ritual of battle; a flashing of spears and the chanting of self-praise to bolster courage for the uncertainties ahead. In the quiet moments of exhausted emotion that follow, the men form silently in their barracks squares, their village streets, their camps in forest and desert; strap on their packs; check their uniforms or smear on the garish paints of war; and move off past the crowds of women, the men too old, the boys too young—past all of these, past the confines of the homeland, out onto the perilous paths, and down the dusty roads that lead to war.

The intervals between these demonstrations and the actual departure for battle may be very short, as is often the case in primitive warfare, or it may extend over many months. Yet, even when the delay is lengthy, there is the sense that something has closed behind one. What lies out ahead is marching, but now it is not boastful measure of close order drill, the war dance, or the unit review, but the quiet, introspective tread of route step. It is time for the soldier to look within himself and ponder his readiness for battle. All of the uncertainties and doubts, the hopes and the sadness of parting, can be conjured in the mind to the steady rhythm of the soft tramp of feet, step after endless step. It is not even necessary that the march be on foot. The rumble of truck tires, the roar of ship's engines, the clopping of the horses' hooves, the helicopter's throbbing, or the quiet hiss of the jet are all conducive to this meditative mood, a muffled, pulsing reminder that one is each moment closer to battle.

At such a time fear can be the dominant emotion—fear of dying, of being injured, fear of showing that one is afraid. Such considerations can be alleviated by concentration on other things, by joking with one's companions, by singing, or group chanting. All are antidotes to personal panic. An even more effective antidote is the march itself, for if the march can be considered a dance conducive to meditation, it is also a conveyer belt carrying troops to war. One cannot very well jump out of the truck, the plane, or the ship. But even a body of troops on foot acts as a sort of container. If you fall out, you will be noticed and may be severely punished. One is strongly impressed with the sense that matters are out of one's hands. For the soldier this may give rise to a feeling of fatalism, but it can also encourage him to relinquish responsibility for actions he may be called upon to perform. Thus marching, with its impressive inevitability, serves the purpose of preparing the soldier for battle.

The time spent in marching is of indeterminate length. For many of the primitive groups, the distance may be only the few hundred yards between the village and the traditional battleground, or it may be an overnight journey.[13] Modern armies may have to travel very long distances in order to reach the field of battle, and the marching in these cases will be accomplished by a variety of means of transportation. Yet, until very recently, even some of the longest distances were covered entirely on foot.

Under whatever conditions the march is made, the common tendency is for the army or group to draw more and more in upon itself, to become more alien to the space and population surrounding it. It becomes an entity composed of many individuals moving along by fits and starts, ever more ready to treat those persons it encounters as objects to be ignored or utilized. This is the case even when these persons are actually or potentially friendly. They are civilians, a part of that other world which has been left behind. At least some of the excesses to which armies are prone can be explained by this tendency to draw in upon itself, severing all real human relations with the exception of its relation to that entity which lies out there somewhere ahead, the enemy. People and places are brushed aside in passing. A church spire appears up ahead; the column constricts, slows down, tramps past the doorways and gardens of the village, catches sight of the gaze of the fearful or the curious. A dog trots along side the soldiers for a while and then falls back. The column moves on and the spire of the church is lost in the distance behind, closed off by the dark block of woods as new fields appear ahead.

The universe closes down to the moving column. Rumors move up and down the line like the eddies and swirls on a stream, "double rations tonight . . . the enemy is in full retreat . . . we're on the wrong road." An officer moves back down the column, looking for evidence of dereliction or simply to give encouragement to tired men. A shout goes up to move off the road to make room for the passage of cavalry, artillery, or trucks. Churning up dust they pass amid the curses or shouts of friendly derision, or just the resigned gaze of the infantry. The vehicles rumble on and are lost over a rise of ground; the column closes back on the road and resumes its march. At intervals it halts for a short break. The men fall out, remove their packs, and lie for a few moments' rest on dusty tufts of grass by the roadside and then, seemingly too soon, are called back to the road.

This moving column has been the common experience of soldiers in all ages, whether the route lies along broad, metalled highways, the mud and dust of country roads, or forest trails. The final goal of such movement is contact with the enemy; the immediate goal, the night's encampment. Entering bivouac, the column sorts itself out into its separate units. Shelter halves are buttoned together and staked to the ground, possibly in neat lines, possibly wherever the individuals choose. With luck the ground will be dry. In the Roman army a routine was long established whereby each night's stopping place was transformed into a model camp with streets and even gates and palisades. Few armies have been so formal. The campfires start for the cooking of the evening meal or the company cookers are wheeled into position, and the men line up to be fed. Men are detailed to forage for wood or food. Guards are posted. Thus the days and nights and weeks may pass for the army, the men bedded down in strange fields by the last embers of dying fires and awaking in the cold mist of the next dawn to fumble for their equipment and resume their march. But there will come a night when other campfires appear on the hills beyond, when one knows with certainty that the goal of all this marching has been reached.

The presence of the enemy has been signaled in many ways through the centuries. For the Maori warrior, it came with the quiet report of the forward scout that the *pa,* the fortified camp, was just ahead. It may have come in the form of enemy campfires well aware of the army's presence. Or, as is so often the case in modern war, it may be marked by the strange emptiness of the landscape. Gone now is the uproar and movement of the crowds of rear echelon units; the only light to be seen is cast by the flickering of the night-firing artillery batteries. The only other sounds are the occasional clinks of someone out there somewhere, digging.

One is caught now at the very edge of battle, deeply enmeshed in the ritual of combat. Whatever the state of preparation of the individual or the organization, there is little chance now that the logical consequences can be avoided. Those tensions, which may have been relaxed during the drawn-out period of preparation and approach, are now again heightened. These are countered by other feelings, almost akin to relief, that one is now committed to a course of action. Certain things can be done. Pickets are set out to guard against surprise, and scouting patrols may bring back more information on the enemy arrangements. Weapons can be checked and cleaned, but the rest is waiting. Shakespeare gives a brilliant evocation of this mood and time:

> Now entertain conjecture of a time
> When creeping murmur and the poring dark
> Fills the wide vessel of the universe.
> From camp to camp, through the foul womb of night,
> The hum of either army stilly sounds,
> That the fixed sentinels almost receive
> The secret whispers of each other's watch.
> Fire answers fire, and through their paly flames
> Each battle sees the other's umbered face.[14]

Not all battles are fought during the daylight hours. Among primitive groups, where great reliance is placed on the ambush and the surprise attack, the night was, and is, often the favored time for fighting. It may well be that night fighting is the most ancient form of warfare, since it does favor action by small groups. Even today, it is the form of warfare most often used by guerrilla armies. However, it is difficult to control larger groups at night, though the Israeli army has demonstrated in recent years that this is possible. Therefore, most modern armies and many primitive warriors as well, have preferred to fight in the daylight hours. Recognizing this preference, the illustrations of battle which follow will be concerned mainly with this more ordinary form of encounter.

The night is the time for preparations. Generals must complete their planning, orders must be issued, and in the early hours the officers and noncoms of the fighting units will begin to rouse their men. Cooking fires are started, equipment is checked and groups of men fall into formation. From the other camp the sounds of similar activities can be heard. Among the Kurulu these beginnings are signaled by the men from the village and allied villages moving in small bunches toward the traditional battleground. The watchtowers are manned, and the warriors gather in knots at the base of the towers, leaning on their spears, eyeing the hill beyond for enemy movement.

In some cases the waiting men will be offered a panoramic view of the battlefield, the folds of the hills, fields and the small patches of woods, and the tiny hamlets, which before the end of the day may assume terrible significance. The Peach Orchard, High Wood, the Huertgen Forest, and Austerlitz lie out there in the morning mist about to be touched and forever marked by history. Forever, of course, is a long time, and most such country places will know their moment of terror and then fade from view, remembered only by the men who fought there, and finally, forgotten. Such overviews of the battlefield are not afforded to all soldiers. Their vision will be obscured by intervening hills or woods or, as was the case for the British at the Somme, by the high parapets of the trenches. For those men, perhaps, the only clear sight they had of that great field was in the first moments after they had climbed out of the trenches and before the German machine guns began their deadly work. By and large, the bird's eye view of the battlefield is reserved for the general and the military historian.

For the man in the ranks, the scene tends to be one of hurried confusion. Tired, busily engaged in getting his equipment together and bolting down a breakfast of half-cooked porridge, hard tack, and coffee, or a cold K ration, the battle envelops him in a welter of disparate sights and sounds. Officers ride up to the commander, shout something, and ride away. The sound-power phone rings, officers gather, the sergeants are called away and then return with tiny bits of information that fit this small unit into some kind of general plan. It does not matter that the officers and men have been carefully coached in their objectives and what they are to do, though this is very often not the case. At the hour of execution, the scene is still one of confusion, and the men will move with puzzled purposefulness as they assemble themselves for battle.

Gradually units begin to move. Artillery batteries may now begin to fire registering shots, or they may already have been bombarding the enemy for hours, even days. The regiments march off to their appointed places in the line. From afar this movement can be seen as brightly colored figures or as small bunches of earth-colored men moving according to some master plan; or, as is often the case, in opposition to some master plan. From within the ranks little can be seen but the back of the man next in front, the rocks and logs which cause the columns and bunches to bob and weave, the branches brushing off the shoulder of the man in front into the face of the individual, the muddy slopes and the tufts of grass which one seizes for support. One hears the muttered curse of momentary exasperation, the heavy breathing. One feels the sweat of fear and exertion, feels also that exhilaration at approaching the unknown which mingles with fear in a curious compound heightening all of the senses of the man in battle.

And suddenly things stop. The unit halts. It is at its appointed place, or what is taken to be that place, though it looks little different from any other place. The unit halts and waits. It may very well be that no sight or sound will reach it to signal that this is the battlefield and that this is the front line. In recent wars this emptiness of the front has been a somewhat disconcerting experience for new troops. Led to expect battle flags, or at least long lines of men and deafening sound, they find, instead, nothing. Birds sing, the sun grows hotter, smells rise from the earth and the vegetation, but no sight or sound— only an eerie presentiment that this is a place of mortal danger. And so the men wait.

In other wars the front of battle has been more clearly defined. Those Kurulu warriors that we left standing around their watchtowers waiting for some sign of the enemy have had their expectations fulfilled. Across the hill the tips of spears and the waving feathered headdresses of the foe appear, rise to full height, and form a line of naked bodies scarred white and red with the paint of war, the tall spears rising far above them in fearsome array down the length of the enemy front. The Kurulu form themselves in a similarly challenging fashion.[15] Ammianus Marcellinus recounts for us the impression made by the appearance of the horde of Persian warriors:

The Persians opposed to us seried bands of mail-clad horsemen in such close order that the gleam of moving bodies covered with closely fitting plates of iron dazzled the eyes of those who looked upon them, while the whole throng of horses was protected by coverings of leather. The cavalry was backed up by companies of infantry, who, protected by oblong, curved shields . . . advanced in very close order. Behind these were elephants, looking like walking hills . . . dreaded as they were from past experience. . . .

So when both sides came near enough to look each other in the face, the Romans, gleaming in their crested helmets and swinging their shields as if to the rhythm of the anapestic foot, advanced slowly; and the light-armed skirmishers opened the battle by hurling their javelins, while the earth everywhere was turned to dust and swept away in a swift whirlwind. And when the battlecry was raised in the usual manner by both sides and the trumpets' blare increased the ardour of the men, here and there they fought hand-to-hand with spears and drawn swords.[16]

A new RAF pilot, at the height of the fighting in the summer of 1940, gives a similar picture of his first exposure to the enemy: "The sky was blue from horizon to horizon and our squadron was climbing to our allocated altitude. Suddenly from the east, I became aware of masses of dots which resolved themselves into aircraft as the enemy formations approached."[17]

These great lines of battle with masses of spears and bodies disfigured and enlarged by war paint, feathers, helmets, body armor, and shields (or even an entire airplane) were an ultimate challenge to the mettle of the foe. In visual terms they declared "we are warriors, larger than life, a machine which is more powerful than its individual parts. We have within our ranks famous fighters who by headdress or by shield insignia you know too well. Come fight us if you dare, or flee while you may." The visual challenge is accompanied by mocking cries, impugning the courage of the opponent. Thus by visual and verbal signs the contestants prepared themselves for the battle ahead.

What is the response of the individual to this martial display? Primarily it is given as the member of a group. Ever since the moment when he began his training as a warrior, he has been preparing for this confrontation, and has been doing it mainly in the view of others. If he has never been in combat he will almost certainly have some private questions about his ability to carry out the duties of his role. Whether he is new or old to combat, he will have feelings of fear for his life and health. He will also be experiencing certain physiological effects stimulated by the situation, changes which will improve his efficiency in battle. In addition to these sensations, he will be conscious of social obligations to the other men of his unit, of their expectations of him, and possibly more dimly, obligations to the society in general.

The ritual activities which he has been carrying out now for so long that they have become for him a way of life, have brought him to this situation. Rational analysis would indicate that it would be much better for the individual to be somewhere else, but the opportunities for such a course have been successively closed off by force, chance, or choice. Being here, he must make the best of it. Beyond this, he may entertain hopes of glory, promotion, and loot, though it is by no means necessary that these expectations be present. The individuals who make up the battleline will vary considerably, from hero to coward, in their reaction to combat. The vast majority will play an intermediate role between these two extremes. However, this variation of attitude will be disguised for the moment by the brave exterior of war paint, uniform, or armor. To the individual the set of men about him seems preternaturally calm and resolute. Under the circumstances he must similarly comport himself and, by so doing, unwittingly sets the example for his like-minded comrades.

The incidences of mockery mentioned earlier may or may not have an effect on the enemy, but they do offer the individual the opportunity to display his courage at little cost. When the foe speaks the same language, it may offer the chance for the exchange of humorous raillery.

It has already been noted that the enemy is seldom in view on the modern battlefield. Thus, it would appear that the visual stimulation offered by the enemy battleline seems to be absent. Actually visual stimulation is achieved by concentration upon the place where he is thought or known to be. The imagination tends to fill these apparently empty places with dangerous men. In the First World War, the occasional sight of the barbed wire and the parapets of the trenches opposite filled this purpose. Eric Leed has also noted that sounds played an even more important role than sight under the restricted conditions of that war.[18] In recent wars a preliminary burst of machine-gun fire, or the fall of a mortar shell, has tended wonderfully to engage the imagination. In any case, once that invisible boundary, the line of departure, has been crossed, one feels, with the greatest intensity, that he is in the presence of the enemy.

Factors other than actual sight or sound can impinge upon the soldier's consciousness. It is said, for instance, that the presence of Frederick the Great upon the battlefield was worth two corps for the work that it did on the enemy's imagination and resolution.[19] The state of mind of the individual soldier may be affected more by the knowledge that he is facing an elite force, whether that force be the Sacred Band of Thebes or the Waffen-SS. Good troops will not be reduced to impotence by such knowledge, but they may well act with greater caution—possibly to their eventual regret.

This initial contact between the two forces does not necessarily lead to immediate combat. They may very well stand facing each other for some hours in the morning light, trying to discern each other's intentions and strength. Among many primitive groups the battle may actually end at this point, with the ineffectual exchange of spears or arrows at long distance. Honor thus satisfied, both sides will retire. Such decampments occur with fair frequency, even in civilized warfare in those cases where one side judges its position to be faulty or its members insufficient for the task at hand. The eighteenth century saw the development of a whole theory of warfare based on the techniques of gaining superiority while avoiding battle.[20] However, since this period of waiting may be marked by cannonading of the enemy, it has often in recent centuries been a period of considerable hazard to the troops, and a time when soldiers have been called upon to show a good deal of bravery. The experience of the Inneskilling Rifles at the Battle of Waterloo, losing over a third of its effectives even before it was committed to battle, is by no means singular.[21] The stoicism of men able to close ranks and maintain position after seeing their comrades massacred by a bounding cannonball seems well-nigh incredible, yet it was rather commonplace. Modern armies have shown similar stoic courage under heavy shell fire.

This waiting, whether one is exposed to enemy fire or not, raises the emotions of the armies to a high intensity so that there is very often an irresistible urge to do something to change the situation. This does not mean that the soldiers are that anxious to get at the throats of their enemies though there are many instances of such bloodthirstiness. It is often simply a desire to change conditions by moving—to get on with it, as the saying goes. The feeling is expressed that it is better to do it now rather than later, though this may not, in fact, be at all the case. It is curiously true that men who have no overweening desire to murder or to test their mettle against the foe, nevertheless feel the urge to attack, or conversely, hope that the enemy will attack.[22]

The morning has worn away, the soldiers are nervous and fretful, when finally the signal is given. Suddenly men find themselves committed irrevocably to closing with the enemy. For the attacking forces, this involves leaving a position of relative, though probably minimal, safety and advancing across an unprotected area to get at the enemy. The defenders are forced to watch what looks like an irresistible mass sweeping towards them: "Suddenly, obliquely to our right, there was a long wavy flash of bright light, then another, and another! It was sunlight shining on gun barrels and bayonets—and—there they were at last! A long brown line, with muskets at a right shoulder shift, in excellent order, right through the woods they came."[23] For either side, as the distance between them closes, the field of vision of the individual soldier is narrowed to that which is immediately before him. This is the supreme moment of warfare. The heroes, the cowards, and the ordinary men alike, are caught up in this action bringing the opposing sides together. Projectile weapons, spears, arrows, bullets, or artillery shells, are taking their toll. The ranks of both sides are torn but reform. The attack continues as the distance is narrowed to yards and then the final few feet disappear and the armies are, as they say, locked in battle.

In reality this often fails to occur. In recent wars the soldier who has hardly seen his enemy since the battle began may find himself pinned down by fire, his unit taking such losses that it can no longer advance. In the wars of the seventeenth through the nineteenth centuries, if the final volleys failed to stop the attacker or dislodge the defender, there might follow some minutes of hand-to-hand combat before one side or the other fell back. At Gettysburg, only a few of the men involved in Pickett's charge actually reached the Union line. Given the close-packed formations of those years, only a few men could be engaged in this close fighting at any one time, and the success or the failure of the few could determine the course of the struggle. As John Keegan has pointed out, these dense formations tended to push men forward so that those in front had little choice but to fight.[24] This was probably even more true in the wars of the ancient world, where projectile weapons were relatively ineffective and the sword was the deciding factor. In primitive wars the contact may have been very brief indeed, honor often being gained by touching the enemy or demonstrating boldly in front of one's own line.

What is happening, in fact, is that two highly disciplined units are breaking down into simple, though murderous, crowds. Under such circumstances control is difficult if not impossible, and the probability of panic is high. When the emotions are so strained, the cry "all is lost" can have massive effect, turning the bravest men into a fleeing herd. Thus, these melees, which are a form of crowd behavior, cannot last for long. The units break off the fight and fall back a few feet to regroup; or, one side may retreat. This is the most difficult of all maneuvers on the battlefield, for a disordered retreat invites the other side to press its advantage. Panicked men, who have thrown away their weapons, are easy victims for a pursuing foe, and it is at this point that so many of the men who died in ancient combat were slain.[25]

Until recent years the battle standard played an important part in war. Capturing standards has been a prized symbol of victory, and men have often performed heroic feats to save the standards. This act did serve the practical purpose in that they provided a rallying point for men in the confusion of battle. As long as the standard was aloft, it gave the soldier a sense of location. Even when he became separated from the men he knew, the sight of the standard signalled that he was not lost, and perhaps also reminded him that he had a duty to perform. Aside from its practical use, the standard oftentimes assumed the character of a sacred object. Men risked their lives to protect it, to pick it up when it had fallen, and often enough to fall themselves in the endeavor. For Americans, one of the most moving moments of World War II was the raising of the flag on Mount Suribachi; the Emperor Augustus mourned the loss of his eagles to the Germans; and even today, in that room of Les Invalides where the flags of Napoleon's regiments are hung, one is requested to remove one's hat.

It is awesome to realize that a set of rituals can carry men forward to this point, where they are willing to stand face-to-face before men they do not know with the intention of killing them. It is true that at that moment, they feel they have no choice. It is also true that the face and the form of the enemy, like their own, has assumed an almost inhuman quality through distortion by hatred and fear, and through the transformation achieved by the wearing of the uniform, the war paint, or the armor. But they are also in this state because they have been carefully prepared and guided in a ritual which allows them to expect nothing else. Some may ground arms and flee, others may fight with a berserk passion which ultimately consumes them. The majority simply fight and fall or survive.

For men in recent wars this type of combat is relatively rare. Modern rifles and machine guns make it difficult to achieve hand-to-hand situations. The fighting may be ferocious and at close quarters, but the opponent will still be out of reach. Despite this, at least through the end of the Second World War, much emphasis was placed on the use of the bayonet. Millions of men were taught the proper method of jabbing these instruments into the body of the enemy while warding off his thrusts. This was usually accompanied by bloodcurdling pieces of advice. Yet, bayonet instructors to the contrary, the weapon was seldom used and its efficacy has been seriously challenged for at least a century and a half.[26]

Many times during the course of the day, victory and defeat will be recorded. The victories of individuals over other individuals, the victory of one small unit, the defeat of another. Both sides will accumulate a number of these small successes and failures, which in their sum will spell victory for the one and defeat for the other. An army can fight rather successfully through most of the day, as the Austrians did at Sadowa, only to have the decision turn against them as evening and the Crown Prince approached. At Waterloo, the British hung on grimly through the day, warding off one blow after the other, finally blunting the advance of the Imperial Guard as Bluecher's Prussians arrived on the field to give victory to the Allies. At Cannae the Roman successes in the center turned to disaster when they found themselves trapped between the great wings of the Carthaginian army. Or victory may arrive, as it does in some primitive societies, with the killing of one man.

In whatever form it comes, victory has been traditionally marked by the ability of one of the opposed groups to take and hold possession of the field while the other is forced to retire. The victory need not be overwhelming; indeed, it may very often be indecisive or even, in some instances, it can leave the victor in worse position than before the commencement of the battle. The concept of the battlefield is in itself interesting, since it is not a clearly defined area. It is an imaginary arena in which the bounds are seen to be the edges of the territory occupied by the two armies during the course of the fight. Yet, in that time it will assume the character of a sacred spot and, for a variety of reasons, may be regarded as such for some generations to come. We have already noted that some primitive groups set aside a particular piece of ground for fighting purposes. In other cases the strategic location will dictate that fighting will occur here at frequent intervals. In still other cases the land will be marked off, and memorials to the action of the various participants will be erected. Such is the case at Gettysburg, where recently much concern has been shown about the encroachment of commercial establishments on the field, an invasion which is considered as the profaning of sacred ground. Even the relatively minor Battle of Tippecanoe is commemorated by the fencing off of the battlefield with little stone tablets to show where each United States soldier fell—yet, it is worth noting that no tablets mark the Indian slain. All this points to the fact that society recognizes something special about these locations and tends to protect them from other use.

The soldiers themselves regard the battlefield as limited, a tangible area for which they can fight and of which they can take possession. Soldiers will treat some geographical feature as the limit which, when reached, marks the end of the battle. The importance of this fact is that, once that goal has been reached, it is only with the greatest difficulty that the troops can be made to move further. Again and again the chances of a truly decisive victory have been lost because the army has simply stopped in its tracks and turned to other activities, such as looting. Indeed, this tendency has offered defeated forces the opportunity to rally and counterattack. In the Battle of Vitoria, Wellington lost the chance to inflict a massive defeat on the French when his army fell to looting and drinking up the abandoned wine. It was on this occasion that the Iron Duke described his men as "the scum of the earth."

There have been various explanations for this failure to carry out the pursuit. Often it is argued that the troops are exhausted, and that darkness would make control of the army difficult. While this is true, it should be noted that a defeated army is no less exhausted and most probably in greater disorder, but this does not hinder its flight. When pursuit is carried through, it can result in terrible casualties for the defeated because they no longer have the cohesion to protect themselves properly. This brings us back to the question of why the victorious army ceases to fight. Leaving aside the arguments from exhaustion and darkness which affect both sides, it should be noted that the individual soldier has a different perception of the battle and its purposes than does the commander or the military historian. For the man in the ranks, the arrival at the perceived limit of the battlefield means that the time has come to reap the profits from the victory. This can take a number of forms, ranging from resting and eating and rounding up prisoners, to looting the bodies of the enemy dead. Under these circumstances the carefully cultivated discipline of the army tends to break down into a loose form of crowd behavior.

This last stage of the battle ritual is much concerned with the dead and death. The enemy slain are stripped of their armor, their weapons of war, and their insignia. At various times in history, they have also been beheaded, scalped, or had their teeth, ears, hands, or penises removed. Prisoners have been slain, held for ransom, reduced to slavery, or eaten. Where the women of the enemy have fallen to the victors, rape, often followed by murder, has resulted. Actions that would never be countenanced in ordinary society are permissible at this time. Though many armies have strict regulations against looting and raping, it is probably significant that such regulation is necessary. Thus, the ritual which began with the training of men in the spirit of murder and self-sacrifice ends, or can end, in the orgiastic dishonoring of the defeated enemy. The organized form of this activity involves the setting up of trophies and the counting of the enemy slain. In classical warfare, the armor of the enemy, together with the captured weapons, was gathered and hung on a tree or post to mark the battlefield.

The casualties, particularly those of the winning side, are subject to a different set of rules than those governing the healthy members of the fighting forces. To be wounded is to be released from the demands of the martial ritual and to pass into another set of healing rites. The fierce appearance is erased by the visible signs of suffering on the faces of the wounded. Bandages and splints make it obvious that these soldier-warriors are incapable of caring for themselves. Very often, both in modern and primitive societies, they will at this point pass into the care of women. During the fighting they, if at all possible, are removed from the battlefield to some protected place. This accomplishes a number of purposes, for not only does it ensure a greater possibility of recovery, it gives assurance to the unwounded that they will be cared for should they also be injured. It also removes from the sight and hearing of the combatants this unnerving evidence of human vulnerability.[27]

Society's treatment of the wounded is to some extent contradictory. For a time they will be treated with full honors because they have given much in the service of the people. However, if their injuries are too debilitating, they eventually become a burden and are shunted off to the back wards of veterans' hospitals, or to the begging class, trading on their wounds for pity and meager charity. With the passage of years, this will become ever harder to achieve. In primitive society those former warriors who are no longer fully men may have an even more difficult time, since these groups may not have the resources necessary to support a useless member of society.

The dead present a different problem. Having sacrificed everything, they are in a position to make extreme demands upon the living. This may come in the form of a call for vengeance, which forms the basis for the ancient blood feud, a demand that enemies be slain so the dead can rest in peace. It may also come in the form of a vow that this shall never happen again. Sometimes the response to the call of the dead is puzzling. In World War I the reactions of the peoples of Europe to the vast losses at Verdun and Somme was the idea that only a final victory could make these deaths worthwhile, and so the struggle continued for another two years.

The dead can strengthen the cause of the living by giving example of the bravery needed on the battlefield, and all the dead are remembered as brave. Furthermore, they will always remain young. Unlike the veterans, both whole and wounded, they will have no opportunity to show the weaknesses of character and all the other undesirable traits of adult human beings. They will always remain as they were at that moment, when they were so violently wrenched out of this life. Indeed, death on the battlefield is the fountain of youth. They shall remain forever young and ready for battle. When next the society decides for war, these battalions of the slain are ready to march with the living. Hallowed by yearly services, their bodies entombed in graveyards reserved for heroes, they remain both a spiritual burden and a source of strength.

Yet, there remains one final step in the ritual of battle, the celebration of the end of hostilities. In those cases, more typical of primitive societies, where the fighting takes place in one day or, at the most, a few days, this celebration would commence on the evening of victory. In modern societies this celebration may well have to be postponed for years, until the end of the struggle. Whenever it occurs it is marked by dancing, the display of of the trophies of battle, military review, and the temporary suspension of ordinary affairs. The Kurulu observe the successful end of fighting in which an enemy has been killed with a period of wild dancing (the etai), in which both the men and women participate. "The men came . . . massed at the end of the field, . . . then charged across it, spears held high against the clouds and long plumes tossing, then broke to form a roaring circle. Some women rushed from the side to mingle with the fringes of the men . . . Ay-HOO, ay-HOO the women wailed, their voices remote in the men's tumult. Just as their grief was deeper at the funerals, their joy was fiercer. . . ."[28] Such displays have their counterpart in the wild celebrations that took place in many major American cities at the end of the Second World War, or in the scenes in London at the end of the First World War. Characteristic of these celebrations is the temporary suspension of ordinary activities and ordinary modes of conduct. Business is interrupted and strangers embrace. These demonstrations mark, among other things, the rejoining of the sexes after the separation of warfare. They also express the essential closeness of the community, the consciousness of which tends to be submerged in the everyday pursuit of private affairs. Lastly, the celebration marks the release of society from the ritual of war. Mourning for the dead may continue, but it will tend to be systematized into annual observances—less and less sympathy will be extended to those who continue their mourning beyond what is considered to be a decent interval.

For the defeated such a celebration is not possible. While many may be privately happy that the killing is ended, the only possibly acceptable public expression is that of mourning for the dead and for the defeated society, mingled often with vows for vengeance. If the society has not been obliterated by the war, this spirit of vengeance often provides the seed for a new struggle. In those cases where the society has been rendered incapable of future military action through enslavement or enfeeblement, a ceremonialized mode of mourning may keep alive its sense of separate indentity. The classic example of this is the Babylonian captivity of the Jews. More recent examples may be cited in the cases of the American South after the Civil War and the Palestinian movements of our own day.

The role of women in the ritual of warfare is a subordinate but necessary one. Women play an exceedingly important part in the initial ceremonies by aiding the process of engendering a warlike spirit and urging the men to participate in the struggle. This may be accomplished in a number of ways; either by cheering on the heroes as they march away, or by shaming those who are reluctant to go. Still within living memory are the British women who distributed white feathers to the "slackers" and sang the cheery ditty, "We don't want to lose you, but we think you ought to go," to the men of the 1914 war. In more recent conflicts, knowledge of the probable costs has tended to subdue such demonstrations, but the sight of women in the uniform of one of the auxiliary services has been used to shame men into joining up as well.

Women also shoulder additional burdens in holding together the fabric of society by filling vacant spaces in the operation of the economy. "War work" has become increasingly important in the era of industrialized mass armies, but women have always had to fill this function, whether for a brief time under the conditions of primitive warfare, or during prolonged sieges. More directly, it was often the women's task to take on the caring for the sick and wounded, extracting arrows, providing bandages, and, perhaps just as important, comforting men for whom fierceness was no longer an obligation.

The most crucial aspect of women's service in war is, however, the role of victim. They are the victims in that they may lose their husbands, sons, or fathers, and will have to take on the chief burden of mourning for them or worrying for their safe return. In their own person, women are the potential and actual victims of war and, perhaps, the most important ones. In recent wars aerial bombardment has reawakened us to this situation, but historically women have been subject to the actions of victorious conquerors. They have been raped, enslaved, and murdered on countless occasions, burned in besieged cities, held for ransom, or forced to watch the slaughter of their men. All of this they must suffer without any real hope of being memorialized for their persecutions. For a society, their loss in large numbers is much more serious than the loss of young men, since only they can assure that society's future. Because this is the case, the protection of women has always been a powerful argument for men entering battle.

Since women, at least potentially, if not actually, are so gravely endangered, they are able to participate wholeheartedly in the celebrations following victory. It is not only for their returned menfolk that they celebrate but also for their own safety and that of their children. Because they have an essentially passive role to play in warfare, it is possible for women to adopt a somewhat detached view concerning the vital need to go to war. They must concern themselves with the cost of war since such glory as may be earned will not fall to them.

The ritual of battle ceremonializes a process of departure and return, in which the participants advance into the territory of the unknown for purposes of undergoing a test. They receive instructions which impart to them the skills needed in the adventure, and they have every reason to believe that it is a mission of the highest degree of seriousness. In this the ritual parallels such rites as those of initiation, and it is worth noting that a man's first battle is called his "baptism of fire." The ritual also reaffirms the cohesiveness of the society in the face of danger. The role to be played by the individual is well-established and is, in fact, the stereotype of the brave warrior, which seldom conforms completely to reality. However, it does transform reality enough to make it possible for battle to take place.

It can be seen that warfare does have its parallels with a number of other human activities. Modern professional soldiers have been fond of comparing war with a sport such as football, but there is an even more ancient and deeper connection with one of man's earliest activities, hunting. The connections with hunting are many. The weapons used in war, at least up to the modern period, were derived from the hunt. The spear, the axe, and the bow and arrow are all weapons known to ancient hunters and were undoubtedly used first for the killing of game. The tactics of the ancient hunters also bear similarity to the tactics of war. The frontal attack, in which animals were driven into some sort of a trap, made it necessary for the hunters to assemble themselves into a line which moved steadily forward so that none of the animals could escape. The surrounding of a group of animals has its parallel in the tactic of double envelopment. Interestingly, these tactics are to be seen not only in the findings connected with early humans, such as the Torralba killing ground in Spain, which dates back to the *Homo erectus* period, but also in the hunting activities of such animals as the lion and the killer whale.[29] In the modern period, as European armies began to move toward a more open formation, the light regiments raised to perform such duties were called "hunters" (Jaeger, Chasseur) and their uniforms were a distinctive hunting green.

The tactics of these once-despised units now form the basis for all modern infantry formations.[30]

Hunting for ancient man was not simply a practical affair. It was surrounded by a great deal of ceremony designed to ensure the success of the hunt. The bear ceremonies of the Siberian hunters include chanting and dancing by the entire community prior to departure. Like war, hunting was, for the most part, a male activity. The hunting party often had to march some distance from the home base in order to arrive at the hunting grounds. There, a camp was established and after further appropriate ceremonies, the hunt would begin. Its successful conclusion was marked by a triumphal return and celebration, in which the meat was divided according to certain ritually established patterns, and trophies of the hunt were displayed. The horns of the deer and the skull of the bear occupied an honored place in the lodgings of the hunters.[31]

Recently, scholars have argued that hunting was, perhaps, the most important formative activity in the development of humanity, a position that has not gone unquestioned.[32] Despite the fact that its contribution to the food supply of the community might often be considerably less than that produced by the gathering of vegetable products, hunting was the honored activity—the sacred one, as opposed to gathering. It is not surprising then that hunting was treated as man's work, while gathering was relegated to the domain of the women and children. Hunting set the style for the society and, it would seem, when it became necessary for the society to defend itself against human predators, the hunting pattern was adapted to that purpose. The parallelism argues very strongly for the antiquity of human warfare—it is even conceivable that the two practices arose simultaneously.

Despite the likeness which warfare bears to hunting, there are also obvious dissimilarities. War is directed only against one's own species; the primary purpose does not appear to be filling the larder, though cannibalism has been a reason for going to war. Nor does the hatred, which so often accompanies warfare, have any part in hunting. Rather, modern hunter-gatherers and our ancient ancestors both give evidences of love and respect for the animals which they killed, or least to the the spirit of those animals. They were necessary to life in a way that is not true of the human enemy. It should also be noted that, although the classical weapons of war appear to have been derived from the hunt, they became specialized to the particular purpose of killing other men. Finally, though hunting could be a dangerous enterprise, the idea of oneself being killed in the process did not play nearly as large a part in the thinking of the hunter as it does in the mind of the warrior.

As we have argued previously, warfare is a human institution like marriage and religion. Its central ritual is battle. But for what reasons has it been so firmly established in society? To answer "defense" is to beg the question, for if it were not similarly established in all or most societies, there would be no reason for its existence. Yet it is also obvious that in a dangerous world, only the foolish go unarmed. Therefore, while protection may be part of the answer it cannot encompass the full range of services provided by the institution of warfare. Like other great institutions, warfare, through its forms, allows humanity to focus on the central mysteries of existence. If marriage emphasizes the sexual union, the miracle of birth, and the continuity of society, and religion draws our attention to those powers beyond our control or even our comprehension, warfare's central mystery is death. Battle is the drama periodically reenacted in which the players are allowed to stand for some time in the presence of death and even be overtaken by it. It differs from the normal occasions of dying by reason of the fact that it is actively courted. During this period the individual is not only placed in danger but is accorded the privilege of being the instrument of death without losing rights in the society. For those moments the soldier-warrior is endowed with godlike or demonic powers. Because he is so immersed in the ritual, he is not simply immobilized by the terror of this power. It is both awe-inspiring and intoxicating, but it is a condition that cannot be long sustained, though from time to time it bears repetition.

To say that battle is a ritual only describes the outer form of this phenomenon. In order to come to a fuller understanding, it will be necessary to examine the inner life of the warlike society, the myths generated by war, and the psychological state of the individual warrior.

3

Orpheus in Piccadilly

EVEN THE WEATHER THAT YEAR had about it a special and memorable quality. Long sunlit days turned the Kentish fields to golden green and the skies above to a blue of startling clarity. In the late spring the hawthorn blossoms had hung like clotted cream to provide a backdrop of almost aching beauty for the grim struggle to protect Britain from invasion. Englishmen, shaken from their moral torpor by the evacuation at Dunkirk and the Fall of France, martialed their limited resources, formed Home Guards by enlisting the services of men who had fought in the other war, frustrated potential parachutists (and many a loyal Englishman) by removing roadsigns, and waited.

The indomitable Winston Churchill noted in a famous speech, "Hitler knows that he must break us in this island or lose the war," and called upon Englishmen to bear themselves so that, if the Empire should survive for a thousand years, people would still remark, "this was their finest hour."

Now all depended upon the Royal Air Force and especially its fighter pilots. Terribly outnumbered, these young men enjoyed few advantages: superior aircraft, the Hurricane and the Spitfire; superior ability, as evidenced by the latest statistics; and the unmentioned, but supremely important radar system of detection. What a sleeping Britain had failed to provide, now had to be compensated for by the courage, skill, and lives of young men from Oxford, Cambridge, the regular RAF, Londoners, men from the north of England, and pilots from the Dominions.

Two, three, even four times a day, the pilots rose to the challenge.

Weary and in thinning numbers, they forestalled all attempts to strike English vitals, and finally, when it seemed that Fighter Command must be near exhaustion, the Germans made a fatal error. Turning from the attacks on the fighter fields, attacks which were beginning to break the British ability to resist, the Luftwaffe struck at London. Though London would suffer, Britain had been saved, the RAF had not been defeated, and the city was nightly demonstrating the resources of courage and moral strength which free men and women harbor within them.

Daily in their sadly torn city, they set out to do their regular work. Nightly in the tubes and the great public shelters, they "took it," while ordinary men and women above performed the extraordinary tasks that were the lot of the wardens and the firemen. Through the winter and the spring, London endured until Hitler, frustrated in his attempt to reduce the English by aerial attack, turned his legions eastward to the assault on Russia. Britain no longer stood alone.

None of the above should be unfamiliar to the reader. It constitutes one of the dramatic turning points of the Second World War and has been retold in greater or lesser detail by hundreds of writers both during and after the end of that struggle. Though it contains errors and omissions of fact, the story is essentially a correct rendering of an historical event, one which justifiably still elicits admiration for the British. It is a story lived for Americans through the nightly broadcasts of Edward R. Morrow and other gifted reporters, so that we have little reason to doubt its authenticity. It is not that which is really at stake here. The battle was fought and it was won. What is of concern is the problem of how the battle impinged upon the popular imagination, and how it was remembered.

There is a rough distinction which historians make between history and popular history. At times it would seem that the dividing line is between those authors who are professional historians and those who are not; though, as Thucydides shows, such a division is not always feasible. When historians make the distinction, it is usually done in an invidious manner. Popular history caters to the common tastes and prejudices, is careless in its research, is filled with errors and misconceptions, and usually sells more readily than the uncontaminated product, not least of all because it is often better written.

But we are not concerned here with professional history. It serves its purpose by painstakingly pointing out the deficiencies of the popular account or by framing new and more penetrating visions of the past. Here we are concerned with a story alive in the writings of gifted men and women and in the minds of millions of contemporaries to whom the mention of "Spitfire," "Me-109," or "Blitz" is enough to conjure up a vision of the entire progress of the battle. What we would like to know is why popular history, with all of its errors, is so compelling and tenacious.

Yet, it is necessary to point out some of the deficiencies in the popular account. Certainly one of the fixed points of the story is the evacuation of the BEF from Dunkirk. The contribution of the small civilian craft and the Dover and Brighton steamers is an integral part of the story, while the contribution of the Navy is noted almost only in passing. Possibly this is a bit strong but when it is remembered that perhaps nine-tenths of the evacuees were rescued by the Navy, one is at least entitled to wonder at the imbalance of the popular account. And what of all of the other evacuations? Nearly as many men returned from fifty other ports as were rescued from Dunkirk. But Dunkirk was the big one. Namsos and the other ports of Norway were remembered with shame; Dunkirk was almost a victory; Dakar, later in the year, has been virtually forgotten.[1]

It seems also to be an article of faith that the Hurricane, and especially the Spitfire, were superior to their German counterpart, the Me-109. Further, it is assumed that the Hurricane and the Spitfire were available in about equal numbers. Actually, none of these assumptions seem to have been correct. In speed, both British aircraft were slower than the Messerschmitt, though both were slightly more maneuverable. Both the Hurricane and the Spitfire carried more guns than the German airplane, and this may have been decisive, though an even greater problem for the German fighters was their lack of range, which allowed them only ten minutes of fighting time over England. About three-quarters of the British force consisted of Hurricanes. The quality of the pilots of both air forces was very good, but the German pilots did have more experience.[2]

One of the curious and persistent myths concerning the Battle of Britain is that the Londoners generally sought refuge, either in the Tubes of the Underground system or in the public shelters. Actually, most Londoners slept in their own beds while only about 4 percent ever slept in the Tubes. Yet, it is the picture of Londoners asleep in the subway stations that remains one of the most vivid memories of the Blitz.[3] This brings up an interesting point. Official history dates the Battle of Britain from July 8, 1940 to October 31, 1940. Popular history includes in its account the disasters of spring, 1940, and the long agony of London through the winter and spring of 1941. Here one feels that the popular account is correct. The retreat, the air battle, and the bombardment, are essentially linked together. It would be difficult to separate artificially all of those events that constitute the time "when Britain stood alone."

One could simply shrug this off as the sort of thing which happens in popular history, with its often nonanalytic ways, were it not for the persistency of some of the errors, and the insistence, despite official disapproval, that the battle did not end on October 31, 1940. One feels that the cup of tea offered to the fireman by some householder was as much a part of the story as Red Leader's three second burst. The feeling is correct, but justifying it requires a further definition of the role of popular history. Traditionally, history not only recorded and analyzed events, but also sang of them. Yet humans need song and celebration. They need meaning that strikes home. With unabashed frankness history has done this in the past—lying about ancestry, using all of the terms of which historians are afraid: "never before . . . finest . . . beyond compare"; singing of some human group's accomplishment for their own delectation and for the inspiration of future generations.

Today the dual roles of history, the bardic and the analytic, have been parcelled out in such a manner that, all too often, the one fails to inform the other. When we speak of bardic history, we are today speaking of popular history to a large extent. It behooves us to ask whether it is simply mistaken history with a flair for the dramatic, or whether the mistakes themselves point toward a structure and a purpose different from, but no less important than, the structure of formal history.

We can return, then, to the mistakes and omissions of popular history. Why, for instance, should the escape through Saint Malo be so largely forgotten? Or Saint Nazaire, or Bordeaux? The answer, though not simple as it sounds, is that that epic stories can carry only so much freight. The essential escape was that of Dunkirk—those which came after, though also dangerous, were not only less miraculous, but went unaided by civilian help. In this summer of 1940, the participation of the whole population, if only as onlookers, was desperately needed.

The evacuations which went before, those from Norway, were shameful—not that the men were less brave, nor the situation less difficult—but rather because at the time, expectations for a successful fight were still high. Later, the evacuation from Norway tended to fit into that period of the war when false illusions still persisted. The evacuation from Narvik and the Dakar failure are particularly interesting. Though the Narvik operation was quite successful, it was abandoned because of its isolated character. The withdrawal, moreover, occurred at the time of the much greater disaster of the fall of France. The Germans, by contrast, recognizing the the difficult nature of this far northern campaign, struck a special Narvik medal. Dakar, coming in September, was unwelcome, unstrategic, and unremembered.

It would seem entirely understandable that a nation would claim superiority for its own machinery. Somewhat less understandable is the fact that years later the superiority would still be maintained. As a matter of fact, one would suppose that the glory of victory would be the greater, if it were assumed that the machines were either equal to, or actually inferior to, the German models. As will be seen later, this claim for mechanical superiority was extremely important to Britain and has been maintained despite certain advantages accruing to its relinquishment.

Probably least understandable of all the misconceptions concerning the Battle of Britain is that dealing with the use of the subway stations. Since at least 1943, it has been known that the vast majority of Londoners did not use the Tubes or any other public shelters, preferring to hide in their own backyard "Andersons," or to remain in their beds.[4] Yet, through the years, possibly no picture of the period has been more widely reproduced that that of Londoners sleeping on subway platforms. A fuller discussion of this problem will be taken up later, but it should be noted here that such a persistent discrepancy between the norm of behavior and that which has been accepted as the general behavior demands an explanation. This cannot be given by supposing that simple mistakes account for the difference.

Again and again one encounters this curious refusal of popular history to take cognizance of established facts. Such a case can be explained by sheer ignorance, yet even among popular authors who are well aware of the facts, the old story holds its power. If then, the mistakes are relatively impregnable against historical demonstration to the contrary, it must be suspected that the mistakes are not simply haphazard ones but that, indeed, they fit into a general pattern of misinterpretation. Or, seen from another point of view, they are integral parts of a pattern of interpretation which has purposes different from professional historical accounts.

One of the clues to this different interpretation is contained in the argument that runs like the proverbial red thread through all the popular accounts of the period: that the British people were morally rejuvenated by the experience of defeat in the spring and the successful resistance of the fall and winter. The defeats made them aware of the depth of their failure, the victories encouraged them to believe that Hitler could be successfully resisted and overcome. More than this, it was possible to create a better England.

There is nothing in the historical record which compels one to believe that England was morally degenerate or obtuse in the period before the beginning of the Norwegian Campaign. One might add that the production program, which provided the margin of victory in the fall, the program for the recruitment and training of pilots, and the program of civil defense, had all been laid out, and were in efficient operation before the crisis broke.[5] One can argue that the will was not there because the British were driven out of Norway and the Continent. But one could argue more cogently that they were outmaneuvered and defeated, an event which can plague even a highly aroused people. In other words, it would be possible to present the events of the spring in terms of military defeat no better and no worse than major defeats of other times and places. Similarly, the victory in the fall could have been viewed simply as a partial redressment of the losses of the spring.

Instead, the military situation is pictured as apocalyptic—a situation demanding not only a reversal of arms, but a reversal of moral stance as well. It is this reversal of moral stance which is the true subject of the popular history of the Battle of Britain. But once the subject is shifted from the plane of historical fact to that of moral transformation, a whole series of changes takes place. Not the least of these is that history ceases to be a passive recounting of the events which have taken place and becomes an active participant in the events which are taking place.

When popular history sings of events and makes them great, it transcends the realm of record and enters that of myth. It is myth with which we are dealing here—sun gods, Jonah and the whale, and all the rest, whether we like it or not. Being modern, of course places a great burden upon us and upon history. We cannot accept mother goddesses, magicians, and incantations, so history must disguise these ancient potions.

This, then, is the secret of popular history. The mistakes are not mistakes but structural elements. If the British forgot the other evacuations, it was because they were subsumed in the one great evacuation from Dunkirk—the successful passage over the waters. The superiority of the weapons assumed magical proportions, while the sleepers on the subway platform were at one with other magical sleepers of mythology. All these things—simplification, magical potency, and mythic adventure—were shared by the people of Britain in 1940. Theirs was an ancient adventure and, dimly aware, both they and we have seized upon those historical portions of the period which best tell its tale.

Thus, popular history is myth. Its purpose is not the elucidation of the factual situation but the demonstration of humanity's emotional and spiritual relation to the universe in terms of a special situation. In its greatest manifestations, the ancient myths are only thinly disguised and the true work of popular history is revealed—to rekindle the ancient relationship of humans to their surroundings. One could ask for worse service from a recounting of the past.

Viewed as a species of myth, the popular history of the Battle of Britain is a heroic saga with a definite theme of death and resurrection. It is very British in the offhand way in which many of the difficulties are mentioned, but no one can doubt that this is a tale of heroism. Nor is it simply a story of heroic adventure in the most obvious sense of being an account of English bravery. Rather, it contains many, if not all, of the elements which one associates with the heroic tales of classical mythology or the myths of other early peoples. Of course these elements are disguised to some extent in language familiar to our age, but never are they really absent.

It must be noted that the myth is complicated by the fact that there are numbers of heroes and that, depending upon the point of view, one person or group may play either a chief or subsidiary role. Thus, Winston Churchill appears both as the embodiment of England defiant (right down to the bulldog look) and as the ancient seer, warning and guiding the prospective heroes. The RAF pilot and his many individual manifestations is either the supreme hero or a gnat harrying the antagonist, while the real hero (from another point of view), the warden or the fireman, prepares for action. Certain divisions can be made: the RAF pilot rules the day, while the wardens and firemen reign during the hours of darkness. Predictably, the heroines appear at night—Dianas in helmet with a blue flashlight. In the day feminine heroes descend underground, Proserpines manning switchboards or moving squadron markers in the Operations Room at Bentley Priory and elsewhere.[6]

There is nothing really unusual about this state of affairs. The shapeshifter is well known in mythology. Neville Chamberlain is magically transformed into Winston Churchill, and his flaccid umbrella becomes a defiant cigar. The long-haired boy of Oxford, concerned only with a rowing blue, becomes the deadly pilot of a Spitfire. The Cockney, depressed but never crushed by industrial civilization, shakes a fist at the sky, and in the wonderful form of a fishwife, takes a charge of a large and panicked public shelter. Nor is the enemy immune to change. The yellow-nose fighter transforms itself into the clown-like barrage balloon figure of Hermann Göring, or the cruel dwarf, the mustached Moloch, and the angel of death.[7]

Though a multiplicity of heroes and heroines exist, and although their adventures follow different tracks and occur at different times, one can still say that the tracks parallel one another and that, in a rough way, a heroic monomyth can be discerned. The story begins with the characteristic darkening of the fortunes of the house of England and calls for the journey of the hero (the English people) into an unknown land. It is ironic that this unknown land is England, but it has become a place magically transformed by the agency of war. Thus, battles take place over Seven Oaks, Maidstone, and the Medway towns—but four miles in the air. Or they occur on London docks with marvelous pepper, sugar, and rum fires raging out of control. It is the City boardrooms ablaze, or sinister mines under Saint Paul's, a bomb exploding waist high in the Cafe de Paris or another laying waste Chelsea Old Church, which is the realm of this adventure.

The hero is encouraged in his quest by the warnings and advice given at the beginning of the adventure by figures of great authority, such as Winston Churchill, RAF instructors, or the training officers of the London Fire Brigade. He is presented with magical weapons like the Spitfire, or a bucket of sand, which guarantee his ability to face the dragons and other unfriendly inhabitants of this magic realm. Like Excalibur and other magic swords, great powers were ascribed to the Spitfire and Hurricane fighters. Even the enemy was reputed to long for these weapons.[8]

In addition to the weapons given him, the hero is also taught certain incantations and magic words, mysterious, yet powerful, which give him protection. "Beware the Hun in the sun," "Keep your sand bucket full," "H.E.," "UXB," "Branch," "angels at 4000," "Blue Leader to Choirmaster," and hundreds of other terms which recur in the popular accounts of the period. They were in common usage among the pilots, wardens, and firemen, and they undoubtedly gave the user some sense of control over very dangerous situations. It may be small comfort to correctly name the airplane which is dropping bombs on your city, but it does give the observer a sense of being able to do something about the problem.

Closely connected with the subject of magical weapons and incantations is the period of instruction which the hero experiences. The pilots, wardens, and firemen, all feel compelled to describe in some detail their training in their various specialties. The instructors themselves are either fatherly or motherly, gentle or fierce, but they are seldom foolish.

Thus armed and instructed the hero plunges into the adventure. For the Battle of Britain this may be said to have begun with the perilous journey over the waters from Dunkirk with the Navy and, particularly, the small-boat men playing the part of Charon. Lest it sound farfetched to suppose that this represents a journey to Hades, it might be well to remember that one of the most characteristic scenes from the Blitz is that of people sleeping on the Underground platforms. Likewise, Richard Morrison, an auxiliary fireman, describes his trip to one of the big fires as "going to a ball in hell."[9] Essentially, the hero withdraws from the world of everyday affairs into the world of fantastic adventure, or to the underworld of the dead, or to the inner realm. The journey has been different for such disparate heroes as Galahad, Gilgamesh, or Ghautama the Buddha, yet in each case a withdrawal from the mundane world is an essential feature of the adventure. In the summer and fall of 1940, English men and women rose in the air, burrowed under wrecked houses for the dead and the entombed, were swallowed nightly by the London Transport Authority whale, or searched within themselves for hidden resources of courage and knowledge which could create a better world.

Specifically, the creation of this better world called for the death of the old and decadent world in order that a new and healthier one could be brought into existence. It meant that the world of privilege represented by Colonel Blimp and the spoiled sons of the rich was doomed. Time and again this theme appears in the writings of the period. The penalty for failure was to suffer the fate of France. The Fall of France (often capitalized) stood as a dire warning to the British of what could happen if they did not transform themselves. In the underworld, the two sides of France, the rotting corpse represented by Pétain and Laval, and the hopeful, spirited side represented by Charles de Gaulle, parallel the often repeated theme of the encounter with the dead brother or sister. France is Enkidu, Eurydice, or the slain Achilles. England is admonished to avoid the frivolities of France in order that the adventure can be carried through successfully and the triumphant return to the world be made. Freedom (often portrayed as the damsel in distress) is to be rescued from the fire-breathing dragon.[10] In the process of achieving this end, the English themselves die and are resurrected, or sleep the magic sleep of the descent into the unconscious. The sleepers in the subway, the pilot falling in flames, or the persons buried under the rubble of their own homes are all examples of this necessary action. Especially poignant were bodies of the young, the rich, and the beautiful carried from the explosion in the Cafe de Paris. The blasting of this night club was symbolic of an end to frivolity and the beginning of the life of stern purpose.

One of the fears of the authorities at this time was that a large number of people would develop a "deep shelter" mentality and would refuse to come out of the shelters after the raids. In fact, this proved to be a very minor problem, but it indicates a fear that the ritual death might not lead to a being "born again."[11]

With return to the world and the announcement of the message, the heroic adventure would be completed. Although this return was not completed during the period under consideration, it was possible by the summer of 1941 to think more readily about a successful end to the struggle. A victory had been won, Britain had not been defeated, and in this sense she did return with the message of hope.

The hero of the Battle of Britain is, in Joseph Campbell's phrase, a hero with a thousand faces. He is one and many, male and female, of high and low rank. Though there does exist an essential unity to the heroic figure, it is also true that separate heroic figures can be discerned. Individual heroes, such as Douglas Bader or Sailor Malan, were numerous, though not all were named. Beyond this there existed the heroic types previously mentioned: the warden, the pilot, the fireman, and the bomb disposal technician, among others. There is a hierarchical relationship between some of these heroic types, so that those of the higher level appear godlike to those below. A corollary to this is that the "gods" manifest themselves only intermittently.

A good example of this godfigure is Winston Churchill. From one point of view, he symbolized Britain's heroic will to survive. Yet, surprisingly, in the popular history of the period he seldom appears. He is most often remembered for the great speeches of May and June, after which he is only infrequently mentioned by those who write their memoirs. One could scarcely say that this was because he weakened, but rather because his august role seldom impinged upon the activities of the pilots, wardens, and others. It was the squadron leader or the sector chief who had immediate impact. For the people in the shelters, the warden assumed this deific role. Wardens checked the shelters but did not stay in them. In one recorded case, a warden who stayed in the shelter to comfort his wife was forced to transfer to another district.

To those on the ground, the fighter pilots were demigods, young Apollos of the daylight hours who drove their fierce cars across the sky and who, often enough, fell to a fiery death. One could watch this progress with detached fascination; yet, like those of the gods of the Iliad, the actions of these men directly affected the lives of those below. A missed assignment might allow bombs to fall on London, though those under the bombs would not necessarily understand the relationship. Sometimes they did, however, as was the case of those villagers who complained about the bombers being shot down on their particular piece of earth. Most often, however, the adventure for the hero on the ground began with the bomb's explosion.[12]

For the pilots, 11th Fighter Group Command at Uxbridge constituted an Olympus from which commands of life and death emanated. The dissonance between the scene at Uxbridge and the squadron aerodromes is worthy of Sumerian or Greek archetypes.

The Group Operations Room was like a small theater. . . . Below us was the large scale map table, around which perhaps twenty highly trained young men and women, with their telephone assistants were assembled. Opposite to us

. . . was a gigantic blackboard divided into six columns with electric bulbs, for the six fighter stations. . . . On the floor below us the movement of all the waves of attack was marked by pushing discs forward from minute to minute along different lines of approach, while on the blackboard facing us the rising lights showed our fighter squadrons getting into the air, till there were only four or five left at "Readiness."[13]

Note the curious, gamelike quality of the Uxbridge command post. Markers appear on the boards as the reports from the spotter stations come in. The commander, Air Vice Marshall Park, and his staff respond with the appropriate moves, and 11th Fighter Group markers are placed on the board. A light blinks off, and they study tensely the remaining lighted bulbs. Switchboard operators, like the Moirai of modern war, relay the command. Certainly the system was a perfectly logical method of handling the complicated command problems of aerial combat, but it also assumed a reality of its own—a tension as involved with the markers on the board as with the planes in the sky which, after all, were now beyond control.

The quality of play can be observed at all levels, though these are games of the greatest deadliness. The pilots follow certain rituals in their contest with the enemy:

By this time I was well out to sea and alarmed to find that I was now the hunted—by six 109s in line astern behind me, queuing up for a chance to shoot. . . . I turned for "home" coastline . . . hoping to find a cloud or two on the way. The Messerschmitts decided to accompany me and took turns having a go, with me evading violently and praying as I have never done before.

One by one they departed as their fuel ran low and I was left with the leader, a most persistent fellow, who finally hit me with cannon and machine gun fire. [I had] ignored one of the principal rules of air combat: don't follow the enemy back home.[14]

The game form of the duel between roughly equal opponents is followed here with the hero possessing the magic sword Spitfire or Hurricane. The contest does not always favor the hero, but this fact only serves to emphasize the danger and magnify the heroism, for even magic swords are not invincible.

On the ground the element of personal battle is subordinated to that of team play. In most accounts the playing board is London, divided into squares known as West Ham, Chelsea, Barking, or The City. A zone defense was employed by wardens, while the firemen moved more or less freely about the city as needs directed. Often enough, conflicts between the players developed. John Strachey reports the case of two wardens arguing over the right to report an unexploded bomb on the border between two sectors.[15] Newspapers took up the gaming spirit, reporting the talleys of enemy aircraft destroyed like sports scores. Someone remarked that this was "the cup finals and we have the home field."

Rivalry between groups could be found among firemen—where the London Fire Brigade showed disdain for the Auxiliary amateurs—or in the aloofness which the specialized rescue squads showed for the regular wardens. Men and women apart were the bomb disposal squads. Engaged in a personal contest against the most impersonal of opponents, these people enjoyed a special place in the ranks of British heroes.[16]

Not to be forgotten in the list of games played by the British during this period was that of sheltering. The game began with the selection of a place which "seemed safe," though often this was simple illusion. Railroad bridges, though virtual death traps, were especially favored by some members of the population. Others used subway stations which might be nearly as dangerous. For many it was the sense of security rather than actual security which ruled their decision. Some found it in the great public shelters, more in backyard Andersons, and most in their own beds.

For those who went to the public shelters, position was everything. Wives or children queued up during the daylight hours to ensure a favorite place when the shelter doors opened. Claims were quickly established and, apparently, enforced. A sort of nightly underground community came into existence, established its own rules, included and excluded, developed traditions, even published a newspaper, and created the unforgettable image of London under siege.

One type of hero, the scientist, remains to be mentioned. Like Daedalus or Wayland the Smith, or Haephaestus, the scientist was isolated and largely unknown. Sir Henry Tizard's and Robert Watson-Watt's contribution to victory through the development of the radar station has since been widely applauded. At the time, official secrecy cloaked their accomplishment, like the rock into which the dwarf retreats after giving up the saphire predicting victory. On the other hand, the achievements of Lord Beaverbrook in the field of aircraft production were widely acclaimed, even to the point of referring to him as a "magician."[17]

It has already been noted that terminology was used for the practical purpose of describing what was happening, but also for the social purpose of establishing an "in-group," who spoke the same language, and for the magical purpose of controlling dangerous objects. It must be recognized that all three functions could proceed simultaneously, so that a warden reporting a bomb falling in the near distance could not only relay the necessary information to the command post, but at the same time could impart to the observer that he understood the process (where the observer did not), and by understanding, controlled it. This interrelated process is brought out rather well in one of Edward R. Murrow's broadcasts describing a scene at one of the London Fire Watch posts:

A stick of incendiaries bounced off rooftops about three miles away. The observer took a sight on the point where the first one fell. . . . Then he picked up the phone and shouted in the gale that was blowing up there, "stick of incendiaries—about 190 and 220—about three miles away." Five minutes later a German bomber came boring down the river. We could see his exhaust trail like a pale ribbon stretched straight across the sky. Half a mile down stream there were two eruptions and then a third, close together. The observer . . . reached for his night glasses and said, "two high explosives and an oil bomb" and named the street where they had fallen.[18]

Though Murrow lacked the expertise to participate in the full mysteries of the fire watch, he did not fail to establish his own membership in an in-group with the well-known signature, "this is London." Murrow's signature was important precisely because it was superfluous. He would have sounded somewhat ridiculous saying, "this is Brighton," but to mention London established his position in the heart of events that year.

The vast amount of jargon was often the only shield and armor possessed by brave men and women. For the fireman to be able to say he was doing "series pumping" or "collector pumping" tended to shield him against the the intensity of the fire or the very real possibility of a building collapse.[19] The terms, the nicknames, were all part of the ritual: "Sheep yelled "Talleyho" and dropped down . . . in the direction of the approaching planes. . . . "O.K. Line Astern . . . Echelon starboard" came Uncle George's voice. . . . I picked out one machine and switched my gun button to "fire." At 200 I opened up in a long four second burst and saw the tracers going into his nose."[20] We participate in this ritual to the extent that we pretend to understand the real meaning of that description. Thus, jargon not only excludes and controls but also permits participation, though often the person presumptuous enough to try to be included uninvited in the inner circle would be rudely thrust aside. Such was the case of one poor cockney (usually a treasured species) who loosely analyzed the problem as one of "them 'igh explosives," only to be contemptuously shut off. Apparently this was often the fate of the "bomb-bore."

Rituals and amulets played their part in the defense of Britain. Early in the summer, the Home Guards had removed all the signs from the highways and had placed defense posts and roadblocks at all conceivable points of peril. At the same time, church bells were silenced to be rung only in case of invasion, so that a sort of Good Friday atmosphere descended upon the land. Earlier, gas masks had been issued and were carried more or less religiously by the people of the larger cities. Although poison gas was never used in the attacks, Englishmen took solace in possessing some weapons against enemy bombardment.

Probably no custom was more rigorously enforced than the blackout of major cities. Stiff fines were levied for the most trivial violations. Constantine Fitzgibbons has suggested that much of this may well have been unnecessary, noting that German pilots stated that they had no trouble finding London, especially on moonlit nights when the streets were wet with rain. The British spoke of the "bombers' moon" and, with good reason, hated it. But even on darker nights, once the first fires had been lit, the bombers had an unexcelled beacon. Since London was so large and so well marked by the winding course of the Thames, it may well have been that the blackout was superfluous. For other, lesser, cities however, it may have been an excellent protective device.[21]

Whatever the merits of the argument against the blackout, it is true that Londoners observed it with an intensity verging on superstition. Certain groups, such as the rescue workers, seem to have been particularly disturbed by any show of light. This concern to make the darkness darker touches those deep levels of the human mind, where the demand for the extinction of light parallels a desire for a kind of personal extinction, or that the old fires of peaceful and civilized society were cloaked so that the fierce fires of war could burn more brightly.

Of the thousands of photographs taken of the Battle of Britain, some few have gained a sort of immortality. In some cases these have been the result of the enterprise and artistry of the individual photographer, but more often they tend to be variations on a few subjects. The most often reprinted photographs are those showing persons asleep on the subway platforms, Saint Paul's in flames, a warden on watch, firemen silhouetted against the flames, and the daylight scenes of destruction. The hazy wing camera photographs of enemy airplanes could be added to this list but, oddly enough, photographs of the RAF from the period are generally undramatic.

Each of the photographs mentioned has been done in a number of variations but the variations are surprisingly few. For instance, no really successful photograph of the subway scene was ever taken from the trackside looking toward the entrance. The different photographs also possess certain common features. Fire is either at the center of attention (firefighters, stricken enemy aircraft, the view from inside Saint Paul's), or it forms a halo (Saint Paul's, the warden). It is, of course, absent from the subway pictures and the daylight scenes of ruined buildings. Human interest is generally absent. There are no human beings in the Saint Paul pictures, the people in the subway are simply indistinct bundles asleep on the ramp. The faces of the firemen are almost never seen, nor does one see the face of the pilot of the burning plane. Wardens may appear as individuals, but not necessarily. The daylight scenes of the ruins may or may not feature individually distinguishable persons. One might make the assumption from this that the popularity of the photographs indicates that humans generally are secret firebugs with a taste for dehumanized chaos. This view, while perhaps attractive to a certain type of intellectual pessimism, has little to do with the subject matter of the photographs.

The pictures of the Londoners sleeping in the Underground stations have a number of important features. They record an aspect of the London Blitz in an unforgettable and even misleading fashion. On a more general level, they depict a modern version of the sleepers in the castle or Jonah in the whale. The act of being swallowed is important in heroic ventures as diverse as those of Hercules and Little Red Riding Hood. In an Eskimo version of the theme, Raven, swallowed by a cow whale, inadvertently breaks an artery and is enabled to escape.[22]

The sleepers themselves are fascinating, since it often is an unusual and even frightening thing to see large numbers of persons asleep. As in the tale of Briar Rose or of Snow White, it is necessary to perform

Underground station. *Courtesy The Trustees of the Imperial War Museum, London*

some heroic or magic deed in order to awaken them. Note that the sleepers are themselves adventurers, taking the measure of the depths, while at the same time they are the object of heroic rescue.

Yet another aspect of the picture is its structure. Since these pictures were always taken looking along the track, the hole of the tunnel occupies a position near the center of the photograph. Emanating from the center are four strong lines composed of the London Transport Authority tile decorations and the tracks themselves. Lastly, the frame of the picture must be taken into consideration. Hence a drawing of the structural elements would look like this:

There is a striking resemblance between this form and the mandalas which C. G. Jung and others have collected, and which are widely used for contemplative purposes in Eastern religions. Not the least peculiar feature of this is the linkage in mandalas between the central circle and the Uruboros, the world snake chasing its own tail, which, in a sense, is what subway trains are doing.

Obviously, one cannot ascribe a conscious intent to create a mandala to the various photographers. Yet, one can reasonably speculate that these photographs appeal, not only to our conscious curiosity about World War II, but also to those deeper levels of the unconscious where the recognition of the profound is immediate and compelling.

Perhaps the most famous picture of the Blitz was taken of Saint Paul's surrounded by the flames and smoke of the burning city. It seemed for a time that the famous church itself would go, but good luck and the diligence of the Saint Paul's fire watch combined to save one of the great landmarks of the city. In the writings of the period, again and again one is made aware of the importance which the English themselves attached to the cathedral. It is always depicted as being at the center of things psychologically, if not geographically. For centuries this had been the case. In the Middle Ages, Saint Paul's was even a center for business activities, and it was from here that Winston Churchill would be buried.

Closely connected with this photograph, though not so famous, is a

St. Paul's (exterior). *Courtesy The Trustees of the Imperial War Museum, London*

St. Paul's (interior). *Courtesy The Trustees of the Imperial War Museum, London*

picture taken from a window in the dome of the church looking out at the city burning. One suspects that, because the two pictures often appear together, there exist connections between the two worthy of investigation. As has already been indicated, Saint Paul's was regarded as being at the center of things, the hub of this London universe at bay. In one sense it could be said that the dome rising above the flames was a symbol to the British of their survival, or possibly of their rebirth amid the travail of war. Were it not for the fact that the British speak constantly of a new England arising from the ashes of the old, this might seem fanciful. Yet the fact that the photograph was highly prized indicates that it had more than ordinary meaning and may well be connected with this longing for a better world.

At another level of meaning, it seems less questionable that the picture has explicit sexual connotations. Thus, it is curious that the sexual symbolism of the companion picture is feminine in contrast to the pronounced masculinity of the first photo. The contradiction is only apparent. The duality of the sexes covers a deeper perception that there is an essential unity in this opposition, and that wholeness is only achieved in this unity. In the *Symposium* Aristophanes speaks of this unity as the previous state of humanity.[23] The Yin Yang symbol of the Chinese expresses this same idea, as do the various hermaphroditic deities of the world's mythologies. Many of the creation myths involve the separation of an original bisexual being into sexually differentiated parts of the universe. The lingam is the architectural symbol of this sexual unity and marks the center of the universe, the hub of creation.[24]

Thus, the sexual symbolism of the lingam (and that of Saint Paul's viewed as a lingam), point the way to deeper levels of perception about the nature of humanity and the universe. In its myths and architecture, humanity continues to recreate and renew these perceptions. Here, in a set of photographs, the very ancient can again be seen. What preceded the first civilizations is now seen as wholly contemporary. It would be inappropriate to speak of superstition here, for what is at stake is an opening up of the mind through the use of symbol and mythology to the potentialities inherent in the human condition.

Photographs of the firefighters have a naturally dramatic quality, which made excellent subject matter for the photographers recording the battle. Perhaps that alone is sufficient reason for their universal inclusion in collections of pictures from the period. Yet, one must ask

London fire brigade. *Courtesy The Trustees of the Imperial War Museum,
London*

why all of the pictures are the same. Shot from behind, the firemen
are almost never seen as individuals, but rather as pygmies silhouetted against giant sheets of flame. The crisscrossing streams of water
from the hoses also seem to be of importance, for they are always
shown. Even the commonsense argument that one should expect firemen, flames, and water at a fire is not an entirely satisfactory explanation, for it should have been possible to take a large number of human
interest photographs. One conclusion is that the real subject matter of
these pictures is fire and water.

The ancient relationship of water and fire as life forces can be seen
in the rituals of many cultures. On Holy Saturday the fires of the
church, extinguished on Good Friday, are rekindled. The paschal candle, adorned with spices, is dipped in holy water, and the waters are
scattered in the four cardinal directions.

The fires of Saturday, September 7, 1940, on the London docks were
oddly reminiscent of these antique ceremonies:

But on the docks themselves strange things were going on as they did on
many a night thereafter. There were pepper fires loading the surrounding air

heavily with stinging particles so that when the firemen took a deep breath it felt like breathing fire itself. There were rum fires, with torrents of blazing liquid pouring from warehouse doors . . . and barrels exploding like bombs themselves. There was a paint fire, another cascade of white-hot flame, coating the pumps with varnish that could not be cleaned for weeks. A rubber fire gave forth black clouds of smoke so asphyxiating that (it) . . . was always threatening to choke the attackers.

Sugar, it seems, burns well in liquid form as it floats on the water in dockland basins. Tea makes a blaze that is sweet, sickly and very intense. . . .

The fire was so huge that we could do little more than make a feeble attempt to put it out. The whole of that warehouse was a raging inferno, against which were silhouetted groups of pygmy firemen directing their futile jets at walls of flame.[25]

The London docks burned like a paschal candle and gave birth to a new race of heroes, the auxiliary firemen. Again, it must be remarked that the regular members of the London Fire Brigade receive rather scant attention, and one suspects that, as in the case of the small boat men versus the Navy, or the warden and the policeman, it was necessary to emphasize the auxiliary over the regular in order to achieve an everyman personification. The myth of the Battle of Britain demanded universal participation, and in way after way that was achieved. Usually, when regulars appear, they act rather as distant and godlike instructors to the neophyte heroes.

The pictures of the wardens and the rescue workers stand in closer relationship to the subway pictures than to those of Saint Paul's or the firefighters. The wardens, those guardians of the night, are often seen as individuals and are little connected with the mystery of fire. The warden's task is to preserve the darkness or the moonlit realm. Women are more often seen in this type of photograph. Like Diana, these women are armed, wearing helmets and semi-military clothing. The rescue workers, on the other hand, appear most often in daylight photographs extracting living humans from the womb of tumbled masonry. Thus, in relation to the sleepers on the subways, the wardens guide them to their descent into the unconscious, and the rescue workers ensure their return. In this sense the scenes of the leveled areas, with rescue workers and mingled women and children, depict the undifferentiated chaos which gives birth to the world of multiple forms.

Taken together, all these photographs reflect aspects of the same transformation ultimately linked to the central theme of death and resurrection which forms the major axis of the entire myth. The wonder world of RAF Apollos and ARP Dianas, scientific Vulcans, the Hecates and Fates of the Underground and the Operations Room, simply serves the central mystery of adventurous descent into the unknown, the unconscious, for a fleeting encounter with the fundaments of the human universe, from which the perilous return marks the end of the adventure.

From every adventure there must be a return and possibly a ceremony marking the end of the exploit. This may come in the form of a washing of the swords or a communal dinner. In the case of the Battle of Britain, the ceremony was performed daily. At the "White Hart" near Biggin Hill, pilots of the 92nd Fighter Squadron gathered nightly to talk and sign their names on the panel reserved for them. Less formally, firemen returning from the flames or wardens ending their night's duties would be offered a cup of tea. "Tea and telling about it" is the title of a photograph in *Frontline*, an official account of the civil defense effort.[26] The cup of tea marked the ceremonial reentry of the hero into the world of everyday life and enabled him or her to recount experiences to the listeners. The encounter with the ultimate is thus transmitted through the agency of a sacred brew to the populace in general. Obviously, this was a reciprocal affair, since both the offerers and the recipients were heroes.

Yet, what can one relate that is important from an afternoon of shooting at enemy planes or an evening of dodging bombs and fighting fires? Some technical notes or advice, such as "beware the hun in the sun" or "keep your sand bucket full," but in relation to ordinary life these messages are as cryptic as those of the Zen masters and usually less applicable. The general lesson of bravery could be learned and reiterated, but courage, unsupported by other virtues, is almost worse than useless. Beyond that, a feeling that a better England must emerge was often expressed. The retelling of the story also brought out other qualities, which relate to some of the unconscious elements noted in the photographs discussed above.

In the years following 1940, numbers of persons committed to writing their impressions of the battle. Much of the early work was, naturally, aimed at influencing world opinion, but is not, for that reason, devoid of value. These records of personal experience had a propagandistic value, but they also appear to have been reasonably accurate reminiscences of a heroic period. Furthermore, the imagery employed in many instances supports the conclusion, already drawn from other sources, that the people of Britain tended to transmute their experiences into mythological terms. Much of the value of the mythologizing comes in the form of metaphors which are here accepted at face value. Thus, if a writer should choose to say that London "suffered," it can be assumed that London is being treated as a living entity. If the writer should claim, as some did, to have "died," this statement can be accepted as true in the same sense that we would accept the testimony of a Beriut shaman that he had died, been dismembered, and then recreated in the spiritual, if not the literal, sense. What is said is absolutely true and helps to merge the particular experience of the Battle of Britain with the most general levels of human experience.

The obvious fact of Britain's isolation was a natural starting point of the thinking of many writers. Such terms as "sea-girt realm" came easily to the pen and assumed a significance that it had not possessed for some years. If one were to suggest that Great Britain was in this period a magic circle surrounded by the world ocean, with the Temenos of London surrounding the the hub of the universe marked by Saint Paul's and the entrance to the underground station, that suggestion would quite well describe the mental picture of the writers of the period. That it also describes Valhalla, Jerusalem, and other sacred locales only serves to show how readily ephemeral fact can be assimilated to a universal mental schema. Edward R. Murrow's "this is London" or the BBC's publication *London Calling* emphasized this centricity. Psychologically, Britain stood at the center of things, a magic realm in which the events of day-to-day life were transfigured. The very process of sleep became a heroic adventure, and a taxi ride was often a journey through Hades conducted by a lugubrious cockney Virgil.

The setting brings to mind the initiation ceremonies of a wide variety of primitive peoples. These ceremonies, intended to conduct the initiated from the profane life of ignorance into the life of sacred knowledge, often featured initiating huts or a withdrawal into the wilderness where the candidates "died" from the old life in order to be born again to a higher life. As the bull roarers often announced the coming of the gods and ushered in the ceremonies, so the sounding of the air raid sirens or the harsh clanging of the squadron phone signaled the beginning of the adventure.[27]

The period of initiation, a sacred season, featured the reversal of societal norms. In England, one of the striking features of the Blitz was the general lowering of class barriers. Persons were more willing to talk without the formality of an introduction; members of one class discovered qualities in members of other classes to which they had previously been blind. The sense of common experience drew the people of Britain together and, though this atmosphere did not last, it nevertheless had some impact upon the subsequent social life of the island. It would seem, for instance, that the determination to create a more equitable society was given further impetus by the shared experience. Members of the lower classes gained a new appreciation of their potentialities through the successful survival of the initiation process.[28]

One of the most explicit recitals of the death and resurrection theme appears in fighter pilot Richard Hillary's *Falling Through Space:* "I was falling, falling slowly through a dark pit. I was dead. My body, headless, circled in front of me. I saw it in my mind, . . . the grinning of the mouth, the skin crawling on the skull. It was death and resurrection. . . . The sickly smell of death was in my nostrils and a confused roar of sound. Then all was quiet, . . . I was back."[29]

It is worth noting that Hillary not only "dies" in this passage, but enters the dark pit and is dismembered. Dismemberment is an attribute of the shamanistic initiation in which the new being is created by reclothing the skeleton with a new and incorruptible flesh. This literally happened to Hillary, since the burns which he received when his plane was shot down made necessary extensive plastic surgery on both his hands and his face. Most important, however, is the fact that Hillary died from the old life in order to be born again to the new and higher life: "It was impossible to look only to oneself, to take from life and not to give except by accident, deliberately to look at humanity and then pass on the other side."[30]

This sense of the value of life could possibly lead to a regeneration of all English life: "Was there perhaps a new race of Englishmen arising out of this war, a race of men bred by the war, a harmonious synthesis of the governing class and the great rest of England; . . . true representatives of the new England that should emerge from this struggle. . . ."[31] This prediction of change was reiterated by many writers. "This war, unless we are defeated, will wipe out most of the existing class privileges. There are every day fewer people who wish them to continue."[32]

But we have certainly taken life to pieces and found out what it is made of. . . . Look how we have come this summer through the deep waters, through the perils and the hazards which all the world thought must overwhelm us, we have not reached the far shore yet, and it may not be God's will that we should ever come there, but we have come far, trusting in the strength we prayed for and that He has given. We must not think of him only as a tribal God, leading *us* only among mankind. We don't know what prayers rise to him among the German people, but if they are prayers of faith and resignation they will be answered, and he will . . . lead them as well as us, to peace and better days.[33]

Such statements scarcely can constitute a program for the reconstruction of the body social, but by reaffirming the mystical unity of humankind they did lay the foundations for willful action to achieve change; and, of course, numerous social changes were effected in Great Britain during the postwar period. The kind of grand conclusions envisioned by Hillary would not be accomplished, and new disillusionments would set in. But these failures should not blind us to the real accomplishments for which this sense of being born again was a necessary prelude.

Just as the writers pledged themselves to a more perfect future, so they faced resolutely their failures of the past. It was widely accepted that Britain had acted pusilanimously in the period of Munich and had failed to prepare adequately for the rigors of war, even after the conflict had broken out. The reason for this failure was that the British lived the living death of ignorance, from which it would be awakened by the initiatory death and resurrection of trial by fire. One does not have to accept this *mea culpa* at face value. Great Britain was better prepared in 1940 than most were willing to admit at the time. Production of fighter aircraft did not increase suddenly in the summer of 1940, but proceeded according to a program that was already well established.[34] However, the new sense of urgency certainly made it appear that a dramatic change had taken place in preparation and production, as well as in the minds of people.

In their struggle to transform themselves (or better, to become truly themselves), the English were sustained not only by the promise of a better future but also by the great moments of the past. Even such an unmystical writer as George Orwell could say: "The Stock Exchange will be pulled down, the horse plough will give way to the tractor, the country houses will be turned into children's holiday camps, the Eton and Harrow match will be forgotten, but England will still be England, an everlasting animal stretching into the future and the past, and, like all living things, having the power to change out of all recognition and yet remain the same."[35]

This organic link with the past as well as the future was much in the minds of the English in the summer of 1940. Such moments of peril and greatness as the summer of 1588 or the invasion threat of the Napoleonic years came readily to mind. Winston Churchill was often linked with the figure of Drake, Nelson, or the younger Pitt.[36] "The idea of writing a book about the defeat of the Spanish Armada first came to me, as it must have come to others, in June, 1940, when the eyes of the world were again turned to the shores of England and their surrounding seas," writes Garrett Mattingly in the preface to *The Armada.*[37] The German airfleets were referred to as air armadas, and Winston Churchill came to personify the defiant attitude of Britain as Drake once had. As the Spaniards of Philip II's time had singled out Drake, so the Germans singled out Churchill as *the* enemy; a role to which Churchill cheerfully acquiesced, or some would say, seized forcefully.

The tendency to simplify and to concentrate upon single figures is well illustrated here. Drake was the leader *par excellence,* though he was not the commander of the fleet which met the Spaniards. Winston Churchill, though the leader of His Majesty's government, did not personally command the armed forces of England. Yet, he created in his person the aura of godlike strength and transmitted this mana to his followers. The techniques which he employed to achieve this superhuman status were many and startling, though none were unknown to mythology. Like Achilles he had the gift of speaking greatly and acting greatly, though he did not die young. His cigar and bowler hat were talismans as unmistakable as Thor's hammer or the lightning bolts of Zeus. He was the ancient prophet calling the British to account for their sins, but he was also the ancient child described as "baby-faced" with "pudgy hands," who often appeared in the strangely infantile "siren suit." He took fierce joy in battle, taunting his foes with mordant wit, yet he could call for magnaminity in victory. Withal, he enjoyed the less stern pleasures of drinking and smoking, exhibiting an impressive capacity for brandy and cigars. He was a jealous god calling *this* "their finest hour," not 1588 or 1805. Finally, like Dionysius, he would be torn apart by his followers in the election of 1945.

The literary record contains a number of subsidiary themes worthy of mention because they point again to the most general levels of human interest. Flowers, colors, the feminine character of the city, and the dismemberment of London, are all subjects frequently raised, although not dwelt upon at great length. The well-known English love for flowers was not to be submerged by the terrors of war. *The Times*, in the midst of more serious matters, still found space to display prominently photographs of crocuses, daffodils, and later in the year, harvest scenes. The writers felt the poignant quality of what seemed to be an overabundance of beauty in such grim times. To many, this familiar beauty was the more noticeable because it was in such danger of being extinguished, so that one might say that England had never been so beautiful. That it also emphasized the feminine amidst the brutal masculinity of war is also apparent. Rape, and the probability of further rapes, were much in the minds of many that summer. Guernica, Warsaw, and Rotterdam had been criminally assaulted, Dame Freedom and La Belle France had been outraged, while London and Britannia prepared themselves for the worst. Like the flowers, because of the imminence of loss, London appeared that year more beautiful and more precious than she ever had in peacetime.[38]

But like a female deity, London was not only beautiful and enticing, she was also terrible. Engulfed in flames she became a death trap for her inhabitants, consuming them as well as inspiring them. Under siege, London tended to dissolve into its various quarters, becoming, as Edward R. Murrow put it, a collection of villages, each with its own focal point. Actually, this had always been the case but the exigencies of war accentuated the already existing situation. Yet, out of this dismemberment and the experiences of self-help, hope for a better, more noble England would arise. Like the terrible mother Tiamat, either London would be divided to create a new world, or she would rise again, phoenix-like, from the ashes of the old.[39]

The myth of the Battle of Britain did not come into being after the battle was fought but was created in the course of the battle itself. It was built in the process of the day-to-day reporting of the news. Elements were added from time to time, while others were discarded. The central points, that England had cast aside the weak and ignorant ways of appeasement and sloth in order to defend righteousness and create a better world, all existed long before the battle was fought. British newspaper and periodical statements from the early days of the war show no tendency toward slackness and, in fact, emphasize the inevitability of victory. In this period (September, 1939, to April,

1940) most competent observers assumed that in the end the superiority of the Royal Navy, the French Army, and the Allied economic position would bring victory. It was an attitude which lacked passionate affirmation, but it was neither weakly held nor unthinkingly arrived at. The English Navy, the French Army, and the economy were magic swords of great power, though their luster was perhaps dulled by long use.

Nor were the British reluctant to accept battle. They knew that Germany could not allow itself to be strangled, so they expected a test of strength, but one which they were confident they could win. When it came in Norway, the British had had a half year to prepare. Thus, Neville Chamberlain could say that Germany had "missed the bus" only a few days before the battle opened. Since the Norwegian campaign was tailor-made for the application of sea power, it was a real shock to find that sea power could not decide the issue. As the British Army evacuated the Norwegian ports, the Labor members of Parliament forced a cabinet reshuffling which brought Churchill to power. Still, the Navy was intact and had inflicted severe losses on the Germans, while in the Lowlands and Belgium, Hitler had now chosen to test the French Army and the BEF.

Again the British and French moved confidently, only to find themselves caught, within two weeks time, in the Fianders trap. Thereafter, a rapid reshaping of expectations took place which resulted in a new picture of the course of the war. Sea power, though still intact, had proven incapable of halting Germany on the continent; the French Army was obviously cracking and would soon be shattered; the British Army had returned weaponless; and economic strength seemed to have deserted the British camp. Under these circumstances the British transferred their reliance to the RAF, the Navy, and the mixed force of Army and Home Guard steeled by a new will to resist. This last factor seems to have replaced reliance on economic strength.

The battles over Dunkirk gave the English people new hope, and they confidently touted the superiority of British pilots and aircraft. Actually, British aircraft losses equaled German losses at Dunkirk, but at the time it was thought that many more Germans had been shot down. The names Spitfire and Hurricane now became household words; for a time it was thought the Boulton Paul Defiant would join this select group, but later actions proved its inferiority, and it slipped into oblivion.[40]

The Fall of France marked the final step in the period of disaster. The British had salvaged respect from the defeat, but the old easy confidence was gone. Through the period of mourning for fallen France which lasted till the end of June, desperate preparations were made for the eventuality of invasion, including the extreme measure of attacking the French Fleet at Oran. By July, the British assumed, possibly wrongly yet confidently, that they were prepared for invasion. One might even say that a script had been prepared. The first essential element for Germany's launching of an invasion was the defeat of the RAF. If this were accomplished, then the Germans would have to cross the channel in the face of a much superior navy and, if the landings were made, the Wehrmacht would have to defeat an army, a Home Guard, and a civilian population prepared to fight to the last. Should even these defenses fall, the British government was apparently prepared to fight from the dominions and colonies.

Thus, successive military hurdles were established, and German failure at any one of these barriers would constitute a vindication of the British hope for victory. One could envision a situation in which the RAF had been defeated but, in which the cross-channel effort had been thwarted by the Royal Navy. The myth of the Battle of Britain would not have been greatly different in such a case. The RAF's contribution would be relegated to that of a valiant defense by a few brave men which bought time for the successful defense of Britain. Undoubtedly, memories of Thermopylae would have been summoned up, or the charge of the Light Brigade, or Gordon at Khartoum. The Navy would advance in such a case to the forefront, resuming its position as the first line of British defense. Thus, the myth of the battle would be different in detail, but the story itself would remain essentially unchanged. Only abject surrender could have changed the story and destroyed the myth.

Perhaps the greatest changes which were made in the British view of the probable outcome of the war involved the subordination of the idea that economic superiority would win the war to the idea that iron will would prevail. However, Churchill's statement that "Hitler must break us in this Island or lose the war" probably indicates a continuing faith that time was on the side of the British. A second major change in attitude was the assumption that Britain stood at the center of things rather than on the periphery surrounding the enemy. In fact, the British throughout the year lasting from June, 1940, to June, 1941, sought to reestablish the peripheral view by emphasizing news from the Balkans and the Middle East, as well as the bombing of German cities. At the end of that period, the task would be accomplished through the German invasion of Russia.

Thus, the English entered the Battle of Britain with a confidence which seemed to surpass rational understanding. So strong was this confidence that it led to claims of victory before such claims were warranted. *The Times* would argue that the victories in the air battles of August 13–19 marked the turning point in the war. This was bolstered by Churchill's statement on August 20 that, "never in the field of human conflict was so much owed by so many to so few." It is probably significant that these words of praise are usually quoted at the end of descriptions of the battle, though they were actually uttered before the turning point.[41] Adding to the British confidence that a corner had been turned was the fact that August 15, widely thought to be the target date for the invasion, passed without incident. By the end of the month, when the most perilous phase of the battle, the attacks upon the airfields and control centers, was beginning, *The Times* was devoting more space to the bombing raids on German cities. These raids, actually of little consequence, were thought to be even more important than the bombing of the invasion ports, though they did satisfy British hopes for revenge.

Few observers at the time saw the German decision to transfer their attacks to London on September 7 as a fatal error. On September 11, Churchill warned that invasion was imminent, and on September 16, church bells were rung in some places in the eastern counties. The rumors of German bodies being washed up on the coast were widespread in the days that followed and continued to be mentioned in the postwar literature, though no evidence of these bodies was ever produced. Most persons considered the attack on London to be simply a new phase in the battle; expectation of invasion continued on into the late spring of 1941. *Time* magazine would head its section on the English struggle as "The Battle of Britain" through June, 1941, though already in March, the Ministry of Information had issued its pamphlet, *The Battle of Britain*, which identified the failure to destroy the air bases as the turning point in the battle and which, significantly, did not deal with the bombing attacks on London and other British cities after the end of October.

A very considerable part of the British reporting of the war was devoted to potentially successful actions. The Bomber Command's attacks on German cities received a great deal of attention, though they had very little effect. The Free French demonstration at Dakar also raised brief hopes, though these were quickly dashed. Most important were the British successes against the Italians and the Italian failure in Greece. The reconquest of Italian Somaliland, the invasion of Ethiopia, and, most of all, the Wavell offensive against Italian forces in Libya, were extensively covered. In fact, there was a time in the spring of 1941 when it might have been thought that the British were on the offensive everywhere.

Little of this was of permanent importance. Yugoslavia, Greece, and Crete would fall in the spring. The Libyan gains would be lost when the then little-known General Rommel entered the battle, leaving only certain names, Sollum, Benghazi, and Sidi Barani imprinted on the British mind. At Tobruk an Australian force would hold out, turning that settlement into a latter day Calais, the capture of which in 1942 would threaten the Churchill government. The Ethiopian and Somaliland campaigns were forgotten. By June, 1941, things seemed nearly as dark as they had in June of the previous year; little intimation existed that Hitler was about to commit the fatal error of invading Russia.

How different all of this is from the story of the Battle of Britain as it came to be remembered. The bomber strikes at Hamm and Berlin were insignificant by comparison with later efforts. They have survived only as attacks on the invasion ports. The fighter sweeps over the French and Belgian coasts are scarcely anywhere mentioned, though the RAF lost as many machines in these attacks as it did in the Battle of Britain. The defense of the British cities and particularly London, which was, in some ways, underplayed at the time, has emerged as an event as important to the winning of the war as the actions of the fighter pilots in August and September of 1940. What this shows is simply that, in the process of writing the history of the period, the British would seek out all significant leads, especially those which were hopeful. In the final analysis, however, the false leads, or those which were not immediately successful, were forgotten. The Beaufighters, the Blenheims, and Benghazi were quietly forgotten while Sptifires, small boats, and roof spotters achieved a kind of immortality as symbolic of the time when "Britain stood alone."

If the myth grew and filled in the details of a predetermined story line, it also faded and deteriorated. This does not necessarily mean that it will be forgotten, though some temporarily serviceable historic myths have suffered this fate. Rather, it means that ordinary people cannot usually long survive as demi-gods, for, as their middles thicken, their glories thin. It is also true that aspirations remain unfulfilled or undergo change. The inevitability of this deterioration seems to be one of the conditions of modern historical myth.

Certainly one of the first signs of this transformation was the rejection of Winston Churchill by the British public in the midst of the very important Potsdam Conference following the end of the European war. On the one hand, it was intuited by the British public that the "better England" envisioned in the heroic years would not be created by a leadership so tied to conservative traditions. On the other hand, it was also quite clear in 1945 that the old British prominence in world affairs was now a thing of the past; that real-world leadership was possessed only by the United States and the Soviet Union. The ensuing years were ones of difficulty and disappointment for the British. The health and welfare programs and the industrial nationalization program were introduced but accompanied by the continuation of a wartime austerity which was finally bitterly resented. The Empire was dissolved in a reasonably graceful manner. Yet, somehow the anticipated bluebirds over the white cliffs of Dover looked suspiciously like crows.

Under these pressures, capped by the real humiliation of the Suez Crisis, a new and mordant vision of Britain appeared, characterized by the writings of that nongroup of authors, the "angry young men." In their stories and plays, it is striking that the antiheroes are typically men who served during the war in posts of no danger, or who did not serve at all. The RAF pilot appears, but only as the successful boob or "crashing bore." In the very fine revue *Beyond the Fringe* one of the skits, "The Aftermyth of War," has the archetypal Englishman, complete with helmet, popping up from time to time with such memories as, "I was in me garden setting out deadly nightshade for Jerry," and always ending with the instruction to his good wife, "Meg, 'ow about makin' a nice cup o' tea." The intention was plain, the idols of the previous generation had to be destroyed. The Battle of Britain had lost its relevance to the succeeding generation.

All of this came as shock to those who had created the "finest hour." One former pilot refused ennoblement when he found that he, an RAF hero, was included in the same Queen's list with the Beatles. Yet, it is also obvious that such things must happen. England's success of 1588 was followed by a long series of disappointments. Similarly, the situation for Great Britain since World War II has changed in ways which were, to some extent, unexpected. While the decline of British power could have been forseen, who would have predicted that London would assume leadership in the world of fashion, or Liverpool in the world of popular music. If the Beatles and Carnaby Street seemed unlikely successors to Spitfire pilots and Bomb Disposal men, they nevertheless captured the world's imagination, and their successors have influenced world tastes.

This deterioration will probably go only so far. The story of the Battle of Britain will be cut and hewn to fit into the continuing story of British development. The memory of what heroes may have become afterwards will recede with time, while their moment of glory remains. Long after the men are gone, the vision of small boats dancing on the channel waves, Spitfires charging dense clouds of fighters, or firemen, wardens, and plain citizens facing the test of prolonged bombardment, will remain like the vision of Drake's ships hurtling toward the menacing crescent of the Spanish Armada. The words too will remain— "never have so many . . .," "Blood, toil, sweat, and tears," "What General Weygand has called the Battle of France has ended . . . the Battle of Britain is about to begin." Above all, there is a good possibility that with all the subsequent disappointments, and despite the fact that Britain has receded from its world position, it may still be said, "This was their finest hour."

4

Band of Brothers

WHATEVER ELSE IT MAY BE, the military is, without doubt, an artificial state of society. Insofar as it has traditionally excluded women, it is obviously at variance with the more normal social situation of humanity. Since there is no room for overage males and male children, it has represented only a segment of human society. In this it parallels other artificial groups, such as secret societies. This is not to say that these groups do not have an important place in the world of humans, but, rather, that these groups at best can play only a partial role in the ongoing affairs of human society. When compared with the family, the hunting-gathering band, the larger tribe, or even the nation state, this abnormality is apparent. It is also apparent that such incomplete societies cannot maintain themselves indefinitely but must depend upon the larger society for their existence.

Perhaps because the military is artificial, it must depend upon more or less rigidly established rules in order to remain in existence. This has led to an elaborately structured and hierarchical order that may or may not resemble the pattern of life in the larger society of which it is a part. In primitive and traditional societies, leadership in the military may embrace the same persons who exercise that leadership in the general society, though this is certainly not a hard and fast rule. In more recent times, this carryover of leadership roles is even more problematical. The military man often finds his position subordinate to that of civilian leadership and, conversely, civilians have often proven themselves to be inadequate military leaders.

The importance of the hierarchical structure pertains not only to the needs of the leadership group, but also to the conduct of battle itself. Asking men to commit themselves to a course of action which runs counter to natural self-protection demands that the controls over these men be very well anchored and accepted by the entire body of the military. The official structure of the military goes far to meet this necessary qualification by imposing a rigid order, reinforcing it with stringent rules for obedience and harsh punishments for any deviation from the accepted norms of action. In many societies the training for the acquiescence to these demands may begin in childhood; in others, the training may be delayed until the individual actually becomes a part of the military. In either case, but particularly the latter, the individual may very well carry into the military attitudes which are at odds with or even in opposition to those of the military structure.

Such a set of attitudes can be very destructive to the efficiency of the military organization, but they can also be the basis for an unofficial structure that will provide further support for the military order. Obviously, if all the members of the military organization were to consider only their own well being, it would be difficult to carry out any military operations. Even if only a substantial portion of the members were to act in this fashion, the results would be devastating from a military point of view. If the individual members are allowed to pursue their own interests to some extent, however, they may find it either to their advantage to remain within the organization; or, they may at least be able to act from time to time in such a manner as to mitigate the worst severities of the military and to hold at bay consideration of the worst possibilities connected with service. An example of a situation which may make it advantageous to serve would be the opportunity for looting traditionally enjoyed by military forces. The striving for glory with the hope that fortune would follow fame would be another such example.[1] Even without these enticements, soldiers have always found it possible to make life in the army less onerous, either by dodging some of the less desirable tasks or by subverting military discipline in other minor ways. Fighting between units of the same army would, on the surface, seem not to be conducive to good military order; yet, this kind of activity can also serve to strengthen the pride that members feel in their own unit. Less strenuous, but still effective, would be the taunting which takes place between different units and arms of the service. Within a unit, complaining has been a traditional and tolerated method of allowing troops to vent frustration. Angry as they may be at the service or some aspect of it, this complaining seldom leads to mutiny. Certainly, that would never be the case where the complaints are focused on relatively trivial matters, which can either be addressed or ignored by the controlling powers.

The military is not only an artificial society in the sense outlined above, it is also an ephemeral society. That is, the membership is constantly changing within a shorter span than the lifetime of any one generation. While it is true that all society is constantly replacing itself, the turnover is much more rapid in the military. Men leave the service for a variety of reasons. Some, though very few, retire; some are killed or die in service; some desert; some are taken prisoner; and others are discharged. In times of peace, the force may be entirely disbanded, or it may be reduced to a small fraction of its wartime size. Alternatively it may retain a considerable size with the capability for enormous expansion when hostilities are resumed. This has been the case in the twentieth century where, typically, the number of men permanently under arms has been greater after the closing of hostilities than it was prior to the outbreak of the war.

The official structures of the military have changed and become more complicated over the centuries, as armies have grown in size and the tools of war have become more varied and complex. A patrol of five or six men raiding an enemy camp may at one time have been the maximum effort that could be mounted by a hunting-gathering society. By modern standards the hundred or so warriors standing and threatening a similar sized group of primitive horticulturalists is so unimpressive that many students of war would argue that such groups have not yet crossed the military threshold. Indeed, with their ritualized limitations on the acceptable number of killed and their tendency to be oftentime satisfied with an impressive but nonlethal demonstration, the activity does not resemble recent modes of warfare. Yet in each of these early instances, the rudiments of structure were already present. The warriors tended to fight individually, but they did mass themselves in an organized front. Raiders acted on principles that would continue to be applicable up to the present day. Furthermore, these early warriors were acting within a structure that was, to them, thoroughly comprehensible and for purposes which were well understood. Even in the very recent past, among peoples who are counted as members of advanced western society, some of these principles were still intact. A man writing of his experiences with a Chetnik group formed in that part of Yugoslavia known as Montenegro explains that the band was organized in the traditional manner, with each village providing one of the four companies that made up this Chetnik battalion. A little further on, he expands upon his hatred of the communists (the Partisans)—it was well known that the (he names a family) were never any good.[2] Ideology had simply become a disguise for an ancient blood feud, but it did have the advantage of making the nature of the struggle intelligible to the individual, and that struggle could be carried out with an organization well know to the participants.

How different is the situation for people entering the modern military organization. They are faced with a hierarchical ordering of units—army, corps, division, regiment, battalion, company, platoon—terms that were probably entirely unfamiliar to them prior to their entry into the service. They will have little idea of how many members make up any one of these units and will probably be quite uncertain of their place in the hierarchy. To the relatively small number of professional military members, and particularly the officers, the order will be seen as natural and, more importantly, as necessary. These people will understand the rules and accept them; they will know the requirements for advancement and be more concerned with this than the majority of the recruits. Since this is their profession and their life, they will see the military as a good and necessary thing. For the temporary personnel called into service by the needs of war, none of this will be readily apparent. This group has to be licked into shape in the school of the soldier, their mistakes and misunderstandings often becoming a source for rueful humor as well as despair for the more knowledgeable.

What is most necessary for new entrants is that they find some place within the hierarchy that they can relate to in a meaningful fashion. Most of the levels of organization are too far removed from the individual's experience to be of much use in this matter. In the years after service, veterans may say that they served with Patton or some other such heroic figure. It sounds well to the uninformed civilian audience, but it really means that the unit to which they were attached was commanded (distantly) by the great leader. In fact, though the decisions of the highest military leaders may have great impact upon the destiny of the individual, the relationship is fundamentally of no day-to-day consequence.

This is not to deny that new soldiers will have a sense of belonging to these larger organizations. They will obviously identify with the nation sending them to war. They will feel—they always have felt—some sense of identity with heroic leaders such as Alexander, Caesar, Napoleon, or MacArthur. Their division patch will give them a sense of identity; the regimental tradition (as in the British Army) may impart to them the idea that they are only the latest in a long line of soldiers who have had the honor of service in this or that glorious unit. But none of these levels quite meets the needs of the individual. The place where military society most directly and constantly impinges upon the individuals, the place where they are most likely to feel "at home," is to be found at the company level.

The company, for many reasons, has long served as the unit level at which most men can feel a sense of belonging. The size of the company, varying from eighty to one hundred and fifty men, compares very closely with the number of men who would be available for service in the widely observed tribal community of about five hundred persons. It has even been suggested that this number of men is about the limit which can be commanded by a single person.[3] In recent times this has not been precisely the case, since the company is made up of subordinate units, the platoons and the squads. Prior to the twentieth century, the companies which made up a regiment tended to be organizational units rather than tactical units, since the regiment itself fought as a single body. In these cases, however, companies could be detailed to act as skirmishers. There is good evidence from the writings men who served in the American Civil War that, although they identified with the regiment, they tended to think first of the particular company within the regiment. Thus, Rice Bull's memoirs concerned principally the experiences of Company D, 123d New York Infantry; or John Worsham's dealt principally with Company F, 21st Virginia. In a very real sense, the company provides a home address for the men in the military.

The company is the place where most friendships are formed; it is the place where the faces are familiar and where one has a greater sense of security, though that in itself might be most precarious. In tribal armies these friendships or acquaintanceships had already been formed in the everyday life of the community. In those armies or organizations which had been formed in a particular section of the country, friendships might be carried into the service; or, at least, one entered the military along with men whose attitudes and dialect were fairly well understood. Thus, in the German Army the recruitment tended to group men from the same regions of the nation. Bavarians served with Bavarians, Saxons with Saxons. In the British Army, regiments were assigned to particular parts of the country and recruitment did tend to come from these areas, though the officers might not.[4] In the American Army, National Guard units were drawn from the different sections of the United States, but, with combat losses and random replacement, these units lost a good part of their regional character. Friendships might also be the result of men having trained together at some basic training center prior to joining the company. Small groups of men, replacements, which entered the company retained some of this identity as members of the same "cohort" and might well retain this identity throughout their entire period of service.

The friendship patterns are also influenced by the official structure of the company. This is more particularly true of the more recent armies, where the functions of the company are more highly articulated than was the case in the past. Friends are not necessarily assigned to the same platoon or squad and, once placed, they will form relationships with persons who up to now have been strangers. But these are the very persons who will assume a monumental position in the individual's life, for they are, more than any others, those upon whom his life will depend. This close dependency may not breed friendship, at least not immediately. These persons are thrown together by function, not because they are kindred spirits. It is even possible for them to work together reasonably well, despite the fact that they dislike each other. This is not commonly the case, but tolerance, rather than close friendship, is common. John Haley, in an appendix to his diary, lists the men in his company often together with acid comments on either the quality of their character or their competency as soldiers.[5]

The platoon, the squad, and the section do channel the relationships which an individual develops within the company. In a sense this relationship is professional, one that is fostered during those hours when the men are working closely together in an effort to establish the harmony that, it is hoped, will lead to success on the battlefield. In the process the individuals will develop an acute sense of where the other members of the squad are at any given point in the exercise. They also begin to see the strengths and the weaknesses of the other members of the unit. This understanding will not be completed until the company has entered battle, for it is a very difficult thing to know how persons will react under the actual conditions of combat. In fact, even when live ammunition is used in the exercise, there will be missing that breathless confusion which seems to pervade military units faced by hostile fire.

Officially, the army tells the men how they are expected to act. There is a whole set of widely accepted virtues and parallel vices recognized by the military. Courage is expected, almost taken for granted, as the primary virtue of the soldier. Under fire he should, as a result of his training, be able to conduct himself in such a manner that he can perform his duties and provide inspiration for the other members of his unit. Cowardice is unacceptable. The punishment is stringent, and death sentences have not been, in the past, uncommon. Officially, there are no extenuating circumstances, particularly if a single act of cowardice results in the failure of an entire unit.[6] At all times the individual is expected to perform the duties which have been assigned to him, even if these duties place him in extreme danger of injury or death. The soldier is expected to act in an honorable manner, though the definition of honor is hazy at best. It certainly includes the injunction to perform one's duty and to act with courage. More than that, the soldier is expected to uphold the good name of his unit at all times. Formerly, officers were ready to fight duels for the sake of personal honor. Failure to give or to accept a challenge marked the man as a coward (and no gentleman).

For enlisted men, duelling has never been mandatory, presumably because these persons, unlike the nobility which made up a large portion of the officer corps, were considered to be beneath honor. Enlisted men often engaged in fights with other units or branches of the service, however, if they felt that the honor of their unit had been impugned. Barroom brawls may not have been considered worthy of being called defense of honor (certainly this was the official point of view), and the miscreants often found themselves placed on charges. Fellow enlisted men tended to look upon these battles in a different light, enjoying and praising the actions even when the participants had ended up in the guardhouse.

Respect was the reward for showing courage, performing one's duty, and defending one's honor or the "honor of the regiment." This goes beyond friendship, for it is quite possible to have respect for a person that one dislikes. Respect pays homage to the person who performs his soldierly duties, whatever his other personal characteristics may be. The braggart, the bully, the conniver, can all gain respect though they may be hated. In exceptional cases the actions of a person or a unit may be such as to gain individual or group glory. While it is widely averred that there is no place in modern war for glory, that attitude has never been shared by all members of the military. Despite the obvious evidence of the cruelty, waste, and horror of modern battle, men are still willing to speak of their military achievements and to wear the signs of these accomplishments—the badges, medals, and ribbons—with pride.[7]

The opposite of glory is shame. Professional military men who have failed in one or another of the tests may find themselves shunned by their former comrades or held up to public notice for these failures. The officer who presumably abandoned the Prince imperial to the mercies of the Zulus and survived rather than dying with him was universally condemned by the other officers, forced to leave the service, and finally left to die in poverty and disgrace.[8]

For the individual entering the service, it is necessary to learn all these things and much more. The first step in the making of a soldier involves a transformation of outlook. He is asked to surrender his freedom of action to the needs of the group, to accept the values of the military even when these run counter to his deepest personal concerns. In the process he will be incorporated into a group and become part of a social cohort which will accompany him through a good part of the remainder of his military career. Traditionally, men would enter the military through the organization which would also be the unit that carried him into combat. Regiments were raised, trained, and committed to battle without any gross transfer of men involved. To some extent this is still the case. Many armies follow the practice of training recruits in a service battalion organically linked to a fighting unit. Other military organizations, and particularly the American Army, have developed the practice of separating the basic training of the soldier from his training as a part of a fighting or "line" unit. This practice has the advantage of standardizing the training given the individual, but only at the expense of disrupting his full introduction into the social fabric of the military society. Cohorts of trainees find themselves broken up when they are assigned to line units, so that a new stage of socialization has to take place. The difficulty of this process is only increased when the placement occurs under conditions of combat. The system also suffers from the fact that it tends to emphasize that the individual is only a replaceable part in a large machine. In this case, efficiency of operation can be purchased at the expense of the morale of the soldiers. This cost may only be minimal, if time exists for the incorporation of the individual into the body social of the organization. If such time is not available, the system may simply be creating a group of lost souls of doubtful military value.

The transfer to a line company is not a simple process of placing the individual's name on the company roster, for he is entering a strange and potentially hostile environment. One cannot be entirely certain what rules will pertain in this new situation, who will be approachable, and whether acceptance is possible. He will probably be accompanied by at least some of the men with whom he has taken his basic training. In this new situation, they will form a cohort of friends and acquaintances that can, to a limited extent, ease the process of transition. However, the official needs of the military will dictate that this cohort be broken up between the various subunits of the company. Thus, they will find themselves parcelled out to the different platoons and squads and forced to make their way in the company of strangers. From the point of view of the new man, this can be very depressing, for he will be simultaneously trying to learn what his duties are (and, thus, fit himself into the new organization), while trying to find out who these new companions are and how he will be required to relate to them.

The process of incorporation also creates difficulties for the older members of the squad. In terms of the official duties of the squad, the question will be asked whether this new member can actually function effectively. This will probably be discussed among them at some length. Often one member of the squad will be assigned the duty of looking after the new member to see that he works as a part of the team in training exercises. In extreme cases it may become apparent that the new man is so incapable that he will be transferred, though the need for bodies is such that this would be a rarity. The new man will also be watched to see if he is socially acceptable. This has nothing to do with his table manners, but, rather, whether he can be included as "one of the guys." In some cases the new person will be immediately outgoing, so that judgment can be passed with the high probability of acceptance. In other cases the new man may be so withdrawn, either from personal characteristics, fear, or depression, that he cannot be drawn out, and will remain for some time a matter of puzzlement or even hostility to the group. He will be the subject of discussion until he decides to open up to the rest of the squad. Possibly, when he does, he will reveal himself to be interesting, or good humored, and, eventually, a valued member of the unit. One of the marks of this progress can be the assignment of a nickname.

Acceptance involves an introduction into the informal structure of the company. The newly arrived will become aware of the friendship groups which already exist within the company, and, conversely, the company will tend to identify the newly arrived as part of a new friendship group. The tendency will exist to think halfconsciously of these persons in terms of their relationship to their own cohort, or singly, if they arrived separately from others. Friendships will continue to exist across squad and platoon lines and even beyond the boundaries of the company, but as time passes, the closest relationships will be established within the platoons and the squads. Other types of informal organization will also exist. Cardplaying and gambling are almost universal occupations in the military, but even here one finds an informal structure. Playing cards for recreation will tend to be carried on habitually between partners or within the same group, such as the squad or platoon. More serious gambling will draw in some of these players from time to time, but the most serious and successful gamblers will tend to separate themselves from the rest of the groups.9 Such games sort out the most aggressive and skillful players in much the same way that sports do. A certain degree of honor and respect will be accorded to the good cardplayer, and athletic skill may be used as an indicator of persons who can fill leadership roles in the company.

Other interest groups will attract members from various parts of the company and beyond. Among the Irish in the American Civil War were a number of men who were members of the secret Fenian organization, dedicated to the liberation of Ireland from British rule. When time permitted, they would hold meetings for the purpose of planning action after the end of the war. In one incredible episode, this involved a meeting of Fenians from regiments of both the Union and Confederate armies.10

Scrounging is another activity that is widely practiced by armies. Typically it is devoted to picking up those things which may be useful for some company activity. This can be accomplished by picking up items discarded by others, by stealing from other units, or by swapping items with other units for those things which are needed. Officially this kind of activity is not countenanced, though it would seem to be condoned by the leadership. In fact, getting things in this way adds excitement and interest to the social life of the company. Stealing government-issued equipment from other units, particularly if the other unit involved is from another branch of the service, is not only acceptable, but is considered to be a praiseworthy adventure.

If there is a presumptive innocence to this behavior, it does have its darker side. Troops encamped on an area without an adequate supply system could actually denude the region. Going into winter quarters involved the need to build semipermanent housing and for this purpose fences, outbuildings, and forest, livestock, poultry, and grain, could be devastated. Civilian populations, whether enemy, neutral, or friendly, could, under these conditions, be placed in serious peril of starvation.[11] Even military operations themselves could be seriously affected. More than one siege had to be lifted because the besieging army could no longer sustain itself on the surrounding countryside.[12]

While much is made of the entertainment provided to the troops by professional actors and organizations, most of the entertainment will have to be provided by the troops themselves. In addition to the card games and bull sessions, the company will periodically pool together its money and its resources to hold a beer party. Drinking is only a part of the attraction of such congregations, though the resultant spirit of conviviality probably makes the accompanying entertainment seem even more witty than would otherwise be the case. The wit is in large part directed at situations and personalities specific to the company. The ordinary rules of military deference are lowered or even overturned, so that the company commander, if he is wise and if he is respected by the men of the company, will allow himself to be the butt of some of the humor. Skits, songs, monologues, and impromptu suggestions from the assemblage all contribute to building a spirit of unity within the company. It is understood that, if the barriers of discipline have been lowered for the evening, they will be back in place on the morrow. The memory of the enjoyment will remain as a reminder that the company is much more than a random collection of men.

Such memories are important to men who have to deal with the realities of military discipline. Traditionally, this discipline has ranged from the harsh to the ferocious. The Prussian Army of the eighteenth century was well known for the brutality of its practices, which were held as necessary in order to make it possible to carry out the the the machinelike maneuvers deemed essential to success on the battle-field. Nor were the other armies of that period and beyond laggard in their employment of savage measures. Execution was mandated for many, even trivial, offenses. Flogging was a regular part of the disci-pline, as was hanging by the thumbs and running the gauntlet. To adjust oneself to such a regimen, the ordinary soldier had several strategies. On the one hand, the man in the ranks (and he was the usual target) could accept without question the correctness of such treatment and strive at all times to avoid incurring the displeasure of his superiors. This, of course, was difficult, both because so many things were punishable and because the background and tempera-ment of the rankers was such that they were accustomed to harsh treatment and were drawn to activities which readily brought it on. In this situation they had to accept the reality of the likelihood of being punished. In response they could feign a kind of disdain, as was the case of the British 58th Foot, known as the "Steelbacks," for their reputation of being able to withstand flogging without flinching or crying out. Since this often involved one hundred or more strokes, it was no slight accomplishment. Less heroic, but to some extent effec-tive, was the method favored by many. The pointed witticism about conditions in nineteenth century industrial towns—"The quickest way out of Manchester? Alcohol"—also applied to the military. The fact that drinking served to bring on as many troubles as it might help one to forget did little to deter the troops.

With the coming of the mass armies of the nineteenth and twen-tieth centuries, there did occur a considerable moderation in disci-plinary measures. If executions did not disappear entirely, they were at least significantly reduced. Flogging and other of the most brutal corporal punishments were dropped in favor of temporary imprison-ment, confinement to barracks, fines, or a dishonorable discharge. Yet there remained a whole host of minor punishments which, though much less painful, were nevertheless aggravating. Improper dress, a less than clean rifle, unshined shoes, or a badly made bed were all subject to punishment. A noncommissioned officer dissatisfied with the performance of the unit could order long marches with full field pack, extra KP, or as Kipling put it, "double drill and no canteen."

Against such harassments the ordinary soldier could protect himself by giving the appearance of compliance while still allowing himself some freedom of action. An extra pair of boots, always shined and never worn, could save him on inspection day.

It is axiomatic that no amount of training will fully prepare men for battle. This is also true of units. A rifle company is fortunate if it has had the time to train itself in proper squad, platoon, and company tactics, so that the men understand what is expected of them and the commander has some idea of which men can be depended upon in leadership roles. The history of warfare shows that this is often not the case. Emergencies can force units into action before they are prepared; others, thinking they are prepared, will discover on the battlefield that they are the victims of antiquated instruction. At Stalingrad, men and women of the Barrikady factory were handed rifles, given a few minutes training in their use, and sent to the front. Almost before they had time to ask whether they could stand the stress of battle, many of them were dead. Not all examples are this extreme, but the French soldiers of 1914, trained to believe that offensive action would always carry the day, learned within weeks of being called to the colors that modern rifles, artillery, and machine guns had reversed the balance so that much of their training was for nought.

Like individual soldiers, units will ask themselves how they will perform in combat. Questions of their preparedness, of the officers' capabilities, of the value of their weaponry, and of the quality of the enemy will be asked. The real answers will only come with battle. Nor will veterans whom they happen to encounter on the way be very helpful. There is a tendency for veteran units to taunt and shout derisive remarks at the newcomers; perhaps, it is just to warn them that the front is a very dangerous place. Heavy artillery regiments that had spent much of the Civil War guarding Washington, D.C., were hurriedly retrained as infantry and sent into the battles of the 1864 campaign. A thousand strong, they looked like brigades to the men of the much reduced and battle-worn veteran regiments. Shouts of warning, abuse, and derision accompanied them into their first battles until they had demonstrated by their fighting and their losses that they were worthy to be called a part of the Army of the Potomac. In Italy, a division went into its first battle with fixed bayonets and drew knowing smiles from veteran observers. Or a seasoned soldier might eye new arrivals and announce to them that "a week from now you'll be dead two days."

A disastrous beginning can, in some cases, ruin an organization. The 106th Division, caught in the first onslaught of the German Ardennes offensive, was destroyed, never to fight again as a cohesive unit, though one of its regiments and other subunits did continue to fight effectively. Fortunately, most units are introduced to battle in a less intensive manner, engaging in skirmishes or standing on a quiet sector, where they are gradually able to accustom themselves to the sights and sounds of war. Even if the first introduction is in a major battle, the unit may be able to survive relatively unscathed, or the unit organization may remain intact even though the losses have been heavy. These experiences, whether difficult or relatively easy, give the company the opportunity to evaluate its performance and the performance of individual members. The first weeks will allow the leaders and the men of the company to see who shows courage under fire, who can be depended upon to perform their duties under difficult conditions, and which ones show outstanding daring. Judgments may be severe. Men who show continuing lapses of courage, or who are somehow never around when fighting occurs, will lose respect in the eyes of other men and may never regain that regard. All of the men may feel fear, but most will be able to disguise it rather well. In the early stages of combat, they may not recognize that almost all men have a breaking point and will have little sympathy for those who reach that point early on.

For the newcomers, battle is not only frightening but also tremendously exciting. All of the experiences are new. The sound of artillery shells overhead or exploding nearby, the rattle of rifle fire and the even more ominous sound of the machine guns have to be absorbed and classified. One must learn quickly to distinguish between incoming rounds and outgoing rounds, and to know when it is advisable to seek cover and when it is safe to ignore such precautions. It is essential to learn the difference between friendly and enemy weaponry or simply even that one is under fire. One frequently runs across mention in the literature of new men mistaking the sound of bullets for bees, or, in one case, the bouncing of spent rounds for crickets hopping in the grass.[13] One has to learn how to react with relative calm under extreme stress; to be able to make a quick analysis of the situation, where the enemy is really located and what terrain features offer the best protection from enemy fire. The excitement of this learning period is remembered by a veteran of the 84th Division: "After a few hundred yards we came under continuous fire . . . but we kept moving. I remember our lieutenant being thrown from one end of a shell crater to the other by a near miss. I remember the wet cold slippery mud, a curious elation and mixture of fear, determination, and a desire for violence as I was captured by the frenzy of the attack. My M1 kicked in my hands as I pulled the trigger time and again, the empty casings and clips arching through the air."[14]

In the first days and weeks of combat, old skills will be sharpened and new skills learned. Patrols will be ordered, and the new men will begin to develop the sense of where each man is, as though they were linked together by invisible threads. House-to-house fighting, getting the feeling of kicking in a door, or covering each other in a narrow street, will become second nature. Steeling oneself to be ready to leave the fragile safety of the wood's edge for the naked vulnerability of the open field is a hard lesson, but one which will come as part of the growing confidence that the soldier develops in this initial period.

Soon, however, other factors begin to make themselves felt. The first of these is that losses are taken. They may be few in number, but over a short period of time they begin to mount up, and, without immediate replacement, the effective decline in the combat strength of the company becomes critically apparent. Wounds will outnumber deaths under ordinary circumstances by three or four to one; however, both work to reduce the strength of the company. Often when these losses occur, they are not spread evenly across the company, but concentrated in one platoon or squad. Friends are lost, and while some of them may return, many of the wounded (and, of course, the dead) are lost to the company forever.

Beyond this, sickness, which is a much smaller factor in the twentieth century than in previous times, will take its toll by removing men from the front for some period of time. It becomes more and more apparent that this society is a very ephemeral one, and soon, even the dullest men can see that, given the continuance of the war (and that does appear to be a given), everyone in the company they knew will be gone. This perception may not have immediate impact because during this early period of combat, the effectiveness of the remaining members is increasing, as is their confidence in their ability to perform their duties. They may even console themselves with the hopeful boast that "the bullet ain't made that can get me," or the more fatalistic, "no use worrying until the one with your name on it comes along." As the number of losses increases, their places taken by new men, the once close society of the company begins to break down a little. The effectiveness of the unit may also be reduced, owing to the inexperience of the replacements, and the slowly eroding confidence of the older men, another important factor. It is estimated that infantry reach their maximum effectiveness after about one month of combat. A plateau is then reached, followed by a falling-off of willingness to take chances or to move aggressively against the enemy. This latter stage is reached at about the third month of combat. Under the conditions of combat in the two great wars of this century, however, it was expected that an infantry rifle company would experience losses of original members and replacements equal to the total strength of the company during this same period. This did not mean that every man of the original company would be gone in that period of time, but it did mean that the majority of them would be gone and that many of the survivors would be less effective soldiers than they had been two months before.[15]

This decline would be marked by a greater concern for one's safety and a lessening concern for the interests of the other members of the unit, especially those who had not been a part of the original group. A loss of hope or confidence that one would survive intact would be noted, perhaps accompanied by an apathy which might well place the person in even greater danger of seeing his fears realized. The excitement of battle, or at least the factors which make it exciting, are still present, but the surviving members of the company are becoming numb to them. At the same time they are becoming ever more aware that the war, or at least their portion of it, is lasting much too long. The feeling grows that there is no way out except for death or a debilitating wound.[16]

Under such circumstances the urge to find some way to escape from the front becomes very strong; but also strong is the feeling that one must not accomplish this in a dishonorable manner. Desertion is punishable by death, assisting a comrade is not. Thus, numbers of men seeking a way out and possibly only half-conscious of their reasons for doing so, come to the aid of wounded men, helping them back to the aid station, although standing orders state that only medical personnel should perform this service. The problem was pervasive enough that Napoleon, in his Order of the Day for the Battle of Austerlitz, stated that "no man shall leave the ranks under the pretext of carrying off the wounded." From the Civil War one veteran wrote: "I have seen five men at times going off during an action with one wounded man. Four were carrying this man as if he were dead, (actually he had a superficial wound in the hand) and one carrying his gun."[17]

And another wrote from World War One that, "after an interval a few slightly wounded men approached, each attended by two or three solicitous friends, one carrying his rifle, another his water bottle and so on. These willing helpers were gently pushed back into the fray."[18]

It is understood that this solicitude is at least as great for one's self as it is for the wounded person. It is worth noting that, in the diaries and memoirs of men who had long service in combat, there is a marked tendency to concentrate on only a very few individuals; possibly one or two friends are mentioned, but very few others. The officers talk little about the members of their platoons; even the sergeants are scarcely mentioned. Enlisted men speak mainly about a friend or two, but very rarely about the squad or the platoon. This is, perhaps, another indication of the tendency to concentrate more on one's own survival the longer one has been in combat.

In previous centuries the rather lengthy time between battles did have the effect of lessening the impact of these perceptions, or extending the time which it took for them to grip the imaginations of the participants. A great battle could have a devastating effect upon a military formation. Some units recorded losses as high as 80 percent in one engagement.[19] But in the following weeks, the unit would have the chance to make good its losses and rest and recuperate from the shock it had suffered. That kind of interval has been denied to combat units in recent wars. Although their losses in any given battle are usually less severe than those suffered in the battles of previous centuries, the impact upon the individuals making up the unit has been at least as great or greater.

In Vietnam, the American military tried to address the morale problem by limiting the tour of duty to one year. This did allow the individuals to look forward to a definite time for release from combat duty. Since men entered a unit at various times throughout the year, however, the tour of duty concept made it somewhat more difficult to establish a sense of unity within each command. Like a train taking on and dropping off passengers at each station, the military unit usually was able to maintain something like its full strength; but, like the passenger train, there was the likelihood that the sense of community would be limited. The chances of creating an informal structure and sense of common tradition between men who lacked a common starting point and stood at different places in their tours of duty were somewhat diminished. Thus, the foundation for the sense of isolation felt by veterans returning singly from that war had already been laid by the conditions of service.

While many things would seem to militate against the maintenance of morale and efficiency in the military under combat conditions, there is much evidence to show that both are, in fact, most often maintained successfully. On the informal side of things, there is no doubt that some of the traditions of the company are passed on to the newcomers, or that they will in their turn begin to create new ones that can be carried forward. For instance, one of the most common ideas voiced by the old members of any company is the assurance given to newcomers that no matter how bad things are in this situation, they had been worse at some previous time. "You may not like this camp and think we're being tough on you here, but you should have seen it back at camp X," or, "this battle is nothing compared to . . . (some previous engagement)." The nice thing about this formula is that it can always be updated so that, even when the memories of the original experiences of the company have been extinguished, other situations will fill that void, and new men can always be regaled with tales from the heroic (or "golden") age of the company. This sense of continuity can be bolstered by the passing on of common phrases tailored to fit many occasions: "hurry up to wait . . . let's get this show on the road . . . this company always gets the hardest jobs," and so on. Songs also contribute their part to the maintenance of the unity and morale of the company, even while the individual members are changing. Some of the songs are bouncy and express the idea that this company is one hell of an outfit:

> Hidy Didy, Christ Almighty, Who the Hell are we?
> Ram bam, Goddam, we're the Infantry.

The German Army had a similar song:

> Zicke zacke, Juppheidi
> Schneidig is die Infanterie.[20]

Other songs had nothing to do with the military but were popular with the troops and are forever linked with one war or another. "Tipparary," "Long, Long Trail," and "Madelon" all bring up memories of the First World War, just as "Lili Marlene" is linked with the Second. Civil War soldiers both North and South had "Lorena" and "Weeping, Sad and Lonely"[21]; the men of the Spanish-American War had "Hot Time in the Old Town Tonight." Some songs lent themselves to parody: "Keep your 'ands Down You Naughty Boy" became "Keep Your 'ead Down Fritzi Boy." Under the impact of combat, the parodies themselves took on a blacker sort of humor. Take, for instance, "Those Mortar Shells Are Breaking Up That Old Gang of Mine," or the German version of the "Happy Wanderer."

> Vieleicht werd Ich bald bei dir sein,
> Annamarie,
> Vieleicht scharrt man schon morgen ein
> die ganze Kompanie, die ganze Kompanie.
>
> (Maybe I'll be with you soon, Anna Marie,
> or maybe they'll bury the whole company tomorrow.)[22]

While many of these songs, jokes, and tag lines would be remembered by veterans in later years, they are essentially ephemeral and do not carry on well in the traditions of the various services. It is necessary for the services themselves to maintain traditions. Some do this very well, others practically not at all. The British Army's regimental traditions are good examples of this conscious effort to maintain morale through tradition even when these traditions are to some extent manufactured. After World War I, the German Army attempted to keep the old Imperial army traditions alive by assigning regimental colors and traditions to the various companies of the Reichswehr. To what extent this was successful is open to question. More successful have been the French Foreign Legion and the United States Marine Corps. In these two instances, the emphasis has been on whole organization rather than any of its parts. Certainly the Marine Corps members were proud to have served in the First or the Second or one of the other divisions, but they have always been first and foremost Marines, as they never forget to tell any and all. The pride and the confidence that is thus engendered works to bolster the combat effectiveness of the Corps.

The informal structure of the military is something of a two-edged sword, since it can work to both support and undermine the official organization. Insofar as it strengthens the morale of the men, it provides support, but, as we have seen, when the older members of the platoon or company shut out the newcomers in combat, efficiency may drop. In some cases the informal friendship structure may actually come to the rescue of a failing official organization. As an example, squad leadership may break down because of enmity between the squad leader and his assistant or because of the failure of the squad leader to command. Sometimes the members of the affected units will simply reorganize themselves unofficially and continue to perform their duties. There may be some loss of efficiency involved, but a total breakdown has been avoided.

Disobedience may not necessarily be harmful to the operations of a military unit. Leaders may have the authority and may, in fact, be charismatic in their role. However, they may not be capable of making wise decisions. In such a circumstance, the subordinate members of the unit may simply refuse to follow orders or else act to stall the execution of the orders. For example, "A major of one of our regiments rode his horse in a tempestuous ride up and down outside the parapet, calling to us to advance. We looked back and could see no one to take our place in case we were repulsed. We determined to hold what we had and not to advance unless with positive orders from someone competent to give them."[23] In this case the decision not to follow the leader was based on a reading of the situation by experienced men (who had had three years of Civil War combat) and probably some knowledge of, and lack of respect for, the major in question. In many other cases a company can go to ground during an attack, and no amount of urging will persuade them to move forward. This can occur in situations where the act of moving forward would be hardly more dangerous than remaining in a position exposed to enemy fire. Furthermore, the failure to move may lose for the unit a chance to take an objective at relatively small expense that will later have to be taken with much greater losses. This is not to say that there are not circumstances when soldiers go to ground after having done all that they are capable of doing, but certainly that is not always the case.

In other ways the informal structure can work to the disadvantage of the objectives of the military. We noted above the way in which friends will help the wounded from the field. Rescuing the wounded who lie out in front of the lines is recognized as an act of bravery, but assisting a man back from the front (thus removing oneself as well) is not. In the case of the latter, friendship undermines responsibility. Numbers of other instances could be raised. On many occasions successful attacks have broken down because the attackers have fallen to looting the possessions of the foe. At Belmont, new troops under Grant, after driving off the Confederate unit, began to rummage through the enemy tents. It was only with the most strenuous effort that Grant was able to regain control and stave off the counterattack. In other cases where looting has been officially allowed, as in the sacking of a city, the individuals can become so taken up with this exercise and the prospects of individual gain that they lose their sense of organizational duties. Napoleon's troops retreating from Moscow were loaded down with loot taken from the city, an extra burden which contributed significantly to the disaster which overtook the Grande Armée.

Such breakdowns of discipline as these are most often only temporary in nature. The troops which went to ground one day, on other occasions would attack with most commendable ferocity. Holding these men to the front would be the concern for the respect of their comrades, which we have already mentioned. This concern for respect was and is a most important factor in the maintenance of discipline. Men may not feel one way or the other about the honor of the regiment, or they may feel that no one at home really knows or cares what they are doing; but the men they serve with do, and what they think is of great importance to most soldiers. Yet, some are not so motivated. Every army has to deal with the problem of desertion. For a variety of reasons, some men will decide that they are no longer willing to serve. It may be that the fear of battle, either as imagined or as experienced, has made them decide that nothing is more important than that they end their connection with the military. It may also be that concerns for happenings at home will work on them to the point where they decide to leave. Whatever the reason, men in every war have taken this option, even when the penalty for doing so is death. Some men desert by surrendering at the first opportunity, although life in the prisoner-of-war camps is often more daunting than death itself. At times desertion can become so prevalent that it can hamper or even destroy the operations of an army. In 1917, Russian soldiers deserted in such numbers that the czar's armies collapsed.

In other cases men, even members of well-disciplined units, may panic and desert the front in large numbers. Usually this occurs because of some unexpected turn in the battle, when fear leads men to believe that all is lost. J. F. C. Fuller's dictum, stating that in every army there is a mob waiting to break out, describes pretty well what happens in the cases of panic. Momentarily at least, all sense of unity has disappeared, and the individuals assume that they are on their own. It is contagious. A few panicked men arriving in the rear areas with news of imagined disaster can precipitate further and even greater flight. It is a curious fact that very often the rout of a unit or an army can begin in the rear as rumor multiplies the magnitude of a reversal which may be purely local.[24]

Finally, there is the case of military mutiny. Usually local in character, it can sometimes, as in the case of the French Army in 1917, encompass a major part of the armed forces. Here, the breakdown of discipline occurs not because of panicked fear, but through the total loss of confidence in the abilities of the leadership or because the leadership is no longer bearable for a variety of other reasons. With mutiny, what had been the informal organization of the military, the friendship groups or interest groups, asserts the right to set aside the official organization in favor of a new organizational structure growing out of the informal organization of the army. If the mutiny is confined to the enlisted ranks of the army, it is most often unsuccessful and is put down with the greatest severity. If the mutiny occurs within the officer ranks, it may have much better chances of success, particularly if the officers leading the revolt are able to carry their own troops with them.

Yet, if there is always the chance for dissonance between the formal and informal structures of the military, there is also the chance for a strained relationship between the military and the larger society of which it is a part. Even in hunting-gathering and primitive horticultural societies, where the warrior class encompasses almost the entire adult male population, this possibility exists. This can best be seen in the rituals which accompany the return of the warriors after battle. Having shed blood, they are very often considered to be ritually dangerous until certain purifying rites have been performed. In those instances where the outcome of the battle has been unfavorable, they may be met with taunts as well as with rituals of mourning as they reenter the larger society.[25] Even after they have been ritually cleansed, they may be treated as separate from the rest of society. In those groups which have created a special warrior class, such as the

Haida of the British Columbia coastal tribes, the warriors continue to be considered dangerous to the rest of society throughout their lives.[26]

Without doubt long service with a unit and the sharing of common dangers did serve to create bonds between the men. These bonds were difficult to sever and created a gulf between the men at the front and those at home. Many veterans of the First World War noted the lack of understanding by civilians of the conditions which existed at the front. Some were affronted by what they perceived to be the self-serving activities of civilians as compared with the selflessness of their frontline comrades. Relieved to be temporarily out of danger, they soon found themselves longing to be back with their friends and, in some cases, did cut short their leaves in order to return.

Rituals of return were not restricted to primitive groups. Both the armies of the ancient Near East and those of the classical period also faced certain purification rites upon the completion of battle or return to society. Sargon of Akkad mentions the washing of the swords as his army celebrated the end of the campaign which led them to the Mediterranean.[27] Roman armies were prohibited from crossing the boundary (oppidum) that surrounded the city of Rome, and the triumphs celebrated by the returning warriors were also religious rituals marking the acceptance of the warriors back into the general society.

While the return of warriors in modern society has been less rigidly marked by ritual, certain evidences of strain between the military and the civil population can be seen. Among the evidences of celebration are the victory parades staged upon the successful completion of war and the monuments erected to mark that success. The Arc de Triomphe and the Siegestor (in Munich) are such monuments. Other, more somber memorials include the various tombs of the Unknown Soldier and eternal flames set to honor the dead.

Yet, while victory is celebrated and defeat is mourned, there are other matters between the military and the civilian population that have to be worked through. Veterans of modern wars are not considered to be ritually impure, but this has not eliminated the nagging doubts and fears expressed by modern societies concerning them. Clothed in the contemporary dress of psychology and psychoanalysis, these concerns are shown by the fear that veterans, having been trained to kill, will not now be willing or able to shed these habits in the gentler confines of civilian life. After each of the great wars of this century, advisories to families on how to treat the returned soldier were issued. Terms such as shell shock and neurasthenia gained currency; outburst of temper or periods of depression were treated as warning signs that the trained killer had not yet been tamed. If the veteran continued to talk about his experiences for more than a few weeks, it was to be considered a sign of serious disturbance and counseling was advised. Much of this was quite silly; society moved rather quickly to a more reasonable approach to the problems of dealing with veterans. Obviously, not all veterans were able to resume normal life at the end of the wars. Some were in serious need of medical and psychological assistance, and this was given with various degrees of success.

In the United States, a more difficult problem accompanied the termination of the Vietnam War and the earlier Korean conflict. Here, the problem was compounded by the fact that the veterans of these wars did not return home in a large group. Rather, they filtered back into society singly and were soon lost in the crowd. For the Vietnam veteran, the situation was worsened by the growing antiwar sentiment, which was especially strong among the members of his own generation. While the veteran of the Korean War might be met with indifference or simply ignored, the man returning from Vietnam was often subject to active hostility. Accused of being killers of innocent children, or strongly suspected of being crazed drug addicts, many of these veterans went through the trauma of losing the faith they had once held in the rightness of what they had done. Some joined the antiwar movement and gained approval from their friends by confessing their sins in such public demonstrations as the "Winter Soldier" meetings. Others chose to dissociate themselves from society and took up a life on its fringes. For more than a decade after the end of that war, this situation continued. It is probably only with the erection of the very moving Vietnam memorial that the attitude of the society began to change.

Men returning from World War One were greeted as heroes, but soon thereafter they began to experience disillusion with the results of the war. Some looked upon their sacrifices as worthless and their experiences such that they could not be understood by those who had not served in the trenches. Thus, after about a decade in which this was little discussed, there came a flood of books expressing this disillusionment, while attempting to convey some idea of the horrors of that war. The term "lost generation" was coined, and veterans of both the Allied and the Central powers began to see themselves as men who, even as survivors, had been destroyed by the war.[28] The following decade saw the veterans warning the new generation of men with slogans like "don't be a sucker." Pacifism became a fashionable position, and students at Oxford would declare that they would not serve king and country in any future war. Not all veterans agreed with these sentiments, just as not all Vietnam veterans saw themselves as discarded by society, but the attitude of disillusionment did strongly affect the interpretation of the "Great War" in the minds of the following generation.

Unlike World War One and Vietnam, service in the Second World War did not seem to arouse the hostility of the troops in anything like the degree experienced in those other conflicts. With minor dissent there was broad agreement on the causes and aims of the war, and, at its conclusion, the belief that it would now be possible to build a better world tended to give an optimistic cast to the attitudes of the returning veterans. Figuratively, the men of this war returned looking forward to a brighter future rather than back toward the battlefields. There was certainly a pride in the accomplishments of the various services and remembrance of the dead, but, remarkably enough, there has never been a national monument erected to the memory of that war. There seems to have been a general agreement to tack the names of the dead onto the tablets set in place for the dead of the first war and to concentrate efforts on the construction of a better society. Soon enough, of course, the perceived threat of the Soviet Union would occupy the attention of the public, and there would be a sense that the weaknesses of the prewar period—the isolationism, the appeasement, and the lack of preparedness—should not be repeated. The shortcomings of this attitude would not be understood for almost a generation.

Perhaps the most enigmatic relationship is that which is maintained with the enemy. In simplest terms, he is trying to kill you and you are trying to kill him, whatever the grander causes of the struggle may be. But other factors are also involved. For one thing, it is necessary that there be an enemy in order for a war to exist. While it seems reasonable to say that one could get on perfectly well without enemies, this has not, historically, been the reality. The wars of primitive peoples bring up the point that for many of these peoples, especially in those societies where warfare and the life of the warrior are highly valued, a way of life would disappear if there were no enemies. It spoils the game if one side consistently fails to appear. The chivalric code of feudal society also depended upon the existence of adversaries. How could one prove one's mettle otherwise? Just as the medieval knight was proud to bear distinguishing marks on his shield, he was also gratified to see the marks of famous warriors in the ranks of his opponents. Even in modern warfare, where famous individual warriors are largely absent, men take pride in saying that they have fought against the best that the enemy has to offer. The fact that this may also create great difficulties for the soldier only reflects more brightly on his heroism.

Thus, in addition to a hatred for and fear of the enemy, there can also exist respect. The same kind of respect that is given to good soldiers in one's own ranks is also given to the brave enemy. One may even have a greater respect for the adversary than for one's allies. In Vietnam, for example, "Charlie" and the North Vietnamese regulars were generally held in higher regard by the American troops than the soldiers of the South Vietnamese Army. Perhaps a part of this respect was due not only to the fighting abilities of the adversary, but also to the fact that, in modern wars, the enemy is but seldom seen. Since he is seldom seen, it is possible to attribute to him an entire range of bad qualities. His bravery is respected, but he is regarded as being, in some way, inhuman. He does not "fight fair," a most curious charge, since the enemy is fighting for his life in a no-holds-barred contest. Often, it is asserted that the enemy soldier is an automaton, incapable of making decisions on his own or operating without leadership. For the most part such charges have little basis, other than as certain myths which exist about the nature of the enemy's society.

At times the chance occurs to develop a closer relationship with the enemy than that allowed by shooting at one another. Taunting contests may take place. For example, the interchange, "Yankee sojer, you die!—Fuck you, you slant-eyed son of a bitch," may not take high marks for witty repartee, but it does establish a sort of dialogue between foes. In the American Civil War, the exchanges led from taunting, to questions of how things were over there, to agreements not to fire on each other, to arrangements for the exchange of needed items, such as coffee and tobacco.[29] In the First World War, there did occur tacit agreements not to fire at certain times (during meals for instance), or to observe a truce while wounded were retrieved. On Christmas day,

1914, Germans and English climbed hesitantly out of the trenches and began to exchange gifts in the middle of no-man's-land. From time to time men in the trenches would serenade the other side, even honoring requests for songs. Such informal assemblies were unacceptable to the commanders, but they continued to take place just the same.[30]

Out of such exchanges would grow a sense of sharing the same interests and dangers. The soldier might live in mortal fear of the power of the enemy and his ability to do him the gravest harm but he also came to realize that the man in the opposite trench was suffering all of the same discomforts, and that he probably had the same concerns for his life as oneself. Out of such a revelation grew a sense of the common destiny of frontline soldiers, a destiny not shared by the rear echelon troops, the staffs, or the civilian population. The respect for the enemy grew out of this realization that he was one's own mirror image.

If the opposing troops had a destiny in common, it might also be asked whether they shared common social origins. An old complaint, heard during the American Civil War and echoed in other wars since, is that war is "a rich man's war but a poor man's fight." Most recently that complaint has been raised in connection with the Persian Gulf War. Historically, there is a considerable degree of truth in the statement. While the cavalry armies of the Middle Ages were dominated by the nobility, the foot soldiers of more recent centuries were drawn primarily from the peasantry of the various European states. This was almost necessarily the case, since the largest reservoir of manpower was to be found there, and it was the group over which the coercion needed to bring them into the military could be most easily exercised. The urban population, both the merchants and the artisans, were able to protect themselves by reason of their greater political power and because, with their skills, they constituted a valuable asset to the early modern state. The armies of the kings were made up of men from the peasantry and from the lowest orders of urban society. Often described as the scum of the earth or the sweepings of society, these men could be drawn into the service for long terms of enlistment, after which they were released to subsist somehow on the ungentle charity of the society. If married while in service (and this was not too common), their children might follow them in their career. With very little hope of rising beyond the noncommissioned ranks and shunned by polite society, they lived as uniformed pariahs: needed but unloved and subjected to the harshest discipline, they could expect either an early death from bullet, bayonet, or disease, or the prospect of being turned out to a meager old age. Their officers were drawn from a class so far above them in the social scale that they seemed of a different world.

With the advent of the mass armies of the late eighteenth and early nineteenth centuries, this situation began to change. It was no longer possible to depend upon the small professional armies for success on the battlefield; or, at least, such became clear with the victories of the Prussians over the Austrians and the French in the last third of the nineteenth century. The American Civil War had already shown the utility of mass armies made up of persons drawn from all sections of society. Although most of the enlisted personnel were still coming from a farming background, urban dwellers were also represented in large numbers. The educated middle class and many members of the political leadership made themselves available for service as officers of the new regiments. These were not professional soldiers, but no group of professionals would have been sufficient to fill the needs of warfare under modern conditions. Modern weaponry, the rifled musket, and a little later the much improved, breech-loading artillery and rifles, made warfare so much more costly in manpower that it became necessary to draw on the whole resources of the population. In the vast wars of the twentieth century, this was even more the case. No longer was it possible, as it had been in the American Civil War, to purchase a substitute to do your fighting for you. Mass conscription was introduced to provide a greater degree of fairness to the selection of those who would do the fighting.

In the First World War, the sons of the middle and upper classes found, in very great numbers, hazardous posts as infantry junior officers. In England, a common way of selecting these officers was on the basis of their public school background or from the students and recent graduates of the ancient universities. In Germany, gymnasium graduates followed the same route, although many of them would serve for a time in the ranks before being commissioned. At Langemarck in the fall of 1914, large numbers of these intensely patriotic, but pathetically untrained, German boys fell before the rifle fire of the small army of British regulars. Soon, however, the ranks of these "old contemptibles" would be riddled, and willing volunteers from all sections of society—from the mines of Wales and Yorkshire, the farms of

Kent, the offices of Manchester, and the small business establishments of London—would find themselves serving in one or the other
of the battalions of Kitchener's New Army. These would have their
real baptism of fire in the terrible Battle of the Somme. With the
introduction of conscription in 1916, those who had not been so ardent
to get in the fight found themselves drawn upon to fill battalions
depleted in earlier battles. Given the social makeup of the United
Kingdom in the early twentieth century, it was impossible to recruit a
major portion of these men from the farming population. Nor could
the laboring sector provide sufficient bodies for the needs of the king's
armies, so that more and more of the burden fell upon the middle
class. This same situation prevailed in the German Army. The French
Army, with a larger percentage of the population still on the farm, did
not have quite the same mix, but everywhere the class structure of
the armies was changing.

Some indication of the class structure of the United States Army in
the Second World War can be gained from the listing, in Leinbaugh
and Campbell's *The Men of Company K*, of the present occupation of
170 former members of that company. It cannot be conclusive, since it
does not indicate the occupation of the person or of his family before
entering service but, on the assumption that such patterns will not be
altered greatly by the military experience, it may be useful. Of the
204 men listed, 34 were killed in action. The information on the
postwar occupations of the surviving 170 men breaks down as follows:[31]

Manual and skilled labor	26%
Office, sales, management	25%
Professional	9%
Business owners	10%
Government, military, postal	11%
Farming	6%
No information	13%

Fifteen percent of the men noted that they had completed at least
some college, and, in other cases where this was not mentioned, it
seems clear from the occupation that the person had completed a
university degree, possibly before entering the service. These statistics indicate that a very large percentage of the members of this company either came from middle and lower-middle class backgrounds or
at least joined this middle group following service. It hardly supports

the argument that the poor and laboring classes provided the vast majority of the men who served in the rifle companies.

Did the very wealthy or members of the most privileged classes of society serve in the more dangerous posts? There is no exact evidence here, but the personal histories of several prominent individuals, such as Presidents Kennedy and Bush, shows that some did seek out dangerous assignments. Although privilege usually brought with it an officer's commission, at least one very wealthy man, Malcolm Forbes, served as an enlisted man in the infantry. One military unit, the 10th Mountain Division, attracted numbers of graduates from Ivy League schools who had experience in the sport of skiing, as well as figures from the sports world and assorted adventurous individuals. Sen. Robert Dole, who came as a replacement officer to the 10th Division, remarked wryly that he couldn't have gotten in to the original group— it was by invitation only.

The system of selection for service in World War II not only eliminated those who were physically unfit, but also tended to exclude blacks, who would have been eligible on the basis of physical and mental fitness but were turned down for reasons (not too carefully disguised) of racial prejudice. Many blacks did serve, and two infantry divisions, the 92nd and the 93rd, were made up of black enlisted men serving under white officers. Other blacks served in separate companies of armor or infantry, and many served in quartermaster trucking companies. Segregation mandated, however, that blacks and whites should not serve together. Prejudice also underpinned the belief that the blacks were not capable of fighting well; this despite the fine records of several black regiments in the American Civil War and post–Civil War period, as well as in World War I. It was only after the end of the Second World War that the services were finally integrated, and blacks were allowed to gain commissions in substantial numbers. Today, after their record of service in Vietnam, no one complains of their lack of fighting spirit.

Wherever they come from, whether from the lowest or the highest ranks of society, the men passing through the military do have their impact upon an official organization which is often unresponsive to their needs. By resistances, either subtle or gross, the men, through their unofficial organization, do effect at least enough change to make life in the military more bearable. To a large extent this unofficial structure does support the needs of the official structure. When it does not, when it, in fact, has a deleterious effect, as in the case of panic or mutiny, the official structure has usually been able to reassert its authority. The larger society of which the military is a part, also has its impact upon the official and unofficial structures. Changes in technology, the social structure, and the values to which it gives support, will all finally be reflected in the military organization. If the official military organization should prove to be unresponsive to the needs of society, or should it act to impose its rigid value system on the society, it may succeed in the short term; but eventually this artificial society will not be able to sustain itself without the support of the larger society. It will be destroyed or find itself altered by the continued pressures from the general society, for it is certain that the military cannot survive without this support. Whether societies will find themselves able to survive without the presence of a military component is another question.

5

Foxholes of the Mind

TROUBLED BY SECRET UNCERTAINTIES: whether they will be able to meet the demands that society will place upon them, whether they have the courage to face the enemy, whether they really want to be away from home; young men stand naked in a line, waiting for the physical examination that will mark the first stage of their assimilation into the life of the army. They will be poked and prodded, questioned, instructed, bullied, herded from one station to the next, and finally, if they are accepted for service, lined up and inducted into the army in a more or less solemn service. Depending upon the gravity of the situation, the physical and mental capabilities for acceptance into the service may be either raised or lowered. In times of grave national crisis, such as a major war, almost everyone will be able to pass the examinations. Even if this is not so at the beginning of the conflict it will become the practice as the need for more bodies evidences itself. At this initial stage of the process, the induction physical, a first valuable lesson is taught. Stripped of their clothing, each individual has begun the process of discovering that he is an interchangeable part in a large and complicated machine. Particularly in the first stages of his training, this lesson will be reiterated constantly.

It has been frequently argued that the purpose of the initial phase of training is to break down the individual completely and to remold him in the image that the military desires. It is true that he will have his hair cut or, possibly, shaved off; that he will be forced to wear exactly the same clothing as all the others; that he will do the same things at the same time as all the others; and that he will generally live under orders over which he has no control. However, it is not in the army's interest to turn out automatons who have lost the ability to act independently. The reason for this is that, once the soldier has been committed to combat, losses will begin to occur, and he may at any moment be called upon to take over the leadership of a small group or to act by himself in the absence of any support. In order to do this, he must still be capable of independent thinking; he must be able, under stress, to analyze a situation, arrive at an appropriate solution, and act upon that conclusion. Understandably, this will not always happen, but the army must hope that it will occur often enough that it can succeed in attaining its goals.

The initial phase of training, "boot camp" or basic training, does aim at instilling within the soldier certain automatic responses, so that he will be able to operate on the battlefield. He must be capable of loading and firing his weapon accurately without having to think through every step of the process, and he must be ready to accept and carry out orders in stressful and confusing situations without arguing the rationality of those orders. To a certain extent these necessities parallel those found in ordinary life; to drive a car efficiently, many of the responses must be nearly automatic, and one has to accept the rationality of the various traffic signals and instructions without questioning the rightness of them. In both of these cases, failure to observe the rules or lack of knowledge in the operation of the machinery could result in injury or death.

There is, however, at least one very great difference between the two cases. In combat, situations may arise demanding that a soldier die in order that the larger purposes of the organization can be achieved. There are not (or should not be) any suicide missions on the highway, though they arise with fair frequency on the battlefield. Not all armies are equally forthright in telling their soldiers of this possibility. The American Army issued a field manual (FM 21–100) to its infantry soldiers in World War II, which does not mention the subject of death at all except for a sample will at the end of the booklet. Other than that, the soldier is informed that he must learn to obey all orders "promptly and cheerfully," show loyalty, and be a team player, so that the purposes of the organization can be realized efficiently and successfully. The qualities needed for success in the army are the same as those needed for success in civilian life; follow the rules and emerge from the army with a clean record and the thanks of a grateful country. Even the oath taken by the individual at the time of his induction speaks only of bearing "true faith and allegiance to the United States; that he will serve them faithfully against all their enemies; and that he will obey the orders of the President of the United States and the officers appointed over him." The occasion of taking the oath is a solemn one, since by the act of swearing the oath, the inductee also accepted the fact that he was now a member of the military, but there was no explicit mention of death. However much the possibility might lurk in the mind of the individual, and however much it might be mentioned by one or another of his training instructors, it was not written down in black and white.[1]

By contrast the oath of the German soldier, the *Fahneneid*, was much more explicit: "I swear before God this holy oath that I will give unconditional obedience to the Fuehrer of the German Reich and People, Adolf Hitler, and, as a brave soldier, will be ready at any time to risk my life for this oath."[2] The German field manual from which this oath was taken went on to discuss the fact that it might become necessary to shed one's blood or to die, as had hundreds of thousands of other soldiers. But this sacrifice is the most honorable form of death possible, since it is a death for the state and the nation of the German people. The writers of the manual recognize that this is a fearful obligation and state that it is not dishonorable to show certain of the physical signs of fear under stress: trembling may not always be controllable. What is not acceptable is that the fear should take hold of the soldier's spirit and, thereby, make him incapable of performing his duty.

Both manuals deal in considerable detail with the everyday demands of military life: preparing for inspection, proper dress, drill, the care and operation of weapons, military courtesy, field craft, and the organization of the army. Where they differ, and where the two armies differed to some extent, is in the emphasis which the American manual places on efficiency, while the German manual concerns itself with moral considerations. The words "bravery" and "courage" do not appear in the American manual, while these qualities are considered the foundation of the soldier's life by the German book. The American soldier is urged to become an efficient member of a team; the German pledges his life for the success of his unit. It should not be inferred from this that the American soldier was unaware of the possible cost of his involvement in battle. Much as he might want to put it out of his mind, the thought of being killed was always there. Probably less than 5 percent of infantrymen were volunteers; aside from the difficulties of life in the field, and the unglamorous nature of infantry service, there was also a strong feeling that the infantryman's lot was a dangerous one. To be aware of the potential for serious injury or death, however, is not quite the same thing as assuming that a duty to die under certain circumstances exists.

How strongly the German soldier felt this duty may be open to question, but no such question arises concerning his superb fighting qualities. On the other hand the fighting abilities of the American soldier, particularly the infantryman, have been questioned. It is averred that he lacked the will to attack energetically, that he was not always stalwart in defense, that his desertion rates were far above those of some other armies, and that he was more prone to suffer mental breakdown under stress. It is taken as a truism that the American Army depended more heavily upon material strength than other armies and that, without this advantage, its performance on the battlefield would have been less than adequate. The infantry has most often borne the onus for these charges. The quality of the individual soldier, his lack of training and discipline, the less than satisfactory abilities of the junior leadership, and the system of furnishing replacements are all noted as contributing to this situation. Even former infantrymen express their doubts and very often rate the German soldier as superior to themselves. T. N. Dupuy's *A Genius for War* attempts to quantify this inferiority by mathematically analyzing a number of engagements between German and either British or American forces.[3] Without questioning his calculations, it is still possible to question his choice of examples. Of thirty of his cases, seventeen deal with battles fought by American forces which had been in combat less than three months. Further, nine of these latter involve troops with just over one month's combat experience, and in two cases the unit had been in combat for less than ten days. It is highly probable that in all of these examples, the German troops were the more experienced. Drawing on the results furnished by Dupuy, Martin van Crefeld's *Fighting Power* tries to analyze why this disparity in performance existed.[4] Much that van Crefeld says makes very good sense. His comparison of methods of replacement is well taken, as is his portrayal of the differences in officer training. In arguing for the greater cohesion achieved by drawing manpower for the units from the same geographical region, however, he fails to note the fact that five of the eight divisions used in the Dupuy study were National Guard formations organized on a regional basis.

An even more widely cited study than either of the above is that of Col. S. L. A. Marshall, *Men against Fire.*[5] There is much that is valuable in this study, which is based on Marshall's experiences doing analyses of small unit combat as soon after battle as possible. Of all of his conclusions, the most notorious is that which stated that only 15 percent of American riflemen ever fired their weapons in combat. Through the years many have tried to grapple with this astonishing finding. It has been alleged that this failure was due to paralyzing fear, distaste for killing, lack of knowledge of the weapon's workings, a training which emphasized marksmanship over the delivery of volume fire, or the general inability of the American infantryman. Only recently has another explanation been offered, so simple in character that it had been overlooked for more than forty years: there is no documentation in Marshall's studies of the small units to back up his claim. Apparently, the question of whether men had fired their weapons was never asked. The officers and men who worked with Marshall on these studies do not remember any questioning on the subject, and it was not part of the program questionnaire.[6] It is probably true that some men did not fire their weapons in a particular engagement, and there may have been some who never fired at all. Many may have fired inaccurately, either because of stress or, in a few cases, because they could not bring themselves to kill another human being. Marshall may have included this statistic because he intuitively believed it to be true, but in assigning an exact figure, he lent to his finding (if such it was) a spurious note of scientific authenticity which has come to be widely accepted as fact.

There are many differences between armies which could be assigned to national character or upbringing; the willingness of the Japanese soldier to fight to the death, the amazing endurance of the North Vietnamese in their movements down the Ho Chi Minh Trail, the iron discipline of the Roman soldier which enabled him to fight so successfully for so many centuries at close quarters. These differences are important and do contribute to success or failure, but, in a sense, they are marginal differences. When measured against the activities of an undisciplined mob, the particular qualities of any well-ordered military organization are large indeed. This is not to say that civilians cannot exhibit bravery. That much was clearly demonstrated by the resilience of the urban populations under the heavy bombardments of the Second World War; it has also been seen in other centuries with populations under siege. Yet men in military formations are different. They do actively seek out situations of danger, either because they are ordered to do so or, at times, through some sort of spirit of adventure. It is often held that men, with the possible exception of a few psychopaths, universally fear battle. There is a truth to this but it is also true that many men are willing to return again and again to the battlefield. The record of the number of British officers in the nineteenth century who, even after being severely wounded more than once or in some cases many times, sought out further service in the small wars of Victoria's reign, gives some indication that war holds its attractions.[7] Robert E. Lee's often-quoted statement, "it is well that war is so terrible—we should grow to love it too much," expresses exactly this attitude.

It might be said that this is all very well for officers, especially generals, but what about the men in the front line? Actually, until this century, officers, including the commanders, were exposed to most or all of the dangers of the battlefield, since control had to be exercised by voice and vision. Even now, officers up to the battalion level will find themselves exposed to most of the dangers of the battlefield. What is true for some portion of the officers is surely true for all of the lower ranks, the noncommissioned officers and men. For higher officers the achievement or the retention of a reputation can be a powerful incentive; but how does the ordinary man react to the various stresses of battle? The junior officers and the sergeants have duties which, though burdensome, also have certain advantages. They must concentrate their attention to the direction of their particular portion of the battle, and they must maintain the image of leadership. These needs can prove to be a powerful support to these junior leaders. To demonstrate composure under difficult circumstances not only serves to steady the troops, but also raises the stature of the leader in the eyes of his followers.

For the lowest ranks, this advantage is lacking. The individual private has only the duties of following orders and of being prepared to act independently in order to save the situation should the need arise. He cannot, under ordinary conditions, exercise command; he can only perform his tasks as a part of the smallest unit (the squad or the section) and look out for himself. Thus, the conflicting impulses of discipline and self-concern can have their greatest impact on these lowest members of the military organization. Assuming that he has had an adequate training in the use of his weapons and the operations of his unit what else does the soldier bring to the battle? Certainly most men approach battle in a spirit of trepidation. There is always the nagging question of whether he will be able to perform adequately. He is also concerned to maintain the respect of the men with whom he is serving. He may or may not be motivated by the great reasons for the war or the reputation of his regiment or division, far less his corps or army. He will also be moved by curiosity. Almost all men, though they fear battle, are extremely curious to see what it is like. "Going to see the elephant" or the "monkey show" were Civil War expressions for this curiosity; "this is it" expressed both the anxiety and the curiosity of the soldier in the Second World War. Many, perhaps all, see battle as a test of their manhood, a test which can be passed by standing on the battlefield—but it does not necessarily entail the killing of another human. While these are not very good reasons for placing one's life in extreme danger, they probably help the soldier to withstand the initial shocks, given the fact that the individual has little choice in the matter.

The initial fears can, to some extent, be stilled by a number of means. Since the great fear is personal injury or dismemberment, this feeling can be transferred to others. The soldier may worry about the potential loss of friends, or imagine the possibility of his unit suffering a setback. If his imagination turns to personal injury, he may think of it in terms of a clean bullet wound to an arm or leg. He may feel himself lucky not to be caught in some death trap, such as a burning tank, a stricken aircraft, or a sinking ship. In any case, the mere fact of being on the battlefield, encountering novel sights and sounds, learning how to distinguish enemy and friendly fire or how to judge the closeness of an incoming round, will occupy his most immediate attention. If he is thrown into an attack the excitement of action can momentarily drown out thoughts of personal injury. This does not mean that he becomes careless, but, rather, that he must concentrate so fully upon the task at hand that other considerations are pushed to the back of his mind. Later, as the squad or platoon is pulled back into reserve, talk of the action may bring to mind the

dangers which he and others have faced—the injuries and deaths suffered by comrades—and at this point, he may begin to think more
fully upon his own vulnerability. At the same time, he will also be
storing up knowledge of what one must do in order to be effective in
battle. Units new to combat will go through the period of becoming
veteran organizations. The individual members will begin to see who
are the most effective soldiers and who need to be watched. For the
replacement entering a veteran outfit, the process will be more difficult, for he must do much of it by himself, and, in the process, obtain
acceptance from the already established group. Some men will help
him in this development, while others will simply ignore him or
parade their own expertice at the expense of his naïveté.

In whatever manner the soldier is introduced to combat, he does, if
he survives the initial period, become more accommodated to it. He
has learned something of what to expect. He becomes more accustomed to living in dirt, wet, cold, or severe heat. He learns that there
is no real solution to the problem of bad or insufficient food and that
uninterrupted or unencumbered sleep is a luxury unobtainable in
these parts. His vision also becomes more narrow. What happens
beyond the bounds of the company falls more and more into the
realm of rumor. He may hear that another company has been hard hit
but will have little in the way of verification. Within the company his
attention is mostly focused on the problems of his own platoon and
squad. For days at a time, he can be out of touch with friends in other
parts of the company. Deaths and injuries to these men are more often
heard about than seen. Suddenly people that he is used to noticing,
who are part of the fabric of the company, are no longer there. The
apparent randomness of death and injury may at first surprise him;
the good and careful soldier is lost, but the company klutz lives on.
He may also be surprised by the equanimity with which he is able to
accept these losses. They hurt, friends and acquaintances are gone,
but the necessity of continuing to function is still there. He finds
himself becoming numb to the pain which, under other circumstances,
he might feel for those who are gone.

Of necessity he has become harder than he ever thought possible.
Things are funny which would formerly not have seemed humorous
at all. The humor is often gross and certainly more grim. A man
getting shot is not funny, but a man who suffers a wound in the
buttocks may become the subject of teasing. This hardening process

accompanies a growth in the skills which are needed to survive and succeed. Men find that they can obey orders promptly, if not always cheerfully, even when these orders place them in positions of the greatest danger. There is little or no sympathy for the man who malingers or who breaks down and is unable to function. The chronic malingerer is useless or even dangerous, since he may not be available when every man is needed. The man who is unable to control his fears, who sits sobbing in his foxhole or in a back corner of some embattled house, gets little sympathy from the others. If he is a long-time veteran, he may receive more understanding, but the man who cracks early on does not. This presupposes that the situation, while dangerous, is not catastrophic. If a unit finds itself overwhelmed, panic reactions may be so general that blame for the breakdown is accepted by all members or shifted off to some impersonal source.

How long the individual can continue to function effectively under the conditions which prevail in combat has long been a matter of debate, and in the twentieth century, as battle has become a more continuous affair, it has become a matter of the greatest concern for the leaders of the military. In the American Army in the Second World War, planning for the number of replacements needed by front-line units was based upon casualty estimates which proved to be inadequate.[8] It had been assumed that, on the average, a rifleman could continue to provide good service for at least a year. Experience in the European theater indicated that under conditions of moderate to heavy engagement, the turnover rate for a rifle company would be about once every three or four months. The fighting in the Huertgen Forest was so intense that companies were reduced to ineffectiveness within days. This same heavy loss rate was also experienced by the Marines fighting on Iwo Jima.[9] These loss rates did not go unnoticed by the individual. He might have become a more efficient soldier and he might have become much more hardened to the conditions of combat, but he also became much more aware of the slenderness of his chances of surviving without injury. Just as the limits of his spacial consciousness had become more circumscribed, encompassing only the company area and the five-hundred yards or so in front of him, so his temporal consciousness was also delimited. Unlike classical drama with its beginning, middle, and end, the war began to seem interminable. The beginning faded ever farther into the past, the end appeared unattainable, so only the middle was left. Like some macabre soap opera, the war seemed destined to continue far beyond the possibility of one's personal survival.

These perceptions tended to lead to a state of depression in which the soldier continued to function, often very capably, but without the sense of hope that had accompanied him upon first entering battle. James Jones has suggested, in a series of notes entitled "The Evolution of the Soldier," that a defense against this depression, employed by some veteran combat men, was the assumption that one was already dead.[10] Jones recommends that anyone entering the armed services adopt this attitude because of the army's need to create replaceable parts (including soldiers), and its assumption that men are expendable. Not every man must pay the full price, but each was potentially liable. Therefore, if one accepted the reality of being dead, one could eliminate the constant worry. In exchange for this acceptance, the soldier could then begin to enjoy each small moment of pleasure that happened to come his way without worrying about what might happen tomorrow. It went one step beyond the traditional "eat, drink, and be merry, for tomorrow we die," to the statement that "we are already dead." Whether this attitude was ever accepted by many soldiers is open to question, but certainly many learned to live from one small pleasure to the next in a world where these pleasures were interspersed with other moments of terror.

The state of depression was very real. It did not mean that every soldier was constantly living without joy, but his outlook was definitely pessimistic. Jones suggested that, in addition to living for small pleasures, the soldier could take refuge in his professionalism. This, he noted, was not the professionalism of the regular officer concerned with his career, as well as with the winning of the war, but rather the professionalism of the man who knows how to do a job well and continues to to perform his duties out of a sense of pride, knowing that he may never realize any permanent benefits from the performance of that duty and may very well not survive its performance.

This suggests that, even in a state of depression, the soldier could continue to act successfully for an indefinite period. In previous wars this had been the case. The soldiers of the Army of the Potomac, even those who had served through all the campaigns, looked forward with optimism to the campaign of 1864, since they believed that it would bring the war to an end. However, after a month of constant and bitter fighting from the Wilderness, Spotsylvania, and North Anna, to the dreadful carnage of Cold Harbor, this initial optimism had changed to the deepest pessimism. The change is reflected in the diaries which some of the soldiers kept. Belief in Grant's ability to defeat Lee faded, and again, as in previous campaigns, the end of the war sank over the horizon of hopes.[11] It should be noted that here, for the first time, these soldiers were experiencing a situation of continuous battle, and one which, for a month, exacted much higher casualty rates than those experienced in the Second World War. Following this period of heavy fighting, there was some relief from the worst of the pessimistic state, though the sense of depression continued. The men at Petersburg could see that an end to the war was coming, but they had real doubts as to whether they would be there to enjoy it.

Psychological studies of the attitudes of the American soldier were conducted during World War II in an effort to get a better idea of what could reasonably be expected of soldiers in the way of endurance. The study looked at motivational aspects as well as actual performance.[12] The findings indicated that the American soldier was not fighting for any of the lofty ideals espoused by the leaders of the nation, though they did recognize the necessity of eliminating the threat posed by Nazi Germany and Japan. Most often the men spoke of goals in terms of "getting the job done so that we can go home." They most definitely shied away from flag-waving or referred to it in ironic fashion. Other motivations included gaining or keeping the respect of the other men in the unit. There was noticeable contempt for the patriot who did not, for whatever reason, put his own life on the line. These are scarcely surprising results, as soldiers in other wars have expressed much the same kind of sentiments. A song from the First World War went, "We're here because we're here, because we're here." In the American Civil War, Northern soldiers by and large were not fighting to free the slaves and, though they felt that the union had to be restored, it was hardly, after the first burst of enthusiasm, a primary factor in keeping them in the fight. The Southern soldier fought because the Yankees were "down here," but his enthusiasm for the Confederacy as an ideal was somewhat more muted. Numbers of German soldiers in the Second World War were motivated by National Socialist ideals. One young soldier relates how he had entered the army as a fervent Nazi and had lost only a part of this enthusiasm after entering battle. But when he was forced to surrender in the fall of 1944, he fell into a state of intense bewilderment, as though everything that he had been taught to believe had come undone. When he raised his arms he felt as though everything drained out of him; that he was an empty shell for some months after that.[13] However, many another German soldier found himself doubting more seriously the cause for which he was fighting.

Well-organized groups of men—many of them in a state of chronic depression—living in conditions of nearly constant danger, heavily armed, and with loyalties directed more toward the immediate group than to the outer society, can pose a great threat not only to the enemy, but to the rest of society as well. Either the group or the separate individuals which compose it can easily begin to act in ways not in the best interests of civilized society—sadly, war itself is one of the interests of civilized society. The history of war is replete with instances of lawlessness, petty or great, committed by the soldier-warrior. The cruelty of an Attila or a Genghis Khan are legendary, but even soldiers of the most well-ordered societies, serving in rigorously disciplined military organizations, can be guilty of illegal, often monstrous acts. Such acts may be committed by the lone individual, condoned by the military leadership, or established as official state policy. These crimes are committed against the enemy, the enemy's civilian population, or neutral populations unfortunate enough to be in the path of the battling armies. Even the civilians of one's own society may be subject to the depredations of the military.

Looting is so commonly practiced by armies that it might almost be considered one of the privileges of the warrior. Petty theft from the homes and property of civilian populations in the war zone is a constant problem. Soldiers will rearrange the furniture between houses to suit themselves, or, in some cases, employ it for the purposes of defense, for there is often a thin line separating justifiable military usage from theft. Money, watches, cameras, anything of value may be picked up by invading armies. The bodies of the dead have traditionally been stripped of valuables, and, in cases where the army is desperately short of supplies, the clothing and boots of the dead may be taken to equip the living. At times looting may develop into a senseless destruction of property, as though the evidences of an ordered society constituted an affront to men living in chaos. As mentioned above, such property destruction may be officially sanctioned. Sherman's March and its accompanying devastation is the most famous American example, though the "Bummers" who tagged along were more interested in looting for their own advantage.

Other instances of officially sanctioned destruction can be seen in the sacking of cities at the conclusion of a siege. In these cases, soldiers who have endured deprivation, frustration, and extreme danger were allowed to vent their fury on the resistant population. The looting and the property destruction were only the prelude to the separate acts of murder and rape perpetrated upon conquered and helpless civilians. Usually the military authorities, recognizing that too long a continuance could lead to a breakdown of the army itself, put a time limit on these activities. After an initial phase of disorder in Berlin and other East German cities the Russian leaders reimposed strict discipline upon the troops. In Vietnam, at the village of Mi Lai, the order to shoot the civilians was given by a junior commander. In this case, the action was a matter of intense embarrassment to the higher command. Initially they covered up the incident, but when the story was made public, they proceeded to punish those of the guilty parties in the lower ranks of the service.

The treatment of the enemy can also cross the line from the legitimate to the illegitimate. This is especially the case in the handling of prisoners. Official policy provides that prisoners should be made to ground their arms and are then escorted to the rear for processing by intelligence units and the military police. For a variety of reasons, this often proves to be difficult or impossible. Units heavily involved in battle may feel that they cannot detail men to guard the prisoners, nor can they trust these prisoners to make their own way to the rear. They may, therefore, simply order them to be killed. Similarly, a soldier who has defended his position to the very last moment at great expense to the enemy cannot always expect fair treatment when he surrenders. Getting past the frontline troops is often the most dangerous time for men taken prisoner. In some cases, a man detailed to take a small group of prisoners to the rear may feel that he has no reason to protect their lives. He may be in a state of shock from losses to his own friends, or he may simply be afraid that the prisoners will turn on him; thus, he may kill them. Often, the treatment of prisoners is motivated by preconception of the nature of these men. On the Russian front during the Second World War, both sides treated prisoners with brutality and callousness. On the western front, the widely advertised actions of some of the Waffen-SS troops resulted in their being killed out of hand when captured by the Americans or the British. This was particularly the case after the details of the Malmedy massacre were publicized. In the Pacific, fear and hatred of the Japanese, as well as evidence of their treatment of American prisoners, led to a situation in which very few Japanese were taken prisoner until the very final stages of that conflict. Those captured were most often killed by the frontline troops.

The treatment of prisoners who did make it to the interrogation centers and the prison camps varied greatly. At one end of the scale would be found the well-ordered prison camps established in the United States for the handling of Germans and Italians captured in the North African and other Mediterranean campaigns. Here, the prisoners were well fed and allowed a considerable degree of freedom in the handling of their own affairs. This was so much the case that in some camps, dominated by still-convinced Nazis, prisoners had more to fear from their fellows than from the guards. Western Allied prisoners in German camps also received generally fair, though rigorous, treatment. On the other hand, Russian prisoners were brutally treated, starved, and in most cases died. Germans in Russian prisons were similarly treated; those who did survive were held for a long number of years following the end of hostilities. Allied prisoners held by the Japanese often received brutal treatment and were subject to starvation and death from lack of adequate food and medical care. It has been argued this was due to the fact that the Japanese were handling them in the fashion sanctioned by their military code for the handling of all military personnel, including their own. It is apparently true that, in some cases, the food allowance for the guards was scarcely better than that of the prisoners. Such treatment has a long and dismal history. The Greek prisoners taken in the campaign against Syracuse were held in quarries under the harshest conditions. Most of those who did not die there were sold into slavery. Very few ever reached their home cities again. At Andersonville, Union prisoners starved and died in great numbers, less from the malevolence than from the callousness and incapacity of the guards and the prison commandant. Confederate prisoners in the North were also badly treated.[14]

Such things are often explicable in terms of necessity, lack of resources, stupidity, or even bureaucratic muddling. Harder to explain are the cases of individual and group action which approach and cross the limits of that which is considered "human." What exactly goes on in the mind of a man who sits down on an enemy corpse and proceeds to eat his K-ration dinner? Or the man who keeps a collection of photographs of badly mutilated bodies? Beyond these examples are the men who pry the gold from the teeth of the dead enemy and fill jars with their collections.[15] The collecting of ears and, of course, the taking of scalps was practiced by both Indians and whites in the savage wars of the seventeenth through the nineteenth centuries. The warriors of the Haida tribe were given to ritual cannibalism. Others, in New Guinea and the South Pacific, hunted heads and roasted their neighbors, and the Aztecs collected prisoners for great annual sacrifices. Many of these acts committed by primitive tribesmen were ritually authorized, while those committed by individual members of modern armies were not. There are numerous instances of bestiality authorized or condoned by modern societies or portions thereof. At Ouradour-sur-Glane, members of the Waffen-SS "Das Reich" Division herded the civilian population of the town into a building, set it on fire, and shot anyone trying to escape. In Russian prisoner-of-war camps, instances of cannibalism have been recorded, and for a time, bands of cannibal prisoners terrorized the rest of the prison population. Beyond these examples—far beyond—are the death camps of the SS. Here the individual brutalities and bestialities of the early concentration camps were replaced by a factory-like operation dedicated to the rationalized destruction of human beings considered unfit for existence in the New Order. Jews, Gypsies, Poles, homosexuals, and the mentally retarded were killed in job lots, the demand for death being so prodigious that new assembly line methods had to be devised. While this did not involve the actions of combat troops, it was planned and carried out by the quasimilitary SS, and it is probable that such a program could only be carried out under the cover of wartime necessity. On the other hand, evidence now coming to light concerning the destruction of human beings under the terror of the Stalin regime indicates that war may not always be necessary for cover or justification.

Often the persons involved in these activities were members of so-called elite units, whether of the military or the police. The Haida warriors were elite, as were the members of the SS, the Waffen-SS, the Cheka, NKVD, and the KGB. They all had this in common: they were above the law (or, perhaps, operated under a higher law not accessible to ordinary humans). Viewing themselves as godlike, they became, in essence, beasts. Holding to some self-serving code of honor or loyalty, such as "Meine Ehre heisst Treue," they became dehumanized. Unfortunately, as the instances of individual behavior by ordinary members of the military indicate, this dehumanization was not restricted to selected groups. There may be, within the individual man, a ghoul. Under ordinary conditions, this ghoulishness will not manifest itself, but the conditions of the battlefield and of war itself are not ordinary.[16]

However reprehensible the actions of such men may be, they do not, in and of themselves, hinder successful military action. One can be a dispicable human being and still be an effective soldier. There is another class of reactions to battle that has long been condemned and often misunderstood. Under the general term "cowardice," mental breakdown in battle has been dealt with as a willful act on the part of persons who are not willing to take their chances with the "real" men serving beside them. Courage or bravery is lauded, while cowardice is, next to treason, the worst of military offenses. For understandable reasons the actions of the coward are not acceptable to the military establishment. It takes needed bodies away from the battle; it can infect the other men of a unit with the same unwillingness to close with the enemy. It can, under certain circumstances, place a unit or even the entire army in danger of defeat and destruction. In an effort to counter the effects of this dangerous attitude, men charged with the offense have been arrested, shamed, or executed. The action of General Patton, striking a man who had broken down, was entirely in the traditional mode of treatment favored by the military.

Yet breakdown is a widespread phenomenon in warfare, affecting men who have otherwise shown themselves to be brave soldiers as well as those who have never demonstrated that quality. Because that is the case, military medicine has concerned itself, at least since the seventeenth century, with methods of countering its effects and returning men to the battlefield. Cowardice can manifest itself in a variety of ways, the most obvious of which is demonstrated by the man who either flees at the first sign of danger, or who avoids placing himself in dangerous situations at all. The self-inflicted wound is an example of one method of avoidance. Some men, finding themselves about to go into battle, will shoot themselves, usually in the leg or the foot. Habitual malingering, placing oneself on sick call every morning, might be considered another. In other cases, a man will simply desert, hoping to find a safe haven away from the battle and from the military altogether. These can all be considered conscious actions on the part of men who find themselves no longer able to stand the stress and the dangers of battle.

Another type of avoidance is not conscious in nature. The training of the soldier places great emphasis on the need to serve loyally and to perform one's duty, no matter how dangerous that may be. The military holds that men may certainly be frightened but that this fear can be controlled through discipline, self-imposed or otherwise. Additionally, men are much concerned about gaining and maintaining the respect of their fellow soldiers; in fact, this may be one of the most effective means of holding them to their duty. Yet, however consciously a man may strive to maintain composure, stress and fear can make it impossible for him to do so. The unconscious can do what the conscious mind will not accept. This can result in an uncontrollable trembling, or more seriously, in instances where the man is unable to move either to attack the enemy or even defend himself. A man, though conscious, may simply huddle himself in a fetal position, weeping, totally lost as an effective member of the unit. He may allow himself to be killed by the approaching enemy rather than take any action to prevent his own death. Sad though this reaction may be, it may be viewed by his comrades with disgust. In some cases, he may be brought out of it by being kicked or slapped, though even these measures are not always, or even often, effective.

An alternative to this kind of uncontrollable action, and one more acceptable in the eyes of others, is the loss of control over the actions of some part of the body. With the best will of his conscious mind, a man may find himself unable to move his legs, or one or both of his arms; he may lose his sight or be unable to hear commands. No physical basis for these conditions will exist, and the only possible remedy is to remove the man for a period of time from the battle. Thus, the unconscious accomplishes what the conscious mind could not. Military medicine began to deal with the problem seriously at least from the beginning of the twentieth century. The Russian army, during the war with the Japanese, began attaching psychologists and psychiatrists to medical units, and, during the First World War, all armies found themselves dealing with large numbers of cases of what was termed "shell shock" or neurasthenia. A variety of treatments were tried, ranging from rest to electric shock. It was found that, while removal from battle was essential, this was less effective the farther from the war zone the man was taken. Many of the most successful treatments were accomplished in hospitals close to the battle, where a man could remain for a short period and then be returned to his unit. Long-term residence in a medical facility far from the line often seemed to reinforce the problems which had brought the man there in the first place.

The condition of "nostalgia," identified and named as early as the seventeenth century, has been observed in warfare since that time. Here a man may, without apparent reason, begin to waste away, refusing food and showing little concern for the state of his health. It received its name because it was accompanied by a longing to return home, and the most effective treatment was found to be the short furlough. It would seem that nostalgia is similar to anorexia, and that it was also known in the concentration camps under the name of the "musselmann" effect, in which certain prisoners simply gave up and allowed themselves to die, even without the ready assistance of the camp guards. It could also be related to the tendency toward temporary desertion noted among Confederate soldiers, who simply left their regiments for a short visit home, after which they returned and were again responsible and effective soldiers.[17]

Suicide as a means of escape from battle would seem to be almost a contradiction. If fear of death is a major cause of troop anxiety, why embrace it in order to avoid it? Yet the fact remains that numbers of men have committed suicide in the midst of battle. One explanation could be that it is a drastic—the most drastic—method of escape from an intolerable situation. Another would be that at least a certain number of men are more disposed to suicide than others and that what they do here, they might have done to remedy some other, to them, intolerable situation. Actively, and with full knowledge of the consequences, may be only one method of committing suicide in battle. Others may seek out particularly dangerous missions and repeatedly expose themselves to death until that goal is accomplished, even though the person may not be fully cognizant of what he is really trying to do. Active suicide can be regarded as a form of cowardice and, as such, be subject to opprobrium. While one might assume that this should not be a matter of concern for the successful suicide, it is, nonetheless, true that persons who kill themselves, as exemplified by their final notes, often show much concern for the ordering of affairs after their deaths. Any charge of cowardice can be avoided by accomplishing the real goal through heroic action. One might wonder, for example, about the state of mind of men performing heroic deeds. At Iwo Jima, 27 percent of the twenty-two Congressional Medals awarded were given to men who covered a grenade with their bodies.[18] Such self sacrifice is indeed worthy of the highest honor, but one may suspect that, at least on occasion, it accomplishes a long sought goal.

Some men may expose themselves to injury or death for other reasons, not all of which can be discerned. An officer may stand up in order to inspire his men to move forward bravely. The captain of an artillery battery serving in France in the First World War tells of the difficulty he had in convincing one of his sergeants, an old regular soldier, to lie down under counterbattery fire. The sergeant was only reluctantly convinced that it was not a shameful thing to do.[19] John Worsham relates an incident that occurred during the fighting at Spotsylvania. While all the others were lying down under the heavy fire, a soldier in an Alabama regiment stood firing his rifle. After a time he stopped firing and began to investigate the contents of a Union knapsack he had picked up. Looking at each article carefully, he selected a number clothing items and then proceeded to undress and put on the new clothes, after which he resumed his shooting.[20] Such total lack of concern for personal safety seems scarcely credible, and Worsham himself averred that he had never seen the like in four years of war. Was the man testing himself or attempting to show his superiority to the men around him? Or had he simply displaced himself momentarily in his imagination from the reality of the battle? At this distance it is impossible to know, but it is one more example of the curious and complex state of mind of men in battle.

For the military leadership, all these aberrations are a matter of great concern. Drainage from the line of battle can occur for many reasons, the most obvious being death, wounding, or illness. But to these one has also to add the nonperformance of men who remain on the line, the "willing helpers" who assist wounded men to rear when such help is not really needed, malingerers, shell shock and battle fatigue cases, and deserters. Based on its experience in the First World War, the American Army tried, through psychological testing, to weed out those unfit for combat duty. In this they were so unsuccessful that psychiatric loss rates for the Second World War were greater than those in World War I. It has been suggested the explanation lay in the fact that, while the army was trying to eliminate the "weak," it failed to realize that all men have their breaking point.[21] Both desertion and battle fatigue reached such proportions for the American Army in the fall of 1944, that the military began to reassess its procedures for handling psychiatric cases and resorted to the execution of a deserter for the only time during the war. With combat fatalities and injuries running well above expected levels, and with the training of replacements, based on these expected levels, not meeting the needs of the army, there was the potential for a real crisis in the continuance of military operations. Virtually all the available manpower had already been either drafted or rejected, with the only remaining large pool being the men just reaching the age of eighteen. The alternatives for resolving the problem included reassessing the men who had already been deferred or rejected, combing out the rear areas for infantry replacements, and somehow finding a solution to the problem of the psychiatric losses. The army had no great success in this last category. The military did learn from the experience of World War Two, however, and in Korea did manage to reduce the number of cases slightly. In Vietnam it was even more successful, though postservice relapses have become a matter of major concern. In any case, the American armed services were less successful than their German and Russian counterparts in dealing with psychiatric losses. Both had far lower caseloads, and both had better success in returning these cases to the front. The German Army's treatment of its psychiatric cases as close to the front as possible may be one of the keys to the solution of the problem. Another was the system whereby men were trained as replacements for a particular unit and were not forced to enter battle as strangers to the rest of the members of the company.[22]

Attempts to analyze the causes of mental breakdown in battle rightly concentrate on fear as a major factor, but there are many other contributing causes which may be only peripherally connected with fear, and some that are more directly connected to the aggressive tendencies within the individual. All of them work in one way or another to direct the individual soldier to concentrate on his own problems of survival to the exclusion of other considerations, such as the goals of his unit or the needs of the other members of the group. Most of these other factors have been a part of military life for as long as we have record and most probably far beyond. In the Egyptian literature a veteran writes, admonishing a younger man who has boasted of being a hero: "You understand how it tastes to be a *mahir* [hero], when you carry your chariot on your shoulder. When you halt in the evening your whole body is crushed . . . your limbs are broken. . . . You are alone, no helper is with you, . . . you determine to go forward, although you do not know the way. Shuddering seizes you, the hair on your head stands on end . . . your path is full of boulders and shingle and there is no passable track."[23] The fear of which the veteran speaks had been caused by the harassment by certain Bedouin tribes attacking the army on its march, but he gives equal weight to the physical exertion needed simply to keep the force moving forward. The long hours of marching over rough country take their toll; clothing turns to rags and ill-fitting boots gall the feet or fall apart altogether, so that many a soldier has marched barefoot.[24] Food is scarce or lacking in either variety or nutritional value. *Coffee and Hardtack*, a fine book on the everyday life of the Union soldier, sums up in its title the staple diet of these men, to which could be added fried salt pork and occasional fruits taken from neighboring orchards.[25] British troops in the trenches of the First World War subsisted on Maconachy (a canned beef stew), often eaten cold, and tea. Even the scientifically designed K-rations of the Second World War lost some of their nutritional value through the habit that soldiers had of trading around or throwing away those parts of the rations that were less desirable.[26]

Even when not directly engaged in battle, the soldier was confronted with obstacles which contributed to his depressed state. A long day's march could involve a great deal of physical exertion. Awakened early to prepare for the march, those troops near the end of the army column might have to wait several hours before actually getting on the road. The packs carried could be very heavy, upwards of seventy pounds, though many a soldier managed to divest himself of the more useless items of equipment. A dry road could be so dusty that men actually choked and were nearly blind from the particles in their eyes. In wet weather these same roads would turn into mires, capable of trapping horses and wheeled vehicles; the foot soldiers might well sink into the mud over their ankles at each step. In the winter, their feet, wet from the snow, would freeze, clothing would freeze, and the soldier could become a casualty without a shot being fired. In summer heat or in the tropics, sunstroke was a constant possibility, and canteens would run dry without the opportunity for refill. For those troops in the rear of the column, arrival at the night's bivouac might be delayed until well after dark, so that many of the men would be faced with a constant lack of sleep.

Physical exhaustion, bad diet, and other attendant health disorders such as diarrhea, were all problems with which the soldier had to contend. In fact, they may have served at times to take his mind off the major question of survival. Other problems would prey upon his mind. Despite the fact that he was surrounded by hundreds or even thousands of men, it was possible to feel a real sense of loneliness. Lack of mail or other contact from home was depressing. Bad news from home could be equally or even more disheartening. The familiar "dear John" letters, which some received from their wives or girl-friends, could produce a state in which the man became separated mentally not only from the support system of his home, but also from the men of his own group. Often enough his friends would rally to his support, but in some cases they would find it impossible to break through the wall of loneliness which the man had thrown up around him.

The sense of isolation could be fostered in other ways as well. Particularly in the wars of the twentieth century, the intensity of the fire could force men and units to spread out to the point where there was no close physical contact. In order to cover the ground at all, platoons and squads might find themselves separated from the rest of the company by many yards or even miles. Under these conditions, a man could find himself guarding an outpost with no other members of his unit in sight. Such a situation could and did give rise to great apprehension in most men. There may have been men who enjoyed operating alone but they have always been in the distinct minority. Sounds, or even the lack of sounds could also heighten the fears of the soldier. In the midst of battle, the rattle of rifle fire, the chattering of the machine guns, the rustling sound of shells overhead, and the explosions became, on occasion, almost deafening. Even when there was no immediate danger associated with the sounds they could be and were, unnerving. At night the sounds were often different, muted perhaps, but forcing the soldier to be constantly alert and edgy. These might be the sounds of "the armourers accomplishing the knights, with busy hammers closing rivets up,"[27] or the muffled clanking of tank treads, or the measured thonk of opposing lonely mortars firing for unknown purposes on unseen targets. It could be some unidentified sound spelling possible peril or nothing at all. On Guadalcanal, an all-night battle was fought with landcrabs, whose stirrings during their nocturnal peregrinations had alarmed a whole regiment. Or it could be the moaning of wounded men lying helpless and dying between the lines, telling out in their final hours the sadness and loneliness of war.

Sights of war, even when not horrifying, contributed to the desolation of the soldier. Some of the sights were bizarre or even surreal. Surreal because, suddenly, awesome events were taking place in familiar surroundings. The peace of the farmyard is invaded by desperate men, as unmilked cows low in pain for the absent farmer. A fight takes place in a department store amidst the counters stacked with men's furnishings and women's lingerie. At Festubert during the First World War, battles took place in the galleries of the district coal mines. Fighting in and around churches was not uncommon, and at the Gettysburg graveyard, a sign announced that the discharge of firearms was prohibited. At Rizal Stadium, the baseball field in Manila, American troops broke through the outfield fence, fought their way across the diamond, the pitcher's mound, home plate, into the dugouts and the locker rooms. The men of two nations with a love for the game must have found the experience very strange indeed.

In the case of the aircrews, the alternation between fighting and rest were more extreme than that experienced by the ground forces. A man might spend several hours in the most desperate kind of combat over an enemy city and return to spend the evening drinking at a pub near the base. Enclosed by the products of the most modern technology for much the day, he would find himself, for a few hours, surrounded by the appurtenances of village coziness. At Lavenham, the 487th Bombardment Group could travel from a world of scientific mayhem to a space from another age, that of the quaintly leaning, half-timbered houses of a medieval cloth town, all within a range of two miles.

Vietnam had its own peculiar circumstances. Troops returned from grueling marches in the bush, punctuated by firefights of greater or lesser intensity, to the schlock paradise of some base replete with a PX. At this oasis all the material bonbons of a wealthy society were available; it was a base where camp shows, bars, dance bands, lights at night, and the appearances of safety belied the fact that, within a space measured in yards, a no-man's-land of barbed wire and booby traps formed a perimeter defense. Here, for a short period in these pleasure islands, troops could rest before again answering the throbbing call of the helicopter, the waiting truck, or the simple order to move out for a patrol. The peace of the base camp was as unreal as the war against the ubiquitous but seldom seen enemy was eerie. Both lent themselves to the sense that "Nam" was surreal, and the troops spoke of their return to the United States as a return to the "World."

Of all the locales in which war has been fought, certainly one of the strangest was that of the trenches in the First World War. Here millions of men lived for years beneath the surface of the earth, their farthest field of vision being that of the sky above. Following the great battles of the first months of that war, the men of the contesting armies dug in until they had constructed two lines of fortifications, running almost uninterrupted from the coast of Belgium to the Swiss frontier. Here, in time, they constructed the equivalent of cities, homes for men providing some slight refuge from the dangers of high explosives. Trenches received names reminiscent of home, such as Clapham Junction or Unter den Linden. Dugouts were created and, in some cases, enlarged to quite incredible dimensions. Some of the German dugouts were wired for electric lights, and panelling was introduced to hide the earthen walls. Even in the ruder dugouts, an ammunition case would be used as a desk, and bunks of wire netting with jute sacking were built. A bit of colored glass from a ruined church might provide a little brightness for the drab surroundings. Nothing, however, could shut out entirely, or even adequately, the reality of the omnipresent danger.

Artillery and mortar fire broke down the carefully prepared trench walls, making constant rebuilding necessary. The winter rains turned the trenches into creeks in which men sank to their knees in mud. Patrols in no-man's-land crept through and around shell holes, sometimes bombing the enemy trenches in the hopes of seizing a prisoner. Snipers waited for the unwary to raise their heads too far above the level of the trench, and rats made their living everywhere, running across the faces of sleeping men, stealing food supplies left out, and feasting on the bodies of the dead. Always there was the stench of decaying bodies. In time the trench lines were improved and multiplied to the extent that it became difficult to find one's way around. They became true labyrinths for the men living in them. Troops entering a new section would often lose their way and struggle for hours just to get into position to relieve another unit. The work here was unending. Caved-in sections had to be rebuilt, and ration parties struggled nightly to bring up supplies. Others spent much of the night repairing and extending the barbed wire protection. Exhaustion competed with anxiety for claim on the physical and mental resources of the men so that, by the time relief came, they were often scarcely capable of making their way from the trenches to the relative safety of the reserve or the rear areas.[28]

As painful and frustrating, at times even as deadly as these experiences may be, they do not constitute what has been termed the "horrors of war." Men can be exhausted and sick without being horrified. In fact, they can also kill without being horrified. Without trying to define horror to the point where it no longer has any application, it can be said that horror is that which causes both terror and revulsion.[29] Situations, which could be viewed as terrifying, can be imagined without causing revulsion or vice versa. A machine gunner under heavy attack manages to maintain his position and kills a large number of the enemy. Throughout the attack he may be terrified though still able to carry out his duties. He has also been very excited throughout the period of the attack, but he may feel neither elated nor revulsed by the results of his work. Another person viewing these same results might be revulsed by the sight of so many dead without feeling any sense of terror.

In the 1812 retreat from Moscow, thousands of men and horses attempting to make their escape across the Berezina crowded onto the flimsy bridge, pushing and shoving so that many fell to their death in the icy river. The scene has rightly been described as horrible, yet one soldier caught in the middle of this madness would write of it later: "Now it is with horror, but at that time it was with a dull, indifferent feeling, that I looked at the masses of horses and people which lay dead, piled high upon the bridge."[30] Many things that are seen in war are gruesome without invoking the sense of horror, or, more properly, what may first be seen as horrifying can quickly become commonplace. Skeletal remains of soldiers from previous battles can cause consternation when they are first encountered. Later, they may be treated with a grim jocularity. A recurrent incident from the trenches of the First World War illustrates this point: a skeleton hand protrudes from the wall of the trench, and the soldiers marching past shake it and make some light remark. This may be a form of whistling in the dark or denying the possibility of horrible consequences, as in the song "The Bells of Hell" (go ting-a-ling-a-ling for you but not for me), which asks in parody of the biblical line, "O death where is thy sting-a-ling-a-ling"?

Of course there is much in war that is horrible. Many of the great battlefields of previous centuries, Borodino, Cannae, and Gettysburg to name a few, were littered with the thousands of dead: corpses blackening and swelling in the heat; the wounded, still not removed from the field, moaning with pain and thirst; wounded and shattered horses screaming; and in the surgeon's tent, the awful work of amputation going on without letup. Survivors, exhausted and shaken, still had to pull themselves together and prepare for the next move in the game of war. There is much in these scenes that is truly horrible, but the impact on the individual soldier may not have been immediate. He may have been too exhausted to absorb it fully, yet it could very well remain in his consciousness for years after the event. It is more likely that the memories of the battle will be fixed upon those moments of terror and excitement when it seemed to the soldier that his life was in extreme peril. These will be remembered without any sense of horror unless some particular detail of the event gives cause for revulsion: in the midst of the fight, a comrade is struck in the head, and his blood and brains are splattered over the soldier. A shell strikes a man, and he is completely dismembered. Such sights are terrifying, repulsive, and memorable.[31]

The battlefields of the First World War, because they were for so long stationary, afforded many opportunities for the horrible. The later wars of this century have not afforded so many scenes of continuing awfulness. The terror inspired by the approach of a tank, or a bomber from one's group exploding under attack from enemy fighters, are momentary visions of horror, but discontinuous since the work of fighting must go on. The view of a battlefield "carpeted" with the dead was less often seen than one might suspect from some of the memoirs. Paradoxically, it was the civilian population of the great cities who were more likely to experience the worst horrors. At Hamburg, the fire storms raised by the bombings of July, 1943, left people with visions of burning buildings, persons catching fire as they ran from the storm, and bodies being smothered in air raid shelters as the storm sucked up the oxygen, then melted in the intense heat. Waves of refugees spread out over the countryside in the wake of these attacks. Finally, even these horrors were eclipsed by the bombings of Hiroshima and Nagasaki.

The cruel fact is that the soldier, in addition to the burden of the pack on his back, must carry these extra burdens in his mind. The disagreeable, the debilitating, the gruesome, and the horrible, have their cumulative impact upon him. Because these are mental images, it is not even necessary that they be actually experienced. The evidence of men who break down at the mere anticipation of combat indicates that vicarious experience can be quite as damaging as the real thing. In fact, it is the real thing, at least for the particular individual so affected. On the other hand, there are men who are able to suffer through all the dangers and cruelty of war without incurring a mental breakdown or even physical wounds. This is not to say that they emerge unscathed, for they may carry with them into civilian life attitudes, memories, and reactions which have been implanted by the military experience. The post traumatic stress disorder (PTSD) that has been so widely noted among Vietnam war veterans is one example. Another, less devastating and seldom identified phenomenon, can be noted among many returning combat veterans. This is the habit, which many of them admit to, of looking at the immediate area around them in terms of military terrain. Often they will find themselves picking out likely cover or the possible locations of enemy positions. This habit may go on for years after the end of a war. It is a different reaction than that noted in the case of PTSD, since it does not result in a traumatic event. It is also not like the "startle" reaction, which some soldiers show in response to a sudden loud noise, or even a softer noise, which reminds them of something dangerous. It is simply a reaction that is there, left over from the war; while not very useful in civilian life, it is a continuing reminder of what they had once been.[32]

From induction through separation, either by death or discharge, the soldier is subjected to a series of stresses of greater or lesser intensity, aimed at the successful prosecution of war. Many of these stresses (or, as he might term them, insults) are not really much more onerous than those to which he might be subjected in daily life. Admittedly, the work can often be hard physical labor and the hours of marching with heavy loads can be long, but these have their counterparts in civilian life. Many men, coming from the background of agricultural labor, actually found the work lighter than that which they had endured back home in their villages, or on the farm.[33] Men coming from the urban background of office work, who might find the physical labor more difficult at first, were at least experienced in dealing with harsh and unfeeling superiors; the Gradgrinds have always seemed to outnumber the Fezzywigs in industrial society. Bad food and hunger were common to the experience of many, and some would eat better than they ever had in their lives. The urban working class, like the farm laborers, were no strangers to hard work, long hours, and sometimes brutal foremen. Even fear, or at least some form of it, was common to all these men. The insecurities of position, jobs, the market, were matters which caused more than a little unease in the hearts of these men. The difficulty was that these endurable stresses were only a prelude to the less endurable stresses of battle. The army might argue that these stresses prepared men for battle and there is truth in this; they were also cumulative, and, when added to the stress of combat, contributed to the breakdown of many.

Most of these men, whether volunteers or conscripts, wanted to serve well, and in this met the first of the requirements of the army for success. They also wanted to survive, and here their agenda departed from that of the military. That they often acted in a manner which ran counter to their individual wants and needs is a tribute to the ability of the military to convince men of the necessity to make great and even total sacrifices. Battle, with its inherent confusion, excitement, and noise, its frequent occasions of mortal danger, its awe-inspiring and fear-inspiring qualities, carried men well beyond the bounds of any ordinary experience. Often tired, often hungry, not seldom sick, soldiers went into battle and exhibited a will and determination which is, to say the least, surprising. If they survived, they learned, and for some time would increase their proficiency. Without rest, however, these abilities would deteriorate. Under severe strain the needs of the individual would begin to reassert themselves, the unconscious mind would begin to discover strategies for removing the man from danger, and breakdowns would occur. It is the contention of many psychiatrists that all men will break down after a period of time, and that that period is becoming increasingly short, as battle assumes a continuous rather than occasional nature. Still, this conclusion remains open to question. Numbers of men did survive for long periods of combat, much longer than the three months or so posited by these medical authorities. Yet, the psychological impact of war is great and is rightly a matter of concern for the military. It has even been argued that the great increase in the lethality and volume of firepower since the end of the Second World War has made it impossible for any man to survive, even for short periods on the battlefield. Whom the bullet does not strike down, the mind may.[34]

The question of how much a man can endure cannot really be answered satisfactorily. Scientific tests can give answers to some questions about the limits of endurance, but the laws of society obviously prevent a full testing of this matter. Soldiers who find their own battle situation endurable may look in wonder at what men in previous ages have taken for granted. For instance, the prospect of close combat with short swords is a matter of amazement and fear for the modern soldier, as is the bayonet charge carried to its logical conclusion. How the men of the American Civil War could stand and fire at one another at close quarters, as they did in the cornfield at Antietam and other drear locales, seems almost beyond comprehension.[35] The hellish living conditions of the trenches of the First World War and the bombardments of long duration there certainly raise the question of how men could endure. But the special characteristics of more modern battle would raise similar questions in the minds of the Civil War soldier, the Roman legionnaire, or the common soldier on the Western Front. The dismal prospect is, as long as there continue to be wars, men will be found to serve. That they will suffer, be wounded, and die, perhaps in great numbers, is certain. That numbers of them, possibly a large percentage, will break under the strain, is also certain.

6

The Action of the Tiger

A CENTURY AND A QUARTER after Darwin published his study of the evolution of species, the concept of physiological evolution is now so widely accepted that any scientific (and even most popular) approaches to biology accept the premise that all animals, including humans, have evolved from other, earlier forms. With some initial resistance, this theory—and it is still officially a theory—has been accepted as applicable to human beings. The physiological similarities are simply too many and too convincing to dismiss. Less convincing, in the minds of many, is the evidence that behavioral characteristics may also have been involved in this evolution, and that humans have been no more immune than other species to the consequences of this inheritance. That people may have instinctive responses which shape their behavior has proven to be a harder idea to swallow. The influences of culture and learning are too great, it is held, to allow any remaining vestiges of instinct to have meaningful influence over the actions of people. Humanity has abandoned instinctive response for the higher planes of learned and reasoned reaction to the problems confronting them. Exceptions can be made for such areas as sexual attraction, hunger, and possibly fear, but even here, the influences of culture greatly outweigh the more primitive impulses. This is particularly marked in attitudes toward the phenomenon of aggression. It is reasonable to ask whether any primal urge to kill one's fellows really exists. Not only do great questions of war and peace hang on the answer, but our own self-esteem as individuals and as members of a species are at stake.

In an earlier chapter, the question of whether warfare is an instinctive response was raised and answered in the negative. War is not an instinct but a human institution which mobilizes a number of instinctive (and reasoned) responses for the purpose of accomplishing certain goals. There is much in human aggressiveness that is instinctive and even necessary to human survival. Aggressive behavior is, in one form or another, characteristic of all animal species. It can be directed either toward other species or toward members of one's own species. It does not necessarily, or even ordinarily, lead to the killing of one's own kind. In other animals, when such killing does occur, it is more likely to be accidental rather than intentional, though there is growing evidence that purposeful killing may not be as rare as was once thought.[1] Most often when these instances of aggressiveness occur, they involve questions of dominance or access to the females, and the contests are carried out between individuals, not groups. The battles between mature male deer in the rutting season would be one example of such aggressive behavior. Such fighting does not constitute warfare, since the results are not usually fatal, nor do they result in a disruption of the social organization. Quite the contrary, they are the foundation of one of society's major organizing principles. Somewhat different is the hostile response shown to individuals entering the area of another group. Here, there may be an aggressive response by more than one of the members of the group, and the intruder may well be killed. Such a reaction approaches more closely the definition of warfare, though the intention of the intruder is perhaps innocent, or driven by curiosity or the hope of stealing some momentary advantage and retreating quickly.

Some of the ingredients of aggressive behavior among animals are worth looking at more closely for the light they throw on human actions. Male animals encountering a male of the same species indulge in a whole repertoire of actions which serve as indicators of their relationship with that individual. If the relationship has already been established, as would most often be the case within members of a group, the actions can range from the dominant to the submissive. Many times the relationship is so well set that a simple motion of the head may indicate which is the dominant animal. If that dominance is to be challenged, a more serious exchange of expressions will come into play. Animals coming into contact for the first time, or in cases of a challenge to authority, are much more expressive. Threat posturing, which can involve the temporary enlargement of the body, will be observed. In four-footed animals and fish, this is most often accomplished by showing the side of the animal to the other. The hairs on the back or other parts of the body may bristle so that the entire animal appears considerably large than would normally be the case.

Cats and foxes arch their backs, and their fur will stand out. It has been suggested that the arching and bristling also indicates a degree of fear. Leyhausen has noted that, in the case of the cat, while the back feet are reacting in an aggressive manner, the forepaws signal caution, resulting in the cat's body arching.[2] This first stage of the encounter may last for some time as each animal measures the other. The teeth may be bared in an aggressive fashion, but the ears may move backward, expressing the fear the animal may feel. Growling, hissing, or other vocalizations will accompany the display, and the two may circle each other, either for the purpose of more accurately estimating the danger, or because there is indecision as to whether to attack or retreat. The attack can come with remarkable suddenness, the fight being savage in its intensity but very often short-lived, the matter of dominance being quickly established. In such a case, the loser will indicate its recognition of this by certain submissive behavior patterns, such as cringing with the ears back, rolling over on its back, or simply by fleeing from the encounter. Very seldom would such contests result in death. In fact, often no fighting at all occurs. The matter is either decided by the simple threat display or left in abeyance. Sometimes the animals, who a moment before were assuming threatening postures, will turn to totally unrelated activities. Among gulls Tinbergen has observed threatening pairs suddenly begin to peck at the grass, as though beginning the process of nest building. This "displacement activity," which brings to an end the encounter, may be the result of the frustration of the animal's original aggressive intent.[3]

One concept put forward by ethologists that has attracted a great deal of attention from students of human political and warlike behavior is that of territoriality. Originally developed to describe the behavior of birds, it has since been observed in fish and certain mammals and gained further notoriety when applied to humans by Robert Ardrey in his book *The Territorial Imperative*.[4] However, there are very real difficulties in making this leap from bird to human. To see the nation state as a logical outcome of the desire to own and defend property, and to see this desire as the manifestation of instinct would seem to go well beyond the limits of the concept as it was originally proposed.

Among birds, territoriality has been analyzed as the action which male birds take to stake out an area for nesting purposes, announcing that claim through specific calls, which have the dual function of warning other males and attracting a female.[5] Once the nesting season is completed this type of activity ceases. As such, territorial behavior is far different from any propensity that men may show for the acquisition and defense of property. Nor has this behavior been definitively observed in many mammals. Numbers of mammals do occupy a certain range of territory for the purposes of feeding, and these ranges may shift through the seasons as the food supply gives out in one or the other of these areas. Ranges can be shared with other species and at various times during the day by members of the same species.[6] Many mammals will mark their progress about the range by spraying trees or bushes or other objects with either urine or the scent from certain glands. "Marking" notifies other members of the same species that the individual has been in this area and may influence subsequent passers-by to seek other locales. This information tends to be very temporary, and the areas marked can vary from day to day.

Both territorial behavior and the habit of marking serve the end of spacing animals through a given area, so that none encroaches on another. It does not necessarily afford each individual with equally attractive nesting or feeding locales, but it does result in enhancing the chances for the survival of a particular group as a whole. Even when a large group is gathered together, the principle of spacing can be observed. Birds sitting on a wire will be separated by about the same space over the entire length occupied. In flight, flocks of birds will also be about equally spaced, so that no matter how they turn, they do not interfere with each other's movement. Schools of fish may turn one way or the other and yet maintain the same distance between individuals. Such behavior not only makes it possible for large numbers of the same species to move together, but also allows signals of danger to be passed through the entire school (or flock) with great rapidity.

Quite a number of these same behavior patterns can be observed in humans. On a crowded street individuals will be going about their different errands, hurrying along the sidewalks, stopping to gaze in shop windows, turning into stores, waiting to cross the street. Some travel alone, others in small groups, some halt suddenly to turn and look for a lagging companion; yet, seldom does one person bump into another and, if this should occur, apologies are usually exchanged. On rare occasions one may see a person pushing through the moving crowd, bumping one person after another so that, from a distance, it appears that a ripple is moving through the crowd. Such an action is so out of the ordinary that observers conclude that the person is either in flight (from a crime?), or possibly demented. Hall has made a close study of this phenomenon of human spacing, showing that it can be observed in all human cultures.[7] He notes, however, that the distance which people maintain between themselves and others varies from culture to culture. The distance is that at which people do not feel threatened. Since it does vary, there exists the real possibility for misunderstanding. If the acceptable distance is rather wide, as it is in North American cultures, a person from one of the Latin American countries, where the acceptable distance is much shorter, may inadvertently threaten (or at least make uncomfortable) a North American companion. Conversely, North Americans, by withdrawing to their own "safe" distance, may give an erroneous signal of hostility or coldness to their Latin friends.

Not all crowd behavior is so benign. Bostonians say that one of the more frightening spectacles to behold is that of shoppers gathered at the doors of Filene's department store on sale day. The pushing and shoving reaches the frenzied stage as the doors open, and the crowd bursts through to rush the counters and tear and pull for possession of the various pieces of merchandise. Such crowd action can reach lethal levels, as it has at some rock concerts, where persons have been crushed against the gates, trampled underfoot, or suffocated by the ferocious pressures of other music lovers. In these cases, the orderly activities of a crowd pursuing separate interests has been replaced by the more aggressive action of a large number of persons trying to achieve a single goal: passage through a narrow space. The pushing and shoving are indications of the heightened level of aggression which, if carried far enough, can lead to panic reactions on the part of all the members of the crowd. This can have tragic results in the case of fire in a theater or restaurant: large numbers of persons pile up in front of doors that refuse to open, where they are crushed or die of smoke inhalation.[8]

Aggressive behavior need not be either lethal or reprehensible. In everyday affairs, men and women do have to pursue their goals aggressively if they hope to accomplish them. The business partner closing a deal or the young man in love will have to act with firmness of purpose, or the young woman pursuing her love may, because of popular prejudices, have to disguise her intentions while still acting aggressively. To accomplish some task, to gain the goal, one must go forth and, in the process, use some of the behavioral techniques common to many animal species, including humans. Bodily enlargement can have its impact, even when there is no actual threat involved. Many sales reps have been able to use their height to advantage; tall hats, padded shoulders, imposing desks and office interiors, can all be instruments used to achieve success. There may not be any conscious intention to intimidate, and when intimidation does occur it may be so subtle as to go unnoticed. Yet, it plays its part in the daily affairs of people.

At a higher level, the aggressive intent does become obvious. Some sections of the population continue to choose to settle differences by fighting. The ostensible causes of such fights are often trivial, the real purpose being simply the establishment of dominance: in the old song, Abdul al Bulbul Amir chooses to start a fight to the death because Ivan has stepped on his toe. Many of the features of aggressive activity seen in other animal species are noted. Opponents will draw themselves up to their full height, throw back their shoulders in order to broaden their chests, and generally take such measures as will increase their bodily size. Standing above a seated opponent can also be an effective method of intimidation.

Aggression may proceed by stages. Verbal abuse, finger pointing, or prodding can be used to raise the hostility of the other party; or, it may succeed in forcing submission without further action. Should the opponent respond in kind, the climactic stage would be set. The fighters may begin by circling each other for some time. This sidling motion can reflect either the aggressive tendency to find the right opening for striking a blow, or it can be interpreted as arising from hesitation and fear. Quite possibly the two antagonists are sending the message to the rest of the crowd to "break this up before we get hurt." Most fights of this sort, commonly referred to as barroom brawls, will, if carried to the level of striking blows, end rather quickly. Either the superiority of one of the antagonists will be established, or the fight will be stopped by the onlookers, or both will realize that they are too evenly matched for either to gain advantage. In this last case, there may actually be more honor gained by the mutual recognition of the each other's worth. In the eyes of the onlookers, they will stand as two brave, strong men; both can garner the plaudits of the crowd and may themselves end as friends.

Even among men who have never struck anyone in anger, dominance fighting occurs. Verbal exchange can take a decidedly nasty, if often brilliant turn, as rivals compete in the game of one-upmanship. Witty thrusts can have more sting than a left jab; memorialized in print, they can have more lasting effect than physical injury. Taunting, finger pointing, and other forms of manual display, as well as spitting and sticking out the tongue, all have their meanings in aggressive display; or, they can be a means of honorable, if not graceful, retreat from a potentially dangerous situation.

Whether or not humans are territorial, groups do tend to create areas where they can exercise at least temporary possession, feel at home, and feel protected from outsiders. Neighborhood taverns are favorite locations for such activity. Strangers dropping into such a place may have to wait for some time before being accepted as a part of the group, and then only if they prove themselves to be truly compatible. Within these establishments there may be an inner circle that is harder to crack. The Stammtisch of the German Gasthof, reserved for particular favorites of the innkeeper, is a physical manifestation of this phenomenon. Other establishments may become the favored hangout of special interest groups, such as parachute jumpers, musicians, sports fans, homosexuals, or Wall Street brokers. Some are even the congregating areas for persons whose avocation is the alley fight.

Marking the place where one has passed, or in which one has a special interest, does occur among humans as well as other animals. The use of spray paint to indicate street gang turf, or as the expression of some anonymous artist, can be seen in any American city. Graffiti can be found on walls the world over and, for whatever reason, there does seem to be some correlation between urination and the urge to write on restroom walls.

Aggressiveness is a very necessary component of survival. It is a means by which the individual can accomplish his goals, whether these be the furnishing of an evening's meal or becoming CEO of a major corporation. Its counterpart, submissiveness, also has its purposes. A proper recognition of when one has been overpowered, outmaneuvered, or placed at a slight disadvantage can save the situation for many people. It can help a person to understand that this is as much as can be accomplished of one's goal, or it may be a strategy which allows the individual to regroup for another try. Submissiveness too has its physical manifestations, which can range from assuming a cringing position to less abject, but still subordinate, postures.

The human smile is particularly interesting in this regard, for it is a most complex gesture. Not only does it indicate a feeling of joy or contentment, it can also be the smile of resignation, or the physical indication of an attempt to ingratiate oneself with a superior. It can be the smile or the smirk of superiority or the grimace of scarcely concealed, but frustrated, hatred. Basically, the smile is composed of two parts operating simultaneously. There is some movement to bare the teeth, although the lips may not actually part. This indication of aggressive intent is contradicted by the movement backwards of the ears, a physical indication of fear among mammals. The interplay of two conflicting instincts, aggression and fear, serves to lessen or deflect any presumed aggressiveness on the part of the other individual. Since it is capable of many gradations, it can be used in greeting friends, showing lack of hostile intent, demonstrating that one's known hostility is being held in abeyance, or showing that one is submitting to the will of the other in a mood of philosophical acceptance. It can be used to give a false signal of good faith, although the acute observer can see through the facade. There are nervous smiles, frozen smiles, smiles of incomprehension, the vacuous smile, and the malicious smile. One might question whether even IBM, with all its cybernetic capabilities, would be able to compute the full range of possibilities inherent in its famous motto.

Aggressive and submissive behaviors adhere to the individual; they are not instinctive group behaviors. Even in the case of a crowd in panic, though the cause of the panic may be shared by all, the reactions are those of separated, even isolated, individuals. *Sauve qui peut* is the cry of one and all. But humans are social animals, and there are numerous occasions in which cooperative effort by the community is necessary. In hunting-gathering societies, a degree of organization is needed so that the women and the children engaged in collecting the plant food and preparing it can do so without useless effort and without collecting those plants which could prove lethal if consumed. The hunting of small animals can be done individually, but for any larger game the cooperation of several males, or even the entire population, will be needed. The evidences of this cooperation can be found far back in human prehistory. At Torralba, in Spain, Clark Howell has uncovered the site of an elephant kill which clearly shows it was the result of a planned drive engaging the services of a considerable number of persons, members of a group of *Homo erectus* hunter-gatherers.[9] To achieve this degree of cooperation, it is necessary to mobilize the individuals of the society for a common effort,[10] and this can be done in a variety of ways. One of the most important of these is the training of the young in the techniques of food gathering and hunting. It should be noted that humans are not alone in this matter. Many other animals, both social and solitary, also devote a considerable time to training the young. Learned behavior is not the exclusive property of human beings,[11] though learning plays a much larger part in the development of the human being than in other species.

Training is only a first step in the process of mobilizing the social group for participation in a common project. In order to concentrate the attention of the members on the problem at hand, techniques which subordinate the concerns of the individual to that of the group will be employed. These can include group dancing, singing, or chanting, or other forms of rhythmic activity. Intoxicants may be employed to induce a condition of enthusiasm (literally to be god-filled) or ecstasy (to stand outside oneself). Yet, such radical measures may only be necessary for the most solemn or momentous of occasions. In more ordinary circumstances, the unity of the group can be reinforced by food sharing, story-telling, or gossip. It is likely that such a level of reinforcement is more common in the preparation of women and children for the common effort of food gathering. This is not because it is a minor activity; food gathering provides either a substantial or a major proportion of the food supply for hunting-gathering groups. Apparently, women are more likely to treat this activity in a matter-of-fact fashion. Men, on the other hand, tend to clothe their hunting activity in an aura of great ceremony. Certainly, it was supposed that this would contribute to the success of the hunt; just as certainly, it enhanced the importance of men's activities and maintained their dominant position in the group.

Mobilization for war followed a pattern somewhat similar to that employed for hunting activities. Causes of various types existed which could provide reasons for armed conflict. In a world of small communities, often numbering no more than thirty or forty individuals, any stranger could be a source of danger, any strange group might infringe upon hunting grounds. Even more important was the fact that such small groups could not provide any assurance of a proper balance between males and females· so that the seizing of women (or the attraction of new men) could become a source of conflict between groups. Another major factor was the prevalent belief that death, any death, was somehow or other the work of sorcery, and that the dead themselves constituted a menace to living society, which could be set to rest by avenging the death. Preparations for war included religious exercises, such as chanting and dancing or the wearing of amulets as protective devices. Painting the body and putting on specialized clothing, often of a most simple nature, had the result of disfiguring the body, making it more fierce and, at the same time, less human. Planning of a more rational type accompanied these preparations. Weapons to be used were carefully selected and checked for defects; a plan of attack was laid out—if a warrior had been instructed by a dream to carry out a raid, the plans for the raid were reviewed by the experienced men of the group to test whether they were viable and whether the leader had the ability to carry it out.[12]

Since these wars of small groups usually had no real economic motivation, and since they were often carried out for the purpose of vengeance or the seizure of mates, it has been held that they really did not fall into the category of warlike activity, but were more in the nature of personal fighting.[13] Yet it must be noted that even a raid or an ambush would involve the full mobilization of the warrior sector of the community, though these warriors were only five or six in number. Otterbein, in his study of primitive warfare, notes a large number of hunting-gathering societies which participated in warlike activities, while relatively few of the still existing groups have professed to be ignorant of war.[14]

Primitive horticulturalists may continue to depend upon hunting for a small part of their subsistence, but basically they have set out upon the path toward a settled agriculture. Their gardens, which may have to be moved occasionally because of soil depletion, produce various forms of root crops which provide the basic foods for these societies. The semipermanent character of their economies makes possible the grouping together of a larger number of persons, though settlements scarcely larger than those of a hunting band are still common. Primitive forms of warfare have been frequently observed among these peoples, and often the causes of such wars do not differ from those of the hunter-gatherers. Capture of women, revenge for the death of a relative, and fear of sorcery each play as large a part in their decisions to go to war as the hope of gain. Capture of land is less prominent as a motivating factor. In style, the warfare of the horticulturalists continues to make use of the the raid by a small number of men, and the ambush, but some of these societies have added to this the confrontation by larger groups of warriors. Often these confrontations will resemble later battle formations, but there is a certain lack of tactical sophistication to them. It may even be totally absent, and many of these societies will limit the number killed in any engagement or be satisfied simply with heroic demonstration.

Two such groups which have been studied while still largely untouched by civilization are the Yanomamoe of the Amazon basin and the Dani-speaking peoples of the Baliem region of New Guinea.[15] Both of these peoples seem to be in a constant state of war with other groups of their general society. Encounters are frequent, and the death rate for each of the groups from hostile action is high. The Yanomamoe live in smaller groups than the Dani, villages of between forty and sixty persons being common. Small, (and, therefore, vulnerable) though these villages are, they maintain a rigorous independence. Alliances are temporary, and today's friend may well be tomorrow's enemy. From childhood the boys are trained to be warriors and encouraged to act aggressively toward women, other boys of their own age, and even toward their elders. They pride themselves on their ferocity and show a great willingness to kill and be killed, even going so far as to practice their death speeches in case they are slain in battle. The typical method of combat is the raid, which can be carried out by as few as ten men. For the smaller villages, this may well be the limit of warriors who can safely be dispatched from the village at any one time and still leave a few to guard the remaining village members. Since the villages are located at some distance from each other, such raids may take more than one day to carry through and must be well planned. The raiding party prepares itself for the mission with a number of ritual observances, such as the singing of the war song "we are flesh-seeking buzzards," which is shouted in the direction of the enemy village. Following this, the members of the party will return to their hut and go through the ritual action of vomiting. The most experienced members of the party will take up the front and rear positions and youths who may be going on their first raid will occupy the center. The departure is timed for the party to reach the point of attack just before dawn, so that an ambush can be established. Rallying positions along the line of march and return are designated in case the party should become separated. Also, if prisoners are taken which would slow the guards, it would be possible to reform and maintain the integrity of the raiding party. The goal of these raids is to kill one or several of the members of the targeted village, or to capture a woman; a general massacre is not usually attempted. On occasion, a "treacherous feast" may be arranged with another group which has relations both with the village and with its enemy of the moment. In this case the third party would arrange a feast for the enemy and during the course of the meal would fall upon the guests and kill them. The members of the instigating group would be hidden outside the host village to capture and kill any that managed to escape. Lesser forms of combat, intended to show the strength and courage of the individual, are to be found in chest-pounding duels, where the challenger bares his chest to the adversaries and invites any one of them to strike his best blow. When the adversary has finished, he must in his turn receive a like number of blows from the first man. Encounters of this sort rarely end in death, though a considerable degree of injury is not uncommon.[16]

The Dani-speaking peoples (to whom the previously mentioned Kurulu belong) employ the raid and the ambush as a means of warfare. The capture of women or pigs, or the killing of one or more members of the targeted group, can all be the goals for such actions. Even chance encounters can lead to fighting and killing. Any man who goes unarmed will be killed without compunction by his enemies. But the Dani also indulge in the spectacular confrontational form of combat in which large numbers, up to a thousand or more warriors, may be involved. This form of battle is a grand spectacle, since the warriors are massed in their finery and are much given to demonstrating their heroism by dashing out in front of the lines to challenge the enemy (often from a rather safe distance) and then retreating to the protection of their lines. The prelude to the battle is marked by challenges shouted at the enemy village. Each group proceeds to the traditional battleground, taunts are exchanged, and the opposed line grow longer as warriors from villages farther away come to join their allies. The battle itself is marked by rushes and retreats of the main bodies, which sometimes devolve into a melee where it is possible for one or a few of the warriors to become trapped. Not-too-lethal arrows are discharged, which cause painful and sometimes fatal wounds, but the killing is generally accomplished with the sixteen-foot-long wooden spears. The battle will continue until one or more warriors have been killed, but the advent of bad weather may call a halt to the proceedings. In this sense the battle, though certainly a magnificent spectacle, is less a battle than a ritual event. The losing side, the one that has suffered the fatality, leaves the field in order to prepare for the funeral ceremonies which will take place on the next day. The winning side returns to its village to join in the *etai*, or victory celebration, with the women of the village. But winning or losing are very temporary situations. The losing side feels impelled to rectify the situation, urged on by the ghost of the dead warrior. Within a short period of time, the day of battle will be rematched so that the balance can be restored.[17]

There is a good deal of conflict within the villages of both the Yanomamoe and the Dani. In fact, the Yanomamoe are so combatative that their villages will divide into opposing groups at frequent intervals, at which time one of the groups will remove itself to a new location. This tends to keep the size of the village relatively small. The Dani are not quite so prone to division, but the most successful of the warriors do take advantage of either their less successful brethren, or those men who have chosen not to fight at all. A man is perfectly free to refuse participation in any given battle, but the man who never fights is fair game for the aggressive men of the society. His women, his pigs, and his other possessions may be taken from him with impunity.[18] Interestingly, outsiders have found that the Dani, who are constantly at risk of being killed and who kill without a thought, are a friendly and relatively joyous people; the Yanomamoe, who live under similar conditions are, on the contrary, quite disagreeable and consider outsiders good only for the giving of gifts.[19]

Despite the fact that many differences exist between the conditions of battle in the primitive state and those under which modern men fight, there are also many similarities. Bodily enlargement and disfigurement, threat posturing, verbal aggression, and the various signs of anxiety and fear are all present on the modern battlefield. The military uniform serves a number of purposes. It serves to identify the person as a member of a particular group; in the eighteenth and nineteenth centuries, the colorful uniforms allowed for identification amidst the dense clouds of black powder smoke which shrouded the battle-field. The various forms of camouflage uniforms worn in more recent years provide some degree of protection for the individual soldiers but also disfigure the body. The shakos of former years and today's steel helmets enlarge and alter the shape of the head, so that the soldier begins to take on an inhuman form. Bodily enlargement is achieved in a more dramatic fashion by placing the soldier on a horse or inside a tank or other armored vehicle. Such a transformation also dehuman-izes the individual rather completely, so the enemy perceives not a man but a mortally dangerous object.

In past centuries the massing of men for the purpose of achieving maximum fire power or shock in the case of a charge, also served the purpose of creating a dehumanized and frightening mass. The oppos-ing individual soldier saw before him this mass without necessarily reckoning that his own group was quite as imposing to the enemy. If discipline failed, he and his comrades around him might well break into flight before the battle was properly joined. Even steady troops could not be entirely immune to the fear inspired by these sights. In modern battle massed groups of the enemy are less likely to be seen simply because modern weaponry has made such groupings suicidal, but an armored assault can have quite the same impact.

Noise, whether verbal or produced by other means, can have a great impact upon the individual soldier, often out of all proportion to the danger it portends. Shouted threats or insults can be used to convince the opposition of the bravery and superiority of one's forces. Taunting is a very old form of aggression and continues to be useful, even under modern conditions.[20] However, the effect of taunting is not only to instill fear in the enemy, but also to arouse anger and stimulate him to fight, just as a well-placed verbal thrust may have a heartening effect on one's own forces. Other kinds of noise may be simply unnerving. The rattling of swords on shields, or the noise produced by an artillery bombardment, can have this result, even when, in the case of the artillery shelling, the impact may not be particularly lethal.[21] It should be noted that, in both of these cases, the act of making the noise can also stimulate the aggressive behavior of the side producing the sound. Thus, rattling the swords or beating drums for the attack can induce a spirit of common purpose in the attacking troops, just as the sight and sound of an artillery barrage can instill a sense of superiority and willingness to close with the enemy.

"Closing with the enemy" is a rather peculiar phrase, since this is what the armies had been doing ever since they set out to do battle with each other. The preparations, the long marches, had all been part of this process which brought them finally into confrontation. Yet, there is obviously a considerable difference between what had gone before and what would happen in the final few hundred yards remaining between the two hosts. Essentially, the two armies are now within what ethologists term the "critical distance," the point at which each of the adversaries is committed to fighting. Within this critical distance, the threat of each to the other is such that the situation can only be resolved by a trial of strength. In the animal world, such contests are often short, with the loser retreating to a safe distance or giving some other physical sign of submission to the stronger. Seldom are these contests lethal, though accidental deaths do occur, and in some cases killing is the objective. More important for our purposes is the fact that these contests are almost universally conducted by individuals, while battle involves groups of men. But, strong as the bond between the soldiers may be, each man must still face the contest on his own as well, so that each will perceive, in part, the enemy group as being stronger than his single self. Throughout the initial stages of the confrontation, during that time when the two forces stand outside of the critical distance, each of the groups and each member of these groups will be weighing the strength and courage of the enemy. The threat posturing and demonstrations, the initial bombardments or futile discharge of arrows at a safe distance, are simply preliminaries to the heart of the struggle. Once within the critical distance, the posturing may take on a different form, restricting itself to animal-like growls, or howls and facial grimaces. The "rebel yell" of Civil War fame is a good example and usually occurred during the final stages of the charge. Concerning grimacing, John Keegan cites a curious order given to the men of the British 40th Regiment during the Battle of Waterloo: "'The men in their tired state' Sergeant Lawrence wrote, began to despair during the afternoon, 'but the officers cheered them continuously.' When the French cavalry encircled them 'with fierce gesticulations and angry scowls, in which a display of incisors became very apparent' the officers would call out, 'Now men, make faces.'"[22] Yet, making faces is precisely what can happen in the moments of battle at extremely close quarters. From the fighting in Gaza (1917), an Australian reported: "Just berserk slaughter . . . the grunting breaths, the gritting teeth and the staring eyes of the lunging Turk, the sobbing scream as the bayonet ripped home. . . ."[23] As we saw earlier in this book, Shakespeare caught the particulars of these awful moments and described them in poetic language:

> Then imitate the action of the tiger:
> Stiffen the sinews, summon up the blood,
> Disguise fair nature with hard-favored rage;
> Then lend the eye a terrible aspect:
> Let it pry through the portage of the head
> Like the brass cannon; let the brow o'erwhelm it
> As fearfully as does a galled rock
> O'erhang and jutty his confounded base,
> Swilled with the wild and wasteful ocean.
> Now set the teeth and stretch the nostril wide,
> Hold hard the breath and bend every spirit
> To his full height![24]

These are not consciously adopted expressions but, rather, are muscular activities which accompany the fearful exertion of fighting at hand-to-hand range. Actually, particularly in modern war, such encounters are extremely rare. They may be the stuff of Hollywood dreams, but most battle takes place at longer distances with the individual enemy seldom seen. Prior to the introduction of firearms, close quarter fighting did occur with fair frequency; when it took place it could be indeed ferocious, but for the individual soldier, the encounter would probably be of short duration, ending either in his death or by his being shuffled aside through the pressure of the dense crowd of soldiers following.[25] The bayonet charge of the age of firearms very often ended with the retirement of the defending force before the final moment or with the collapse of the charging troops from the volume of defending fire. As Ardant du Picq put it, "Each nation in Europe says 'No one stands his ground before a bayonet charge made by us.' And all are right."[26] There does seem to be a marked reluctance to kill at close quarters, at least as long as there is any choice in the matter. Soldiers prefer to maintain some distance from their enemy and some, brave enough to face enemy fire, either avoid returning it or fire over the heads of the opposition.

For the cavalryman in the age of horse, the problem of closing with the enemy was complicated by the fact that he was dealing not only with his own reactions, but with those of the horse as well. The instinct of the horse not to charge or jump a hedge of bayonets held by well-disciplined troops formed into squares, as they were at the Battle of Waterloo, reinforced the perception of the rider that, although he appeared most formidable astride his horse, he was still heavily out-gunned. As a result, cavalry charges against steady infantry tended to end either with the rider pulling up short or circling around the foot soldiers.[27] In the twentieth century, armored vehicles, which appear so overwhelming to foot soldiers in the open field, have found themselves in great difficulties in confined spaces, such as village or city streets, and have often been put out of action by daring antitank teams.[28]

The crew-served weapon tends to create a special circumstance for the soldiers involved. Unlike the rifleman who, in going to ground, does not thoroughly disable the other members of his team, the members of a crew must function together more closely because they are tied to a single weapon. In both world wars, observers commented on the greater steadiness of the heavy machine-gun crews, and artillery-men have long been noted for their devotion to their guns. In the latter case, members of a gun crew have shown great, even suicidal bravery in the defense of their guns or in attempts to disable the weapon so that they cannot be of use to the enemy.

Crews of vehicles, such as tanks, airplanes, and ships are, of course, even more thoroughly tied to the service of their weapons. Since, in the case of aircraft and naval vessels, their major opponents will be other such craft, the process of dehumanizing the enemy is even more complete. The enemy is an Me-109 or a battle cruiser of the Lion class. The enemy is the instrument. During the First World War, a sense of individuality was retained in the person of outstanding fighter pilots, who were identified by the distinguishing marks on their air-craft. Many a lesser pilot would go to his death largely unknown, despite the personal markings. There were many famous pilots in the Second World War, but they tended not to elicit terror as individuals, though they might be celebrated by the press of their own nation. Certain very effective groups were well known to the enemy, but as the "yellow-nosed fighters," the "Abbeville Kids," or the "Bastards of Brunswick." But here the reference was more to the airplane and to the group than to the pilot. In naval warfare, more important than the prowess of the individual commander in the minds of his opponents was the type of ship(s) commanded. Thus, a battleship clearly out-classed a cruiser or a destroyer, and the lesser ships in such an encoun-ter could only save themselves in such a meeting through flight.

Massive and powerful though these weapons are, however, they are also very vulnerable. It is surprising to the man on foot to see a monster tank suddenly begin to burn; if it is the enemy's, there is a feeling of gratitude as well. Only if the tank is one's own is there real concern for the occupants. For all these weapons—tank, plane, or naval vessel—there may come a time when the the weapon itself becomes the greatest danger to the occupant. Attention is turned from the enemy to the salvation of the craft (or, if that is impossible, to the craft's abandonment). Fire and explosion are the great fears and the latter may quickly follow the former:

The right wing . . . was wrapped in flame from the wingroot to about six feet from the tip. We had bought it. It was all over. The alarm bell! Find it! . . . During emergency practice, I could never find it but by a miracle my fingers were quick to touch it. . . . Bail out! Bail out! . . . I had all the time in the world, or so it seemed to me. Everything was framed in slow deliberate acts. What took me seconds to do, I remember as interminable dreamlike events. . . . Smoke was beginning to drift out of the bomb bay, and was being sucked up through the shattered top turret. . . . It was over. If she blew, she blew . . . I looked for the pull ring on my chute pack. I made sure I had my fingers wrapped around it when I tumbled out head first from the falling plane.[29]

For naval crews the sense that the stricken ship is the enemy is even more immediate. Those who serve below decks will never see the opposing forces, and until a shell or torpedo strikes, they will be thoroughly involved in performing the same tasks ordinarily required of them. When that occurs it becomes terribly apparent that danger lies in the flooding of the ship, an explosion of steam from the boilers, or, most sudden of all, the explosion of the magazines. Fire fighting, or the closing off of holes ripped in the hull of the ship, becomes the most important order of business. When those emergency measures fail, then flight, with the hope that their compartments have not already been sealed off. For the deck crews the sight of the wreckage of what had been the bridge or the gun turrets can be terrifying, but they too will have definite procedures to follow in dealing with the emergency. With these men too, particularly if their own stations have been damaged or destroyed, their major tasks will be involved with saving the ship and with saving themselves from the dangers posed by the burning vessel.

Curious reactions have sometimes been noted in emergencies of this sort. Aboard the *Yamato* during its last suicidal mission to Okinawa, with the ship under heavy attack from American dive-bombers, Ensign Yoshida found himself carefully wiping the seawater off the chart table. Other men in other parts of the stricken ship would sit down and get drunk on saki.[30] This tendency to turn away from the matters at hand, or to perform totally inappropriate acts, has often been marked. Soldiers in the midst of battle will suddenly begin looting. Others, assuming that the battle has been won or that their tasks have been completed, may lose all sense of danger and open themselves to counterattack because they have neglected the most rudimentary precautions. Something like this reaction can be seen in the animal world, where two furiously competing individuals may suddenly stop and take up a completely unconnected activities. Screaming gulls may turn to pulling up patches of grass, or the snarling cat may become engrossed in licking its paw. Such "displacement activity" is puzzlingly inapplicable but may be a method of resolving unbearable tension. Copilot Bert Stiles, on bomber missions over German territory, would find himself daydreaming and totally oblivious to the potential dangers until called back to reality by the pilot.[31]

Excitement, fear, and the press of fellow soldiers can create a strong sense of confusion in the individual. Even such a positive-thinking man as Theodore Roosevelt confessed (at the Battle of Las Guasimas): "It was a most confusing country . . . and I had an awful time trying to get into the fight and trying to do what was right when in it; and all the while I was thinking that I was the only man who did not know what I was about. . . ."[32] Crowding a large number of soldiers into a constricted space can also create confusion and in some cases lead to panic. A few days after the incidents which created such confusion for Colonel Roosevelt, Private Post of the 71st New York found himself being pushed along a narrow trail with elements of several other regiments in a rush to get these men into position for the attack on San Juan Hill. Spanish bullets firing into their midst were causing heavy casualties, and they were totally unable to retaliate. An officer by the side of the trail had broken down and was irrationally calling for men to bury a young lieutenant who had been killed. In this case, although the men finally arrived at their destination in a disordered state, it is surprising that they were not panicked.[33]

Fear and crowding can even have a surprising effect on the tactics of armies. Thucydides, discussing the Battle of Mantinea, says, "All armies are alike in this: on going into action they get forced out rather on their right wing, and one and the other overlap with this their adversary's left; because fear makes each man do his best to shelter his unarmed side with the shield of the man next him on the right, thinking that the closer the shields are locked together the better he will be protected. The man primarily responsible for this is the first on the right wing, who is always striving to withdraw from the enemy his unarmed side. . . ."[34] In modern times men have not borne shields in battle, but the still-present habit of crowding together has been widely marked. The common cry of the Second World War, "Spread out! One mortar shell could get you all," reflects this habit of soldiers to seek a spurious safety in numbers closely packed. The men huddled close together may not be panicked, or even overly frightened, yet they do find a greater comfort level in knowing their comrades are very close by. In this instance, crowding does not lead to antagonism but, strangely, is gratefully accepted. The alternative of being so widely spaced that there is not even visual contact can be a very disconcerting experience.

A soldier's perception of the limits of the battlefield provides another instance of a response that would seem to reach beyond the borders of rational thought and may be in some way instinctive. We do know that certain primitive warriors, including the Dani-speaking Kurulu discussed elsewhere in this chapter, set out restricted areas, agreed upon with the enemy, on which battles would be fought. In a sense these became the playing fields for the game of war. This did not preclude the use of other areas for the purpose of ambush, but the designated areas held pride of place. They were, as Huizinga has proposed, sacred areas, not to be used for profane purposes.[35] While we no longer have designated areas for battle, individual soldiers do recognize certain features of the landscape in front of them as being the objectives to be reached during the day's fighting. Of course, more distant objectives, such as the enemy's capital, are also in their minds, but the immediate goal may form for them a sort of temporary limit beyond which they are often reticent to move. It may only be a part of a broader battlefield, but for the moment the restricted space in front of them is the focus of all of their attentions. In some cases, a section of the landscape that had previously been ignored will become an objective and, thus, part of the circumscribed area and the object of intense struggle. This happened on the second day of the Battle of

Gettysburg, when the Little Round Top was seen to be a key to holding the field. In other cases, it may be the banks of a river or a ridge of low hills, but the individual soldier sees it in terms of a limit toward which he is advancing and beyond which he will not be required to move. This may contradict the thinking of the commanders, but it does represent one of the impediments a commander faces that makes troublesome the pursuit of the enemy.

Sorting out those responses which are instinctive from those which are not is, in a number of these instances, difficult. Examples of such difficult instances include startle reactions in response to noise, the baring of teeth, and the habit of huddling together. Other responses that may be instinctive include the habit of soldiers to hunch forward in the attack in much the same way that people do when walking in heavy rain. The use of dancing, singing war songs, and marching in rhythm, may also have its intoxicating effect upon the soldiers; in lieu of these, soldiers have historically made use of a variety of intoxicants to bolster their resolve. There are classic signs of submission, such as raising the hands or bowing before a captor, which may also have an instinctive base. As has already been pointed out, it is not the intention of this study to prove that war is an instinctive activity, but rather that it is a human institution which marshals a set of instinctive responses, primarily that of aggression, to the achievement of social ends.

Closely associated with the question of instinctive response and warfare is that of the antiquity of the institution. Many observers have held that warfare is really the product of civilization; that there can be no true warfare that is not governed by economic needs. It is supposed that, in societies where there is no property ownership, there can be no fighting to seize the neighbor's goods. When it is admitted that fighting does take place between hunting-gathering groups, it is alleged that this is not really "war" but, rather, falls into the category of a blood feud. It cannot be war because, among other things, so few persons are involved (and, thus, the "military horizon" has not been achieved).[36] Admittedly, fighting among hunter-gatherers and primitive horticulturalists does not involve any large number of persons, but it does involve a large percentage of the participating societies. It must also be noted that the cost of these struggles is not minimal. Despite the fact that the battles may conclude with the loss of a single life or, sometimes, with no loss of life at all, they can, if repeated often enough, be a major cause of death in the society.

The weaponry of war in the recent period is so specialized that it most often has no use away from the battlefield. Historically, this has been less true. The spear, the club, the sling, and the bow and arrow, were also the major implements used for hunting. Ancient armies might modify these weapons for use in war, but they remained recognizably hunting instruments. It is even true that the tactics of the battlefield have their parallels in the techniques of cooperative hunting. Surrounding the quarry, hunting from ambush, the preparation of special traps and pits, the cooperation of hunters in the stalking and killing of large animals, have long been a part of man's repertory of skills, and the transfer of these skills from the field of hunting to that of warfare or vice versa proved exceedingly easy:

Until recently war was viewed in much the same way as hunting. Other human beings were simply the most dangerous game. War has been far too important in human history for it to be other than pleasurable for the males involved. It is only recently, with the entire change in the nature and conditions of war, that this institution has been challenged, that the wisdom of war as a normal part of national policy or as an approved road to personal glory has been questioned. . . . It may be that killing other humans was a part of the adaptation from the beginning, and our sharp separation of war from hunting is due to the recent development of these institutions.[37]

In his study of the warfare practiced by primitive groups, Keith Otterbein included ten communities who lived at the hunter-gatherer level. Of these ten societies, two of them (or 20 percent of them) did not have a record of offensive warfare or military organization, although the Copper Eskimos did defend themselves in the rare instances when they were attacked, and the Dorobo killed any strangers entering their mountain territory.[38] Of the other eight groups, five were either continually or frequently at war, though this warfare was very limited by reason of the size of the groups (seven of the ten groups lived at the band level of organization). Only two of the fighting communities had warriors that could be considered professional (and, in one case, these warriors formed the nucleus of an otherwise nonprofessional military organization). The other six depended upon nonprofessional warriors. Warfare tended to be loosely organized and, in most cases, could be initiated by any member of the society. In battle, both the line formation, employing projectile weapons, and ambush were favored, although ambush was somewhat more popular. The weapons used by these warriors included both the projectile (spears and arrows) and shock (close combat weapons—stabbing instruments and clubs) types. One of the groups used only the shock type of weapon. It may be supposed that the employment of the projectile weapons favored a warfare in which demonstration of prowess rather than actual killing was highly prized. It probably also contributes to the low casualty rate shown by the five groups, for which evidence on this subject exists.[39] Major reasons for going to war included revenge, and, to a lesser extent, plunder (including captives) and trophies. The seizure of land for hunting was cited in only one case.

Although the ten groups cited in the Otterbein study were hunter-gatherers and were, for the most part, organized at the band level of society, their methods of warfare did not differ substantially from those of the Yanomamoe or the Kurulu primitive horticulturalists. As was the case with these agricultural peoples, dominance or seizure of land played little or no part in the causes of the hunter-gatherer wars, and revenge assumed a prominent role. Thus, there would appear to be a considerable degree of congruence between the practices of the hunter-gatherer groups and those used by primitive agriculturalists. It can be argued that using groups studied in the modern period, or using such information as may have been furnished by classical sources, offers no certain evidence about the practices of prehistoric humans. Admittedly, these practices could be relatively modern aberrations from a tranquil past, but the continuity of military weapons from the hunting background does offer some reason for suspecting that war may be an institution of some antiquity. The stone spearheads discovered in prehistoric sites, as well as some of the other implements could have served the purposes of combat as well as the hunt. Evidence of violence has been reported in skeletal remains dating as far back as *Australopithecus africanus* though this conclusion has been strongly contested.[40] The reports of cannibalism seen in the bones from Krapina have also been cast into doubt.[41] Yet, it is most difficult to believe that humanity, so given to violence throughout recorded history, so prone to kill the stranger, has suddenly, after spending peacefully 99 percent of its time on earth, discovered the joys of lethal violence.

7

The Coordinates of Chaos

O NE OF THE GREAT TENSIONS that has always existed in warfare is between the fact of confusion and the need for order. The apparent and real chaos of battle almost always works to the disadvantage of the commanders by negating the control necessary for success. At times a lucky break occurring during the struggle will lead to eventual success, though only if the commander is able to gain sufficient control to exploit the unexpected turn. Thus, at Remagen, the quick action on the part of a small unit to seize the bridge, coupled with the temporary confusion on the part of the Germans, allowed higher command to breach the Rhine defenses. Ordinarily, the results of confusion are not so positive. A U.S. Marine general, speaking to a forward unit during the opening phases of the recently concluded Persian Gulf War, warned that the unit would find battle most confusing, noting that the first rule of war is Murphy's Law—"if anything can go wrong it will go wrong"—and its corollary—"it will go wrong at the worst possible moment."[1]

The need to impose order for the purpose of avoiding confusion (as much as that is possible) has traditionally led military leaders to create an artificially high degree of order in the daily lives of the troops, an order marked by rigidly scheduled routine, a hierarchical organization of the army, and a mathematical standardization of units and procedures. The Roman camps laid out each night with geometrical precision, the rigid battle order of the Macedonian phalanx, the numbered loading steps for the preparation of the military musket, as well as marching in step, are all evidences of this concern to maintain a rigid, indeed mathematical, order. The rhythmic beating of the drum, it was hoped, would somehow hold at bay the chaos always threatening the military unit.

The elimination of aberrancies has been the constant concern of the leaders and planners. Tactical rules, drilled into the troops through repeated exercises, would allow them to perform in anticipated ways on the field of battle. Weapons, and the proper use of them, have been constantly refined. The science of ballistics, perhaps the most precise of the military procedures, has a history ranging back to the very dawn of warfare. The eye-hand coordination needed to hit a target with a spear is something that could only have been learned through continuous practice and attention to the minute details of the act. Hitting a moving target is an apparently simple act (though difficult enough to achieve) that must have had a long period of evolutionary development, even before the moment that prehistoric humans began to use the implement for hunting and warfare. For a long time, the hurling of projectiles would remain more an art or skill rather than a science. The judgment of the man in charge of the catapult or the ballista in estimating the probable tension needed to place a stone of uncertain weight onto the desired target was not easily learned. With the advent of gunpowder, the cannoneers, working with weapons and projectiles still only crudely manufactured, had to estimate the amount of powder needed to overcome the loss of power due to windage (the space between the ball and the barrel of the cannon) and still fire effectively. Science and technology came to the assistance of the gunners so that the trajectory of the ball (and later the shell) could be planned with an ever-increasing accuracy. Mathematics became the grammar of violence. Most recently, computer technology has enabled artillerymen to fire at and hit missiles approaching at supersonic speeds.

Less obviously spectacular, though no less important, is the military science of logistics. Armies in the field have very seldom been able to live off the land; they must bring forward a part of or all their supplies, ammunition, and replacements. Planning for these needs can become almost impossibly complex, since a breakdown in any part of the system can lead to the failure of the whole enterprise. "For want of a nail" is not an entirely facetious maxim. Logistical operations are so important, it has been argued that Alexander would be considered one of the great commanders of history based alone on his ability to maintain his army in the long marches from Greece to

India. It is not enough to reckon crudely the amount of ammunition or food that the army will need for a given number of days of operation. The means of transportation must be provided and the fuel for that transport, whether it be hay for horses or gasoline for trucks, must be brought into the equation. The proper supplies must be sent to the appropriate unit; ammunition of the wrong caliber is useless, and it may be that not all units of the army possess identical weapons. All of the many items of equipment must be preplanned and brought forward in the proper order. Mistakes do occur, confusion will persist; that large armies in the field are supplied at all is a minor miracle; or, at least, it represents a tribute to the administrative abilities of those in charge of supply.

Attempts to achieve the kind of mathematical precision aimed for in the field of ballistics and logistics have proven less successful when applied to infantry. Historically, the need to achieve a massing of power while retaining maneuverability did lead to the organization of infantrymen into blocks, as in the case of the Greek and Macedonean phalanxes or the Roman legions. In the early modern age, after a long hiatus, when infantry again became the decisive arm on the battlefield, men were again formed into blocks, first of pikemen and then, with the more general introduction of gunpowder, of fusiliers, musketeers, and finally, riflemen. As long as the weapons used were muzzle loaders, with their necessarily lengthy process of reloading, coupled with a short range of accuracy, formation in compact blocks continued to be the only means by which a sufficient volume of fire could be delivered. In addition, the introduction of the bayonet provided the infantry with a shock weapon which could be employed for fighting at close quarters. In all these cases, the armies were subdivided into discreet units, each of which was capable of functioning independently so the army would not become an unwieldy mass impossible to maneuver with any efficiency.

Moving masses of men in tightly ordered blocks is possible only when some form of close order drill is imposed, so that each man in the mass moves in conformity with his neighbors and at the same pace. To perform these maneuvers on the barracks square was one matter, but to maintain these formations over rough or uneven terrain was only achieved through long practice and iron discipline. To hold these formations under intense fire from the enemy calls for a kind of resolute behavior that is almost impossible to imagine. Yet the history of the many battles fought during these centuries shows that it was possible. Not only did men maintain the integrity of their units, but these units were maneuvered, often with great efficiency, over the battlefield. Perhaps inspired by the machinelike behavior of the men and the near mechanical operation of the army in maneuver, some eighteenth-century writers came to believe that it would be possible to construct a geometry of war, a set of theorems and rules which, if inflexibly followed, would render victory certain.[2] Not surprisingly, this happy formulation failed the test of practical application.

Napoleon's dictum that "God is on the side of the big battalions" does not imply that any military unit will become better simply by growing larger. Ten thousand men in a single unit are not necessarily more powerful than ten units of a thousand men each. The latter may be, probably would be, more maneuverable. Provided that there is adequate communication between the leadership of the ten smaller units and if they acted in a coordinated fashion, they would be more than a match for the large, unwieldy mass. In fact, ten thousand men in a single, unarticulated unit is not a unit in the military sense at all; rather, it is a mob. On man cannot command ten thousand without subordinate commanders to relay and enforce his orders at various locations within the horde. Armies have always understood this and have organized themselves in discreet units of manageable size. "The Roman legion of the imperial period contained ten cohorts, each subdivided into three maniples. There were two centuries in each maniple, and the century—in practice eighty strong—was formed from ten eight man mess units *(conturbernia)*."[3] The Spartan army of the late fifth century B.C. had, as its major tactical unit, the *lochos* of 100 men divided into 2 units *(pentekostyes)*, and each of these was divided into 2 platoons *(enomatiai)* of 25 men each, which were themselves composed of 3 squads of 8 men and a leader each. Four *lochos* made up a *mora* commanded by a *polemarch*; the Spartan army consisted of 6 of these latter.[4] The basic unit of the Macedonian phalanx, the *syntagma*, was composed of 256 men organized in 16 ranks and 16 files. Each file of 16 men made up a mess unit.

In the modern era, perhaps at first heavily influenced by the writings of Vegetius, units of roughly parallel size developed. By the Napoleonic era, line companies of infantry numbered about 140 officers and men; between 6 and 8 companies made up a battalion, of which there were 3 to a regiment. A considerable degree of change occurred in the composition of these units as the army adjusted itself to the changing conditions of both war and the quality of its recruits.[5] Infantry regiments of the American Civil War were supposedly made up of 1,000 men divided into 10 companies. In practice the companies might, at the time of enlistment, contain no more than 80 men. In battle these regiments soon found themselves reduced to an average of 300+ men able to perform active service. Mess units in the Civil War armies seem to have been formed by 5 to 10 men clubbing together. Company strength of the European armies in the late nineteenth and early twentieth centuries varied between 150 and 200 men, with 4 rifle companies making up a battalion.[6] The increase in the power and rate of fire of the modern breechloading rifle forced these armies to move to an extended order formation, with the result that what had formerly been mess units became the tactical units of section, squad, and platoon, numbering about 5, 10, and 40 men, respectively. It is suspected that in those armies where the size of the company approached 200 men, the enlargement was done with a view to maintaining a ready pool of replacements in anticipation of casualties.

Not only has it been the practice to break down masses of men into manageable units but, as often as possible, these units have been uniformly armed. Thus, the Macedonian *syntagma* armed its men with the thirteen-foot pike known as the sarissa, though the men in the rear ranks may have been armed differently. In all the ancient armies, lightly armed troops, such as slingers, were seperately organized to act as skirmishers or to perform other duties. The advantages of uniform armament are obvious, since differently armed men in close formation would find it difficult to coordinate the operation of their weapons. According to the Bible, the tribe of Benjamin went so far as to organize a unit of left-handed slingers.[7]

Whatever the army or the sophistication of the weaponry, there do seem to be certain numerical constants that crop up. Infantry companies again and again are reported to number about 100 men or to range between 80 and 120 men. The Spartan *lochos* and the Roman century fit into this range, while the Macedonian *syntagma* was so designed as to be divisible into two sections of 128 men for purposes of extending the line. Battalions of about 500 to 800 men are also common, though in some cases units of the same size have been termed regiments.

Ordinarily, in the present century, the battalion has been composed of four companies numbering about 400 to 500 riflemen. In the Roman army of the Imperial period, the *cohort* was composed of six *centuries* for a total of 480 men. Lastly, the groups of messmates of the older armies and the comparable squads of recent armies contain about the same number of men (5 to 10 or possibly a few more). Actually, the modern squad is divisible into sections of 4 or 5 men, which was also a fairly common size for a group of messmates.

It has been argued that the reason we often see military units broken down into subdivisions of the one hundred or so men is that this represents the limit that can be efficiently controlled by one man. In fact, particularly in the recent period, it has become necessary to appoint lower-ranked commanders to handle platoons and squads which make up the company. From the point of view of the man in the ranks, the company comander and his subordinates represent visible authority. Beyond the company level, that authority tends to become shadowy; the battalion—and, even more, the regimental commander— is not someone that the private in the ranks would even consider engaging in casual conversation; they are simply unknown except as distant authority figures. The company commander stands in more direct relation with his men, and this is more observable in the case of the platoon leaders and sergeants. As was noted earlier in this book, the company is the soldier's home address, and, to a greater or lesser extent, the company is family.

There may even be more to this constancy of numbers than the matter of efficient control. Primitive man did not ordinarily live in large groups; the average size of these groups and the consequences for primitive military organization may suggest that there is more continuity between primitive and modern warfare than is often thought to be the case. Joseph Birdsell's studies of Australian precontact dialectical tribes has led him to conclude that there existed a strong tendency for these tribes to maintain a population of about five hundred members. In cases where a tribe had been diminished for any of a variety of reasons, they tended to recover to the five hundred–person level, while significant expansion above this number would lead to a "budding off" of parts of the dialect group so the "magic number" could be maintained. Since these dialectical tribes were hunter-gatherers, they did not ordinarily live in one large settlement but, rather, tended to live most of the time in groups of about twenty-five persons.[8] Birdsell contends that these numbers should also hold true for the

Pleistocene as well as for the more recent periods. This position was supported by Louis Binford, whose studies on paleolithic cave dwellings indicated that those dwellings were each capable of providing shelter for about twenty-five persons (250 square meters of floor space).[9] The importance of these figures for the study of warfare is that a group of about five hundred persons can be expected to contain between eighty and one hundred adult hunters or to furnish about the same number of warriors, if we assume that primitive and prehistoric groups did engage in warfare. The number of adult males capable of hunting or fighting in a group of twenty-five persons would range from four to six. The correspondence between these figures and the average number of soldiers in a company (one hundred) or the half-squad (five) is intriguing. It can at least be speculated that one hundred is not only about the limit that can be effectively controlled by one man, but that one hundred may mark a limit for effective cooperative action. Four to six men, or possibly a few more, may actually be the ideal size for effective action in hunting or war; fifteen or so such groups may be the maximum that can work together effectively. Beyond this level, cooperation will be between similar-sized units grouped together by some higher authority. Again, referring to Birdsell, there is evidence that among dialectical tribes, the marked tendency exists for the dialects to diverge somewhat after surpassing the five hundred–person level, and that at about two thousand persons, the odivergence becomes so great that communication is difficult. If there is a connection between these tribal-sized figures and the continuing composition of military forces, then one can see that the four groups of eighty to one hundred hunter/warriors putatively furnished by the four tribes of five hundred persons would correspond rather exactly to the number of riflemen making up a modern battalion.

Of these numbers the most significant may be the group of five to ten men. Ten Yanomamoe raiders, including some juveniles, set out from a village of about forty persons; nine Kurulu warriors, expecting battle, gather at the base of a watchtower on the edge of the traditional battlefield. Eight Spartans form a mess unit, sixteen members of the Macedonian phalanx eat together; the Roman *conturbernia* comprises eight men. The men who eat together fight together, and in modern armies, they are quite likely to fight as a separate unit rather than as single members of a larger mass. Infantry sections and squads range from four to twelve members; RAF and Luftwaffe fighters flew in "finger four" formation—two pairs each of leader and wingman. Bomber crews of between four and ten men were used by the various air forces. Four to five men made up the machine-gun and mortar squads, while the U.S. Marines divided their rifle squads into three fire teams of four men each for the island fighting.

Enumeration is one of the inescapable facts of military life. Issued a serial number upon their induction to military service, the new recruits find themselves placed in a numbered training company, lined up, and instructed to count off and to perform other tasks "by the numbers." SOP (standard operating procedure) was "Null Acht Funfzehn" (0815) in the German Army. The pieces of equipment are often known by number: Mark Four, M-1, F-15, and in those units where there are liable to be many men with the same last name, they will be numbered; thus, Robert Graves in his memoirs of life in the Royal Welch Fusiliers would speak of O-nine Morgan. Once the initial phases of training are completed, the men find themselves transferred into numbered units ranging from 1st Division to the fabled 1344th Messkit Repair Battalion. Until the Cardwell reforms of the 1870s, the regiments of the British Army were numbered rather than named; even today the number "22" can be seen on plaques in Chester for the Cheshire regiment.

Some counting is carried on by individuals for their own personal gratification or, perhaps, to build their reputations as redoubtable warriors. The Plains Indians adopted the practice of "coup counting," that is, touching the enemies in battle with the coup stick. That this practice took the place of killing could be considered an indication of admirable restraint on the part of these societies, though it did not entirely eliminate the practice of killing in battle. In aerial combat fighter pilots counted their kills; leading aces became heroes in their homelands, though not all went to the length of Baron von Richtofen, who had trophy cups made for each of his victories. A more grisly example of the habit of enumeration was the decision of the American forces in Vietnam to keep a body count of enemy killed as a means of determining the progress of the war. In actuality, the body count is a very old institution, the first recorded instance appearing in the first recorded description of a war: Entemena slew [the Ummaite forces] up unto Umma (itself); . . . his [Ur-Lumma's] elite force . . . (of) 60 soldiers he wiped out [?] on the bank of the Lumma-girnunta canal. [As for] its [Umma's fighting] men, he [Entemena] left their bodies in the plain [for the birds and the beasts to devour] and [then] heaped up their skeleton [?] piles in five [separate] places."[10] Admittedly, this is not a very precise reckoning, but that is a problem which has dogged body counts throughout history.

Counting enemy losses may give the commander some idea of how well he is doing in battle, but this is counterbalanced by the accounting which must be taken of losses to one's own forces. Modern leaders have come to reckon on a percentage of losses which is acceptable for any given operation: 3 to 5 percent may be within the acceptable parameters set by the military; 30 percent is not. The "seriousness" of these percentages is subject to change; if a decisive victory is won with high losses, the losses might be worth it. The Allied forces were willing to accept very high losses on D-Day, if a landing could be achieved. In this particular example, the casualties were lower than expected, but the costs of the continuing battle for Normandy were above the predicted levels, with the result that something of a crisis developed for the combat units.

Loss includes not only the killed and the wounded, but also a number of other diminutions in force, all of which contribute to the declining ability of a unit to continue operations. In any attack there will be a steady drainage from the front. Men are killed and wounded; some persons, despite orders to the contrary, will assist the wounded to the rear. Others will drift back from the front on errands mainly important to themselves. Under heavy fire the men will go to ground. If they cannot be made to move forward again, they are effectively lost, at least temporarily. It may well be that the resistance is such that continuing the attack is useless, but more than one operation, which stood a good chance of success, has been defeated by the refusal of men to move.

Sickness has often reduced the number of men available for the day of battle. In fact, until this century disease has always been the major cause of losses to the strength of an army. Even today it is a continuing, though much less important, problem. A host of other factors contribute to the reduction of forces available for the fight. Modern armies, with their vast array of weaponry and other equipment, demand that a large number of soldiers be involved with the maintenance of this machinery and its resupply. Guarding the lines of communication is necessary, and, in hostile country, may absorb a considerable part of the combat units. Troops in training, persons involved in the maintenance of morale, troops in transit—all are unavailable. Gen. Leslie B. McNair, commander of U.S. Army Ground Forces in World War II, bemoaned the fact of the large numbers of men going from here to there but, seemingly, never arriving.[11] Beyond this, some armies follow the policy of leaving a certain percentage of the combat troops out of battle, so that they will be available to reconstitute the unit in case of catastrophic losses. A swollen headquarters force may be a source of comfort to some commanders, but this also serves to remove troops from the front.

For the men at the front, there is the further question of how long they will be serviceable. Besides being killed or wounded, the front soldier faces the probability that his efficiency will decline over time, so that he may finally be more of a liability than an asset. The length of this period has been the subject of much discussion, and the study of past actions and wars has not really resolved the question. It does seem obvious that men will not endure forever the stresses of battle, and the military appears ready to accept the axiom that all men have a breaking point. Whether this will occur within a few weeks or months, or whether it will be possible for men to operate efficiently even after years of combat is still debated. Studies by American teams of psychologists in the Second World War seemed to indicate that after three to four months of combat, those men who had not been killed or wounded would be rendered psychologically unserviceable.[12] This was, of course, an average; some men did, in fact, continue to fight effectively for years. On the other hand, some collapsed in their first experience or even before they had been committed to battle. Given the intensity at which it is posited that all-out war in the future will be conducted, observers have reckoned that the ability of men to withstand the stress will be greatly reduced even from the levels of the Second World War.

Whatever the reasons for the loss of men in battle or their unavailability for battle, these losses do occur, and some calculations have been made as to the average turnover time for a combat unit. As mentioned earlier in this book, it has been estimated that, in battle of moderate levels, an infantry rifle company will experience 100 percent turnover of personnel in a period of three to four months. This does not mean that every man will be replaced but rather that losses, for whatever reason, will equal the total strength of the company. Officer losses will be particularly high: the average length of time that a platoon leader was able to remain in combat during the Second World War was sixty-two days.[13] In previous centuries, when battle occurred only sporadically, the endurance time of the individual soldier was much longer. The daily loss in battle, when it was finally joined, tended to be much higher.[14] but the period of time between battles was, on the average, much longer, and the men were given that time to recuperate. In the campaign of 1864, the Army of the Potomac found itself in almost constant combat, from the Wilderness to Cold Harbor, and the morale of the troops dropped precipitately.[15] The extended order of battle adopted by all armies under the impact of increased effective firepower tended to reduce the daily loss rate while at the same time increasing the number of days of continuous combat.

The huge losses that have been a part of modern war have led some observers to regard primitive restrictions on losses as being a sign of greater rationality on the part of aboriginal men. A battle which is fought only until one man has been killed is certainly dangerous enough, but ending it at that point preserves all of the rest of the contestants and serves to maintain the ritual character of warfare. However, if this rule is extended over time, the results may not be so beneficial.

As noted earlier in this chapter, in the case of two groups of five hundred persons, about eighty to one hundred warriors will be available at any given time. If the losses are evenly distributed between the two groups, the frequency with which these ritual engagements occur could have an important impact upon each of the societies. If these battles were fought at intervals of two months, the expected loss per year would be three for each society. If the warriors could be expected to be available for combat between the ages of fifteen and forty-five, however, this would add up to 180 days of combat for the surviving warriors, with a loss to each community equivalent to the total strength of the warrior group at any given time. If battle were joined only once a year, the losses would still equal 15 percent of the average strength. Thus, losses in ritual battle alone would have a considerable impact upon the societies. One could add to this the loss of manpower through debilitating injuries in battle, the haphazard killing of women and children, and losses from disease or accident. With these consideration taken together, it is not at all certain that warfare has become more dangerous to society than was the case under primitive conditions. That at least has been the situation until the introduction of such weapons of mass destruction as the atomic and hydrogen bombs.

Primitive warfare does conceive of all adult males as being potential warriors. In some cases the prosecution of war is given over to a more specialized group, which might be considered to be a professional military organization. It would appear, however, that most hunter-gatherer groups which have any military organization at all tend to rely upon the abilities of the entire adult male section of the population. With the appearance of civilized societies, military responsibility has been generally handed over to a more restricted membership. In the Greek city-states, though it might be the duty of all citizens to serve in the army, this was contingent on their ability to supply their own heavy arms and armor, a qualification that tended to eliminate the poorer citizens. These latter could and did serve with the light troops or as rowers in the navy. Still, a large section of the male members of the society, slaves and other non-citizens, were not obliged to serve. In Sparta the unique situation existed in which one portion of the society, the Spartan citizens, was armed against the suppressed portion of the society, the helots. In Rome, a general citizen militia was transformed over the centuries, particularly after the establishment of the Empire, into a professional force that did not engage the services of the rest of the citizenry.

Medieval warfare presented a more extreme example of this restriction of warfare to a small portion of the community. Armed knights, for the most part members of the noble classes,[16] carried the responsibility for defense as the infantry groups of the earlier medieval period proved less and less effective. The era of gunpowder brought the infantry back onto the field as a significant force and opened the bearing of arms to a broader section of the society. Yet, until the wars of the revolutionary period at the end of the eighteenth century, there was no real notion of general military responsibilities. Following Napoleon's downfall, most of the European armies reverted to the employment of small professional forces. One exception, Prussia, was regarded as militarily backward for its reliance on military conscription. It was only the success of the Prussians in the series of wars from 1864 to 1871 that led the other nations of Europe to resume the practice of peacetime conscription.

Yet, even modern conscription systems did not result in a total mobilization of the relevant adult male sections of the population.

The United States, for example, mustered into service 10 percent of its total population for the Civil War (Union forces only), 5 percent for World War I, 12 percent for the Second World War, and slightly less than 5 percent were inducted into service during the Vietnam era. Other nations, Germany, Russia, France, and England, did mobilize larger portions of the population during the First and Second World Wars, and their losses were heavier, though, with the exception of the Soviet Union, the deaths did not exceed 5 percent of the population.[17] In fact, few wars of the modern period have resulted in a death toll that would place the survival of the entire society in danger. The Paraguayan War, with the loss of some 25 percent of the total population, is a gruesome exception to this rule. Yet, while a somewhat lower percentage of adult males serve in the military than would be the case in primitive society, a larger portion of the civilian population has been placed in danger by weapons' developments of the twentieth century. Non-combatants in some numbers have always been at risk: cities have been put to the sword and populations have been taken captive, but seldom have such large numbers of persons been endangered.

Curiously, while the nineteenth and twentieth centuries have seen a great increase in the size of armies, there has been a noticeable decline in the numbers of frontline troops, not only relative to the entire size of the army, but also in relation to the the size of the population. In the American Civil War approximately 80 percent of the Union Army, or about 1,700,000 men, was comprised of Infantry. Not all these men saw combat, but as many as half of them did. In World War I, an estimated 800,000 infantrymen were committed to battle. In World War II, seventy-three infantry divisions each contained about 3,200 riflemen (or about 230,000 for the entire army). To this should be added the replacements, the mortarmen and machine gunners, the runners, the specialist troops of battalion and regimental headquarters, the men of the armored units, the combat engineers, aircrews, and certain other specialist groups. In total, it is estimated that no more than 800,000 men saw direct combat action in the Second World War, and this figure would appear to be no larger than the figures for either the First World War or the American Civil War. As a percentage of the total population, it represents a decline from 3.6 percent to 0.8 percent to 0.6 percent over the period from 1865 through 1918 to 1945. The figures for American involvement are admittedly lower than those for other nations, such as Germany or Russia, but combatant figures for any modern state pale by comparison with figures for any primitive society, where the majority or the totality of the adult male population would be expected to engage in direct warfare.

This thinning out of the forces engaged on the forward edge of battle has resulted in, or been made possible by, a greater abstraction of violence. I mean "abstract" here in the sense that the direct confrontation and killing of the enemy has begun to recede into the background. The empty battlefield, commented on by many observers, is one manifestation of this development. Another, noted by John Keegan, has been the tendency for the officer class to delegate the direct tasks of killing to the "other ranks." In recent wars this has been carried to the point that some officers, even those fighting in the front lines, no longer carry weapons.[18] Even the ordinary soldier is today only very rarely involved in the direct killing of his opponent. Hand-to-hand combat, like the bayonet charge, is a very rare occurrence and has been so for more than century. Killing at a distance— using high powered rifles, machine guns, mortars, artillery, or aerial assault—is the much more likely scenario. In the bombardment of cities, this abstraction is carried to an even higher level. The trajectory of the missile, whether guided or free falling, is calculated to achieve the desired result. "Targeting" becomes the causal factor. Casually, with a perhaps necessary touch of callousness, we speak of "collateral damage," which includes, of course, civilian casualties.

George Orwell commented acidly on this tendency to hide the naked truth behind a cloud of abstract words but there is reason for this.[19] As deluding as the words may be, they do allow commanders to think more calmly about what is being done. To be able to visualize the battle as the movement of well-ordered troops, to imagine the invisible tracery of howitzer shells arcing through the night sky toward intended targets, to imagine the enemy reacting intelligently and predictably to one's own movements, all assist the commander in making his plans. Good leaders know that what happens on the sand table, or on the screen of the computer, is only an approximation of what they hope will take place in battle. They also know that, if truth is the first casualty of war, the second is the plan of battle. The well thought-out ambush prematurely uncovered, the ritual battle formation of the primitive warriors, so much like a form of dance, breaks down as warriors suddenly find themselves too far forward and entrapped by the enemy. Roman legionnaires charging victoriously into the middle of the front are cast into confusion and despair as the great wings of Hannibal's army close around them. The geometric forms of regiments flow smoothly forward and disappear into the smoke of battle, searching blindly for the foe while the commander awaits for some word of their progress. Orders are misunderstood or not clearly given; runners become casualties, and radio or telephone communication breaks down. Sophisticated weaponry falls victim to mud or sand. Troops are landed on the wrong beach. Everywhere common fear and berserk courage take charge as Murphy's Law rules the day.

From its origins on, war has involved the attempt of humanity to impose order on chaos. This institution which marshals the forces of some of deepest human instincts, which gives free reign to both fear and aggression, brings on a reversion to that imagined earliest condition of humanity in the state of a free and violent nature. Lest disorder overwhelm the world, humans must also control this violence and bend it to their purposes. In pursuit of this goal, they have called into service all the techniques by which they have been able to understand and control the natural forces of the universe. Whether these be an understanding of the will of the gods or a knowledge of the physical universe or the techniques of controlling fellow humans, they have, at various times, summoned each of the them for assistance. So religion, psychology, geometry, mathematics, and theoretical physics have marched to war. Sadly, the result of the use of these tools of order has only been to increase the violence and worsen the condition of chaos.

8

The Long March:
Preservation and Change

THROUGHOUT THIS STUDY it has been argued that warfare is a practice with very ancient roots. All the examples of warfare discussed thus far, however, have either been drawn from modern battles, the battles of primitive agriculturalists, or those of hunter-gatherers either presently existing or known from written accounts. Paleoanthropologists have rightly questioned whether it is really possible to tell anything about the behavior of early humans from analogies which draw on recent events. It is probably not very surprising, then, that they continue to develop concepts of behavior which pay close attention to ancient environmental and physiological conditions but which arrive at conclusions not entirely removed from those achieved by analogies.[1]

Perhaps the place to begin is with the appearance of *Homo erectus* some 1.6 million years ago on the plains of eastern Africa. To search farther into the past involves discussion of the place occupied in evolution by a variety of hominids and hominoids, about which there exists considerable present disagreement among paleontologists. This is only somewhat less true of *Homo erectus*, but some things do appear to be more or less certain.[2] By this stage early man was fully bipedal, tools either of stone or other materials were in use, and the diet was formed of both plant and animal foods, though it is not certain whether *Homo erectus* had become a true hunter or relied on scavenging. The condition in which offspring are born considerably less than fully developed, made necessary an extended period of care for the young and greater assistance from the adult male. It is assumed that food sharing by the immediate family, and possibly the community group, was practiced. These communities probably numbered between twenty and forty persons; in them, the labors were divided, with the women and young children charged with gathering plant food in the vicinity of the base camp, while the adult males ranged more widely in the search for animal food. Because of the patchiness of food resources in the savanna environment, the competition from other animals, both herbivores and carnivores, and the energy demands of *Homo erectus*, who must be classified as a rather large mammal, the groups of these hunter-gatherers tended to be spread rather thinly over the African continent.

None of these characteristics were peculiar to *Homo erectus* alone. Other hominids and primates had adopted a terrestial way of life in the savanna. Meat eating is practiced occasionally by present day chimpanzees; communities of small bands can also be noted, though food sharing is very limited or nonexistent. Present day primates are neotenic, though the period of development after birth is more limited than that of present day humans and probably shorter than that of *Homo erectus*. Important differences can be seen, however: the cranial capacity of *Homo erectus* was larger than that of preceeding hominids, and at some point in its development, *Homo erectus* began to use and eventually to make fire. One investigator claims to have found in skull impressions evidence of both the Broca and Wernicke areas, which are related to language. Others have shown that there was some development of the larynx, but whether or not these would add up to the capacity for speech is far from established. Still, it may be inferred that communication of some sort, either by vocalization or gesture, was practiced.[3]

The advantages which this species enjoyed over other hominids may have been marginal, but they were sufficient to allow it to gain supremacy. By one-and-a-half million years ago, *Homo erectus* was the sole surviving hominid. Within another half million years, the species would begin expansion from Africa into the Eurasian continent, spreading all the way from Morocco to Java and eventually to the north of China as well. There is a good deal of controversy regarding whether or not the species ever entered Europe. The earliest inhabitants there have been classified variously as *Homo erectus* or as one or another early grade of *Homo sapiens*.[4] In the process of this move out of Africa, the small bands of hunter-gatherers became more widely separated than ever as they dealt with the problems created by colder climates and more widely spaced food resources. Actually, they seem to have stayed close to the southern edge of the Eurasian land mass, only entering the colder regions late in their history. A stone tool culture, the Achuelian, was developed and remained the hallmark of Homo erectus from the time of their emergence to the time of their ultimate disappearance two hundred thousand years ago. Other evidence shows that they probably built shelters,[5] learned the use and the making of fire,[6] had the ability to coordinate action with other groups for the hunting of large animals,[7] and involved themselves in certain types of ritual activities. It should be noted that, in the passage to the various parts of the Eurasian continent, Homo erectus demonstrated a very considerable adaptability in terms of using plants for food, and, in the forested regions of Southeast Asia, they apparently took advantage of bamboo as a material for tools.[8] Although their accomplishments in stone tool manufacture were relatively unspectacular, and although we have only the most shadowy evidence of progress regarding their imagination, Homo erectus must be credited with establishing or continuing a good part of the groundwork for the evolution of the human species.

The evidence for the history of Homo erectus is sparse. Of the millions or possibly billions of individuals who lived during the life span of this species, remains of less than one hundred have been found. For the most part, these remains consist of partial skulls, lower jaws, isolated teeth, and a few assorted bones. One virtually complete skeleton has recently been found, that of a juvenile male. Yet, from this small collection of materials, paleontologists have been able to derive a remarkably extensive picture of the life of this species. Microscopic inspection of the teeth give some idea of what types of food were eaten, the muscular structure can be inferred, even the length of pregnancy has been estimated.[9] Some post cranial skeletal parts of a female giving evidence of a lingering disease have suggested that the person was cared for during the final months of her life.[10]

For the purposes of this study, it must be asked whether the remains give any evidence of violent activity. Given the episodic nature of violence and the paucity of materials for investigation, it would be reasonable to suppose that nothing would be found. Yet, surprisingly, the bones do contain signs indicating the use of deadly force. From the Ngandong site (400,000 years BP [before the present]) in Java, skull 7 shows a large area of damage which has been interpreted as "a partly healed wound perhaps inflicted by a blunt weapon."[11] Ngandong 11 shows a number of pits on the vault of the skull, which have been seen as the result of blows delivered at the time of death.[12]

Such evidences of violence are not unique. During the period ranging from 400–300,000 years ago, the Steinheim skull, that of a female in her mid-twenties, is heavily damaged on the left side from the effects of a blow with a "blunt instrument" undoubtedly resulting in her death. The head was then severed from the body.[13] At Vertesszoelloes (400,000 years BP), cut marks have been been interpreted as signs of cannibalism.[14] In the cave at Krapina (75,000 years BP), a group of skeletal remains were found that were originally suspected of having been subjected to cannibalism. This conclusion has been refuted but leaves the suggestion that the persons were purposely killed.[15] The Shanidar cave contained the fossils of a number of persons, one with the left side of an eyesocket crushed, another with a large scar resulting from a blow, and a third who had been fatally stabbed.[16] From a more recent period (7,200 years BP), thirty-eight skulls were found, in the Offnet cave, which had been been cracked by bludgeoning and then decapitated.[17] Finally, Fontbrigona cave (9) (6,000–7,000 years BP) revealed six individuals—three adults, two children, and one person of indeterminate age—who had been cannibalized. This is the earliest known instance in which solid proof has been offered of the practice, though, interestingly, there is no definite evidence for the victims having been cooked.[18]

Given the fact that the total of all hominid fossil collections is not that large, this number of instances of violence is significant. Since, necessarily, only those cases in which the cause of the fatal injury is visible from the skeletal remains are included in this summary, it may be suspected that violence was an even more frequent occurrence. The question remains, though, what sort of violence is illustrated here? A number of alternatives can be suggested: domestic, ritual, accidental, intracommunal quarreling, and, lastly, warfare. It is quite possible that, as a cause of violent death, warfare would have played a relatively minor role, since its occurence is likely to have been even more sporadic than that of the other occasions for lethal activity.

One cause for the probable low level of hostile activity between groups is the fact that the hunting-gathering way of life demands a good deal of territory for the satisfactory survival of individuals and groups. The reasons for this include the patchiness of resources (that is, not all areas provide equally good sources of either plant or animal food). Competition for available food would come not only from other human groups, but from other animals as well, both carnivores and herbivores. Furthermore, the seasonality of food resources necessitated a migratory existence. Because of these conditions, the human groups found themselves spread thinly over the usable areas of the Eurasian continent. Estimates of the amount of territory needed for the annual support of an individual range from 10 km² to 80 km² and even higher. For a band of 25 persons, this would necessitate areas from 250 to 2,000 square kilometers. A study from Poland of Mesolithic hunting groups estimates that an area of 47,000 km² was occupied by between 600 and 1,500 persons. The area used by the occupants of the Star Carr site in Yorkshire has been estimated to range from 80 km² to over 300 km² for a group of 20 persons. However, Star Carr was a winter season camp and would, therefore, in all probability, represent only a portion of the band's annual territory.[19]

Granted, hunting techniques of the Mesolithic period differed considerably from those of the Paleolithic. Regarding the plant food resources, the weather conditions occasioned by the continued glaciations of the later Pleistocene impacted the gathering possibilities not only in the colder regions, but also in Africa, where a drier climate (and, hence, a sparser vegetation) paralleled the advance of the glaciers in the higher latitudes.[20] Yet the population density cannot have risen much past the lower limit of one person per 10 km², if it ever reached that level. Thus, it can be assumed that, during much of the year, the small hunting bands would have had few occasions to meet other human beings. The conditions of annual survival, and the human feeding strategy which had evolved, mandated that the search for food be carried out by small groups. The band was a very efficient feeding unit, dependence upon larger animals made group hunting advisable, and the unreliability of the hunt made gathering a necessity. Both males and females shared in the responsibility for the group's well being; the four or five adult males not only hunted but provided protection against predators. The females gathered the plant food, at times trapped small animals or participated in animal drives, and were the primary caregivers.

As was noted before, however, the hunting-gathering band cannot assure its own generational survival, since there is no guarantee that a balance between male and female offspring will be achieved. At some time contact would have to be made with other bands for the exchange of mates. Whether such contacts were initially hostile (as in the case of wife stealing), it can be assumed that in time a larger exchange group of twenty or more bands would be formed, providing a stable balance of males and females. Such exchanges would have been much easier for groups sharing a common set of signals, vocalizations, or language. At times some of the bands making up this larger group might also cooperate in the hunting of very large animals. Howell has suggested this in connection with the hunting of the elephants discovered at the Torralba site.[21]

Groups having a common interest in mate exchange, and probably sharing other customs as well, would also have a common interest in protecting their territorial range. Under ordinary circumstances, these ranges might very well have been secure, but alterations in climate conditions which reduced the plant food supply or changes in animal migration patterns, could lead to a situation in which the larger group would be forced to seek out new territories or in which a group of strangers would seek to enter the group's territory. At this point hostilities could well take place. They might be restricted to threat posturing and other belligerent behavior, which would be sufficient to ward off the strangers or force them to make room, if it were their territory which was being invaded. Quite possibly stronger measures would be needed, and actual fighting or even killing could take place. The fact that early humans were capable of lethal violence, and the long history which violence has had since that time, makes this a distinct possibility.

Threat to the food supply and the attempt to resolve the problem by trespass on a neighbor's territory can be described as an economic cause for war. Yet, it is known that primitive warfare has involved incidents in which no economic reason can be seen. Wife stealing or revenge for some previous injury or death have also been occasions for hostilities. Such events can be considered the conscious and immediate causes for a conflict but leave in question the reasons for the existence of the institution of warfare itself. It has to be asked whether war served in some way to maintain the human species. To ask that question places warfare in the same group with a number of other human institutions, such as food sharing, the marriage system, and a panorama of activities, customs, and beliefs that define a human culture and differentiate it from all others.

Each of these institutions tends to make use of ritual. Meals are served in a particular manner. This may involve rules to define which persons received the most honored portions of the food or to establish those times appropriate for a ceremonial feast. Marriage laws establish who may marry whom, with incest (somewhat variously defined) being universally forbidden. The forms by which the union is sealed can be widely different but share the common quality of legalizing the union in the eyes of society. The customs of each particular society and, perhaps most important, the beliefs of the society serve to establish what is truth, what is acceptable, and for many, what is human.

Each of these institutions is linked to a basic drive: food sharing to hunger, marriage laws to sex, and belief to fear. Each serves to regulate the satisfaction of these basic drives. Food sharing directs that the human animal shall not simply seek out his or her own sustenance with no concern for others. It serves as a major factor in the bonding of the family group and meets the needs created by the longer period required to raise the human young. The sexual drive can be satisfied in a bewildering number of ways, but the rules of marriage establish the means by which the individual family units can be linked to the wider group of society. The world is a mysterious and dangerous place so that fear could become an overwhelming and debilitating concern. Belief attempts to deal with this fearful condition by addressing it and trying to provide explanations. In the process it creates a community of more or less like-minded individuals able to cooperate for purposes central to the preservation of the society.

In the process of accomplishing these various tasks, each of the institutions has set in play a series of behaviors (or has codified existing behaviors) which, in turn, have evolutionary consequences. Food sharing helps seal the bonding between male-female-children units and with the small group of other family units, consisting of related males or females and their spouses, which constitute the band level of society.[22] As has already been noted, this level of human organization may provide for the annual survival but cannot guarantee survival in succeeding generations. The rules of marriage provide the means for linking one band with another so that stability is attained at the level of about five-hundred persons. In turn, shared belief, common signals, vocalizations, or language provide the cement holding together this larger group. Some of these larger groups might be linked together by commonly shared communication styles and beliefs but, as has been observed in living hunter-gatherer societies, these devices tend to break down into local dialects and differing customs and taper off at about the level of two-thousand persons.[23]

Cultural boundaries create not only compatriots but strangers as well. Dialect differences, various beliefs or customs, all provide reasons for exclusion and in many cases, murder. In the world of primitive people, the stranger was to be feared and, therefore, shunned at the very least. It was in this gap that the institution of warfare found its place. If the ritual of battle confronted enemy with enemy it also presented the opportunity for looting, rape, and the taking of prisoners, and it is the latter two possibilities which tie warfare together with the other great institutions. The exclusionary quality featured by the other institutions carried with it the distinct possibility that the separate groups (and here they should be considered as constituting separate gene pools) could evolve in different directions. "Without gene flow, it is inevitable that there will be speciation."[24] Warfare provided one means by which the gene pools could be interconnected, and though this is probably not the only way, it is one of the more common. One connection between warfare and gene flow is obviously rape, for it has been a recurrent theme of warfare down to the present day. One finds generals alluding to it as a primary reason why men fight.[25] It has occurred in most or all of the wars which have been fought, though it has been an uncommon happening in some of them. From the point of view of gene exchange, it can only have importance if conception results, as it has undoubtedly in many cases. Even more importantly, it would be necessary for the child of such a union to be able to mate in the society into which it was born. This has never been assured. Several things might take place which would prevent the passing on of the new genes. The prospective mother might be killed by her own kinsmen, the child might be killed at birth, or, having been born and raised, it might prove unacceptable as a sexual partner for physical, social, or economic reasons.

Rape, though it is the sexual consequence most often noted, is only one of the possible means by which the exchange of genes can take place. Prisoners can be taken. If they are able to get past the tests of instant killing by the capturing troops, or the festivities involving the torture and sacrifice of prisoners which could follow the conclusion of a successful raid or war, they might be able to enter into the life of the capturing group. Men, women, or children surviving the hazards of capture could, on occasion, find themselves accepted into the new society to the extent that they would be considered partners for marriage (or, at least, concubinage). Whenever this did occur, gene exchange would be possible, and the new patterns would enjoy some chance of survival in the new gene pool.

Another possibility that might take place in boundary situations would be the decision by an entire band to transfer from one large group to another. This could arise as the result of conflict with one or more of the bands of its original group. It might also result when a band, weakened by conflict, disease, or losses through accident, joined with a party, possibly similarly weakened, of the stranger group.

From the point of view of the great institutions, warfare completes the linkage begun with the family group. The band too small to sustain itself without recourse to outside members is enabled to extend into the larger society of culturally similar groups through the agency of marriage. The society, bound together by a variety of common observances, was yet too small to prevent the radiation of many groups into possibly fully differentiated species. Warfare either prevented or delayed this from happening by introducing new members into the society, violently but at times effectively. This introduction of new persons or genes could only occur, however, on the condition that the new arrivals were accepted into the family groups. Thus, the relationship of the institutions is circular, spreading outward until it turns back in on itself. One must imagine a situation in which the constant jostling of warfare affected the gene pools of the small local societies in an ever-widening circle, so that a common species was maintained.

The dominant effect of these behavior patterns was conservative: to maintain the species by the constant intermixture of the genes. The active agents in this process were marriage and warfare; food sharing and a common culture provided the field in which this activity could occur. It is true that the system allowed also for the transmission of genetic material which could effect some evolutionary change. The changes which did occur, however, were, in effect, channeled so that the genus *Homo* remained in the hunting-gathering niche which it had carved out for itself. Wolpoff argues that the primary function of gene flow is to change the frequency of existing alleles in the gene pool rather than to introduce new alleles, thus providing a continuous source of new combination possibilities upon which natural selection can act.[26]

All species that exist or have existed at some time in the past are (or were) subject to a wide variety of pressures which could threaten their continued survival. Climate has always had a great formative effect upon living organisms; those well adapted to life in a tropical climate could disappear with the onset of a long period of severe cold. Competition from other species for available food has driven some to extinction. Still others may have become so specialized that they were incapable of adjustment to changed circumstances. Yet many other species have proven able to adapt to change, even when the adaptation has resulted in rather startling changes in the species themselves. Evolutionary theory, simply stated, argues that continuing pressures will act as a selective device to favor those members of a given species that exhibit some quality that makes for an advantage, though in the long run these advantages may be temporary. These qualities are governed by the genetic makeup of the individuals, which can be passed on to the next generation. Fundamentally, at any given moment, all of the potentialities of a species are contained in the genes of the species' population, though only a fraction of these potentialities will be realized since the possible combinations are always much greater than the number of actual members of the population. Some of these combinations will be lethal and would not be transmitted (or, at least, would result in a diminished capacity to survive and procreate). Others may create advantages in mating which lead, in the longer run, to some evolutionary dead end. In a large population, subject to random mating, the tendency would be to favor certain genetic combinations, with other less favored genes carried by some smaller portions of the population or, perhaps, lost through failure of transmission.

Species are not static. Changes in gene structure can take place through mutation. Most of these mutations will probably not prove advantageous and will either continue to exist as minor characteristics of the genetic pool or be altogether lost. Some few will prove to be either immediately or eventually advantageous, in which case they can affect the makeup of the entire species over time. Not only are species not static, they also do not necessarily remain in a situation where random mating can take place throughout the entire population. In the process of entering some niche favorable to its survival the species may begin to spread out geographically to the extent that separate genetic units are established. This division may also be achieved by some behavioral change which could be related to habitat, such as woodland versus plains, mating times and courtship practices, or even certain changes in physical appearance of the individuals, such as size, color, or the types of signals used. In such cases the individuals would continue to be capable of mating and producing viable off-spring with otherwise differentiated members of the species, but these behavioral and minor physical differences would make that occur-rence unlikely. In extreme cases the differention may proceed to the extent that mating will no longer be possible, and a new species will have been established.

Under such circumstances of separation, particularly if the sepa-rated populations tend to be of small size, greater differentiation can take place. The process of "genetic drift" can lead to the rather rapid elimination of certain genes and the favoring of others. This could lead to a dead end, to the splitting off of a separate species, or to the maximizing of the impact of any mutations which might occur. If isolation is not complete, any changes taking place in the smaller populations could be transmitted to the neighboring genetic pools, even when the contact was very tenuous. It is, thus, possible that changes taking place in small, semi-isolated units could be transmit-ted by way of the "stepping stones" of other genetic units, so as to affect the entire species population. Conversely, the semi-isolated could be maintained as a member of the species through contacts in the other direction.[27]

The possibilities for the isolation of hunting-gathering groups was considerable. In the case of the Mesolithic hunter-gatherers of Poland cited above, the radius of their territory would have been about 125 miles, and the distance between the centers of two such adjacent groups would have been about 250 miles. Admittedly, this may have been an extreme example; in nearby Czechoslovakia the territories occupied appear to have been much more compact.[28] One may also wonder about the degree of contact which could have been main-tained between the African and Asian groups of *Homo erectus*. The model that has been presented here is certainly a simplification of what did, in fact, exist. One could posit a number of variations of the theme of the nuclear family, but it would be difficult to avoid com-pletely conclusions for its necessity in some form. Similarly, the impor-tance of hunting could be variously rated: in some societies, gathering would provide much the greatest part of the food supply. The further question of whether a decline in the importance of hunting would result in a male population more given to peaceful pursuits, or whether it would result in a transfer of energies to the field of intraspecific conflict, is open to debate. It can be argued that we have no hard evidence of the existence of warfare in the fossil record. There is no spear point stuck in the rib cage of some unfortunate combatant, for until the very late period there are no remains of wooden spears. No paintings of warfare are to be found prior to the Neolithic period. Yet, despite these evidential deficits, all of the parallels between hunting and warfare—all of subsequent human history—creates the strong suspicion that warfare was practiced by early beings. That it probably had such a long existence also suggests that it served some important function in the maintenance and evolution of the genus *Homo.*

The long history of humans on earth gives evidence of both preservation and change. From East Turkana, 1.6 million years BP, to Choukoutien, 300,000 years BP, the species *Homo erectus* shows a remarkable degree of stability. Yet, despite the conservatism evidenced signs of evolution exist in both the Asian and the African specimens. Whether this was a result of regional evolution, as posited by Wolpoff and others, or whether it was the result of intrusion from the west with a consequent gene flow between the two populations is a matter of considerable controversy within the scientific community. The majority opinion holds that *Homo sapiens* first developed in Africa and spread from there to the other areas of the globe.[29] The physical evidence for an African origin is certainly more abundant. Skulls and other skeletal remains of archaic *Homo sapiens* have been found in a number of African sites, from Klassies River cave in the south to Jebel Ighoud in Morocco. Tool kits markedly superior to anything possessed by *Homo erectus* have also appeared. Even more convincing is the startling evidence that all living humans can trace their ancestry to a single female, who lived approximately 200,000 years ago.[30] A number of the fossils discovered in Africa and Europe have been termed as either *Homo erectus,* with evidence of some evolutionary change, or early grades of *Homo sapiens.*[31]

In Europe, two forms of *Homo sapiens* would finally emerge, *Homo sapiens neanderthalensis* and *Homo sapiens sapiens.* Neanderthal man has undergone a considerable reapraisal since the remains were first discovered and diagnosed as those of a much deformed idiot. It is presently understood that he was a remarkable physical specimen with a brain capacity equal to that of modern humans, though of slightly different conformation. In fact, he showed a life of the spirit far in advance of anything previously seen. Grave sites at La Farrassie and Le Moustier indicate a concern for the honoring of the dead. The decorative arts began to make their appearance, though in nothing like the quantity or quality associated with the later work of Cro–Magnon man. Whether he should also be included among the ancestors of modern humans has been and is being argued, though majority opinion says not.[32] Specimens of *Homo sapiens sapiens* have been dated to about 100,000 years BP, and by 40,000 years BP, this species had come to dominate (and, indeed, survive) as the only representative of the genus *Homo*.

These modern beings were taller but less physically robust than *Homo erectus*. They had a larger brain, made better tools, had fully developed languages, and a much richer imaginative life. Yet in many respects they remained very close to the ancestral form. The basic community continued to be that of the hunting band, a group of about twenty-five men and women, together with their children, working to provide the means of survival both by hunting and gathering. These communities continued to be spread very thinly across the land. Their languages, rituals, and marriage customs could bind together a limited number of such bands in reproductively stable communities but served to differentiate and even to isolate these entities from similar communities. The question of how these communities were able to maintain genetic coherence was the same as it had always been, and it is suggested here that one of the answers was the same: the pursuit of warlike activities.

This leaves unanswered the question of why war has continued to survive in an age when the transmission of genetic material is accomplished much more frequently, efficiently, and without consequent loss of life by such relatively peaceful means as trade, urbanization, or long-distance travel. The answer would seem to lie in the new conditions which were introduced as consequences of the agricultural revolution. For the first time, immovable properties, as distinguished from traditional hunting and gathering areas, became the focus of group attention. This transition created a source of wealth, in the form of land, animals, and personal property, which had formerly not existed. Economic gain as a cause of war really came into being with the introduction of farming. At the same time, the settled conditions created by agriculture offered the possibility of bringing together larger groups of people who could be organized by new leadership for a variety of purposes, including that of war. The traditional habit of war, which had served a very different kind of function during the millennia of hunter-gatherer existence, was employed to new ends. Wars of conquest, slaving raids, battles for the control of local governments, all now became functions of armed aggression. The military forces themselves now grew in size. The five or ten men of the raiding party, the eighty to one hundred men of the primitive tribal assembly now becames armies in the sense understood by modern students of the subject. Over the period of the several-thousand-year transition from hunting-gathering to the agricultural way of life, the military threshold was crossed.

The original function of war was not actually obliterated, however. Wars of conquest and concomitant large scale introduction of slavery did result in a continuing mixture of populations. In the ancient world of both the Middle East and the Roman Empire, and even more obviously in the conquest of the Americas, new populations reduced and replaced the original inhabitants or became intermixed with them over a period of centuries. Yet, in the process of serving the new functions assigned to it by society, war has become more of a menace to the continued existence of society. It is not, however, alone among the great institutions in this respect. Every one of them—food sharing, marriage and kinship relations, cultural customs and beliefs— have all undergone transformations and taken on new functions with the coming of agriculture and the growth of urban civilizations. Not all these transformations have been beneficial. One could easily speak of the destabilizing effect which agriculture and urbanization have had upon a species adapted to a hunting-gathering niche in the natural world or, even more, of the impact upon the rest of the environment. We have scarcely begun to come to grips with the consequences of this destabilization. Solutions to the problems of war, overpopulation, the wasting of resources, and the conflict of beliefs, are not yet in sight, though it is at least fair to say we have begun to realize that we must look for them.

Notes

1. The Living Museum

1. Buffy Sainte-Marie, *The Universal Soldier*, (Woodmere Music, 1963).

2. William Broyles, Jr., "Why Men Love War," *Esquire*, Nov. 1984, 55–58. See also his book *Brothers in Arms*, especially chap. 19.

3. Sue Mansfield, *The Gestalts of War*, 4.

4. *The American Heritage Dictionary*, 24–25, 1518.

5. The literature of animal behavior studies has grown rapidly in the last quarter century. The classic works of Nikko Tinbergen and Konrad Lorenz have been augmented by a large number of studies of many different animal species.

6. In the process of studying hearing loss in prison populations, researchers discovered a very high percentage of prisoners who had suffered some form of head trauma. Carol C. McRandle and Robert Goldstein, "Hearing Loss in Two Prison Populations," *Journal of Correctional Education*, vol. 37, no. 4 (Dec. 1986): 147–54.

7. Edward T. Hall, *The Hidden Dimension*.

8. Keith F. Otterbein, *The Evolution of War*, 39–44.

9. Robert Ardrey, *African Genesis*, 22–29.

10. The types of cannibalism referred to are those practiced in the recent past by certain groups in New Guinea and other primitive areas, not those which occurred in extreme survival cases, such as the Donner party incident.

11. For a discussion of the techniques used by wolves, see Erik Zimen, *The Wolf: A Species in Danger*, 218–19.

12. John Keegan, *The Face of Battle*, 16.

13. These statements are taken from personal conversations with a B-24 pilot and an infantry rifleman.

14. Johan Huizinga, *Homo Ludens*, 89–104.

15. Samuel A. Stouffer et al., *The American Soldier: Combat and its Aftermath*, vol. 2, chap. 3.

2. THE MASKED BALL

1. For example, the Koranic injunction, "Exert thyself [*jihad*] in the pathway [*Sabil*] of the Lord," provides two words, *"sabil,"* which as "fountain" is used to describe the charitable act of providing drinking water, and *"jihad,"* which has been taken as the word for holy war.

2. Boys as young as nine served as drummers during the American Civil War.

3. Otterbein, *Evolution of War*, 19–23.

4. Napoleon A. Chagnon, "Yanomamoe Social Organization and Warfare," in *War: The Anthropology of Armed Conflict and Aggression*, ed. Morton Fried et al., 109–59; Peter Mathiessen, *Under the Mountain Wall*, 14–15. A recently published study of the Yanomamoe, Kenneth Good's *Into the Heart*, was not available to me at the time of this writing.

5. See, for instance, the treatment of Katczinsky (but not Corporal Himmelstoss) in Erich Maria Remarque, *All Quiet on the Western Front*, or the depiction of Sergeant Worley in Edmund Blunden, *Undertones of War*.

6. Orders to form up for the execution of a deserter are frequently mentioned in the memoirs of American Civil War soldiers. For instance, see John W. Haley, *The Rebel Yell*, 243; Thomas F. Galwey, *The Valiant Hours*, 143–45; also B. H. Liddell-Hart, ed., *The Letters of Private Wheeler*, 68, 151.

7. "Tageslohner der Schlachtfeld," in *Vier Jahre Westfront* ed. Fridolin Solleder. 82; see also Eric J. Leed, *No Man's Land*, 113.

8. Moses Hadas, ed., *The Greek Poets*, 175.

9. Philip Caputo, *A Rumor of War*, 12. In the TV adaptation of the book, this chant is changed to "War is killing! Killing is fun!"

10. In fact, Aristodemus did choose not to fight. Herodotus, *The Persian War* 7.229.589. For Yanomamoe death speeches, see Chagnon, "Yanomamoe Social Organization and Warfare," 131.

11. It is quite probable that Boris was being diplomatic here. His real concern was to insure his control over the Bulgarian Church.

12. Homer, *The Iliad*, 52–53.

13. Mathiessen, *Mountain Wall*, 9.

14. William Shakespeare, *Henry V*, act 4, chorus, lines 1–9.

15. Mathiessen, *Mountain Wall*, 13.

16. *Ammianus Marcellinus*, vol. 2, 461–63.

17. Richard Hough and Denis Richards, *The Battle of Britain*, 234.

18. Leed, *No Man's Land*, 131–32.

19. Similarly, Robert E. Lee and Stonewall Jackson exercised such an impact on the minds of the men of the Army of the Potomac.

20. Not all military leaders agreed with this elegant type of strategy. Such leaders as Frederick and the Marshal de Saxe did favor bringing the enemy to battle, and de Saxe was much disturbed by the tendency of cavalry to pull up short and fire ineffectively at infantry formations.

21. Keegan, *Face of Battle*, 128.

22. From the letter of an Illinois sergeant: "We lay there about eight minutes and yet it seemed an age to me, for showers of bullets and grape were

passing over me. . . . Twice I exclaimed aloud . . . *"My God, why dont they order us to charge!"* Quoted in Bell Irvin Wiley, *The Life of Billy Yank*, 70.

23. Leander Stillwell, *The Story of a Common Soldier*, 45. This is an account of his experience in the first moments of the Battle of Shiloh.

24. John Keegan, *Face of Battle*, 99–105.

25. Most recently this has been seen in the wreckage along the highway outside Kuwait City where Iraqi soldiers, fleeing in assorted military and civilian vehicles, were caught and destroyed by aerial bombardment.

26. Numbers of soldiers in the American Civil War questioned the usefulness of this weapon, as did Private Wheeler in the Napoleonic era. Battlefield surgeons also noted the extremely low number of wounds caused by the bayonet, but this was sometimes explained away by arguing that most bayonet wounds were immediately fatal.

27. It is one of the greatest fears felt by soldiers that they might be wounded and left to die unattended. Even under the improved conditions of modern medical evacuation systems this can happen. Robert Goldstein tells of being severely wounded in the Normandy battles and remaining without help for twentyfour hours, although he was inside the American lines during the entire period. Robert Goldstein, personal communication.

28. Mathiessen, *Mountain Wall*, 88.

29. Female lions use a system of hunting which involves the driving of the prey by one lioness into an ambush, where another lioness is waiting. Killer whales which attack sea lions have been observed surrounding and driving their quarry toward the shallow waters, where they are then caught.

30. Peter Paret, *Yorck and the Era of Prussian Reform*, 28–31.

31. The bear cult, or at least parallels to it, have been discovered as early as the Neanderthal period. Cave bear skulls have been discovered, and at least one skull was pierced with other bones in a ritualistic manner. See F. Clark Howell, *Early Man*, 126–27, for an illustration of this arrangement and a further description of bear cults in the succeeding periods, 153–54.

32. Nancy M. Tanner, *On Becoming Human*, 23–28.

3. ORPHEUS IN PICCADILLY

1. Peter Fleming, *Operation Sea Lion*, 150–55. 338,226 troops from Dunkirk, 35,000 from Norway, nearly 200,000 British and Allied troops from other ports such as Calais, Boulogne, Saint Omer, Brest, Cherbourg, Saint Malo, and Saint Valery were rescued. In addition, 22,656 civilians were transported from the Channel Islands, and another 15,000 were moved from other parts of Europe.

2. There were many suggestions that the German planes and pilots were inferior. See, for examples, *The Times*, 31 May, 1940, p. 6; *The Times*, 26 Aug., 1940, p. 24; letter, *The Times*, 4 Oct., 1940, p. 5; Ministry of Information, *The Battle of Britain*, 52. For a less one-sided view, see J. E. Johnson, *Wing Leader*, 36.

3. British Information Services, *Frontline*, 67. Constantine Fitzgibbons, *The Winter of the Bombs*, 16–17.

4. British Information Services, *Front Line*, 67; Fitzgibbons, *Winter*, 145. See also *Punch* cartoons from the period, many of them showing people either in Anderson shelters or in their own beds.

5. Hough and Richards, *Battle of Britain*, chaps. 4 and 5, 53-80.

6. Ibid., 116-17; see also the recollections of Edith Kup, a plotter at Debden, in Ibid., 352-53.

7. The English cartoonist David Low was particularly skilled at depicting the enemy in this fashion. See David Low, *Low on the War*, 17, 47, 58, 59, 93, 94.

8. Adolf Galland, *Die Ersten und die Letzten*, 97.

9. Maurice L. Richardson, *London's Burning*, 83.

10. Low, *War*, 24, 35.

11. Fitzgibbons, *Winter*, 160.

12. Graham Wallace, *R.A.F. Biggin Hill*, 132.

13. Winston S. Curchill, *Memoirs of the Second World War*, 362-63.

14. Sgt. Pilot Robert Beardsley DFC, quoted in Hough and Richards, *Battle of Britain*, 341-42.

15. John Strachey, *Digging for Mrs. Miller*, 77.

16. Richardson, *Burning*, 30ff. On looting by rescue squad workers, see Fitzgibbons, *Winter*, 257-58.

17. Hough and Richards, *Battle of Britain*, 49, 51, 102-103.

18. Edward R. Murrow, *This Is London*, 199-200.

19. Richardson, *Burning*, 141.

20. Richard Hillary, *Falling through Space*, 132-33.

21. Fitzgibbons, *Winter*, 26.

22. There are a number of myths about sleepers: Sleeping Beauty, Brunhild, Frederick Barbarossa, Snow White, to name only some of the most famous ones. Swallowing myths, such as those mentioned, are also rather frequent.

23. Plato, *Symposium, The Great Dialogues of Plato*, 85-89.

24. For a discussion about the lingam, see Joseph Campbell, *The Masks of God: Oriental Mytholgy*, 169ff. For a discussion on bisexual gods, see Joseph Campbell, *The Masks of God: Creative Mythology*, 204.

25. Richardson, *Burning*, 25-30.

26. British Information Services, *Frontline*, 70. See also Strachey, *Mrs. Miller*, 97; Fitzgibbons, *Winter*, 235.

27. Mircea Eliade, *The Sacred and the Profane*, 186-97.

28. "The Mood of Britain," *The Times*, 5 Oct., 1940, p. 5; "News from the Depths," *The Times*, 27 Sept., 1940, p. 2; Murrow, *London*, 144, 146, 153, 160.

29. Hillary, *Falling*, 141.

30. Ibid., 222.

31. Ibid., 156-57.

32. George Orwell, *The Orwell Reader*, 270.

33. Margaret Kennedy, *Where Stands a Winged Sentry*, 250-51.

34. Undoubtedly the sense of urgency after Dunkirk did lead to the faster production of fighter aircraft. For the period June through August, the planned number of fighters had been 611. The actual number produced was 972. The increase was accomplished by concentrating the efforts of the aircraft indus-

try on fighter types at the expense of other types, although trainers, etc., could not be entirely neglected because of the need to produce pilots for the fighters. The basis for this increased production was already established well before the crisis arose. See Hough and Richards, *Battle of Britain*, 102. See also Basil Collier, *The Defense of the United Kingdom*, 42, 68, 78, 95, 112, 120, 128.

35. Orwell, *Reader*, 270.

36. *Punch*, 4 Sept., 1940, p. 237. The cartoon shows Drake standing behind Churchill.

37. Garrett Mattingly, *The Armada*, v.

38. See also, T. Hay, "Let us Have Flowers Too," *The Listener*, 16 May, 1940, pp. 978-79; *The Times*, harvest photographs throughout August, 1940.

39. Murrow, *London*, 183. For a discussion of Tiamat, see Joseph Campbell, *Masks of God: Occidental Mythology*, 75-85.

40. It is possible to trace the development and transformation of the story of the year 1939-1940 in the pages of the newspapers and periodicals of the time. See Stratigus, "The War Surveyed: The Test of 1940," *The Spectator*, 5 Jan., 1940, p. 7; "Marking Time" *The Spectator*, 22 Mar., 1940, p. 401; "The War Surveyed: Norway, The Third Phase," *The Spectator*, 26 Apr., p. 586; "A Decisive Hour," *The Spectator*, 13 Sept., 1940, p. 260. *The Times* struck a similarly optimistic note at the beginning of the year: "The outcome of the first few months of limited fighting is, then, that the Allies have assured themselves . . . that they cannot be defeated," 1 Jan., 1940, p. 9; "Confident of Victory," *The Times*, 5 Apr., 1940, p. 8; "A Miracle of Deliverance," 5 June, p. 7; "The wasted years are come to reproach us for past levities," 6 June, 1940, p. 7; and so on through the year. On the Boulton Paul Defiant, see *The Times*, 31 May, 1940, p. 6, praising its brilliant performance over Dunkirk.

41. In the 1966 movie, *The Battle of Britain*, these words were flashed on the screen at the end the film.

4. BAND OF BROTHERS

1. Even a common soldier, Bastot de Mauleon, was able to garner 5,000 francs in ransom from knights he had captured. See Maurice Keen, *English Society in the Later Middle Ages*, 138.

2. Manuscript shown to me some years ago by the author.

3. John A. English, *On Infantry*, 4.

4. For instance, in the well-known case of the Royal Welch Fusiliers in the First World War, neither Siegfried Sasoons, Robert Graves, nor R. C. Dunn were Welsh.

5. Haley, *Rebel Yell*, 284-88.

6. The question of individual failure will be taken up in another chapter.

7. Bill Mauldin, *Up Front*, 135, speaks of the almost secret pride he takes in his medals. James Jones mentions the special pride taken in wearing the Combat Infantry Badge.

8. David Clammer, *The Zulu War*, 192-203.

9. Among the gamblers there were some that were undoubtedly professionals. Men with this kind of skill often refused to play cards with the men

of their company simply because they had to maintain the trust of these men in combat.

10. Galwey, *Valiant Hours*, 244–45.

11. For a good study of the impact of occupation, see Myron P. Gutman, *War and Rural Life*.

12. As Gutman points out, local areas under occupation were often able to make up food shortages by trading in one of the markets not too distant from the occupied zone, although the prices might be considerably higher. Ibid.

13. Galwey, *Valiant Hours*, 42.

14. Harold P. Leinbaugh and John D. Campbell, *The Men of Company K*, 42.

15. Stouffer, *American Soldier*. vol. 2, 284–89. A particularly good account of the typical experience of a rifle company is given in Bruce Eggers and Lee M. Otts, ed. Paul Roley, *G Company's War*. In addition to the narrative, "Appendix I: The Reckoning" (261–66) gives a listing of the company losses from all causes. During seven months of war 625 men served with the unit whose TO strength was 193. Of the original members only nine survived the war without injury or absence. All of these were headquarters personnel.

16. Richard A. Gabriel, *No More Heroes: Madness and Psychiatry in War*, 85.

17. Galwey, *Valiant Hours*, 218; David Chandler, *Campaigns of Napoleon*, 422.

18. J. C. Dunn, *The War the Infantry Knew*, 51.

19. Bruce Catton, *Glory Road*, 322–23.

20. Quoted in Wolfgang Borchert, *Draussen vor der Tuer und Ausgewaehlte Erzaehlungen*, 67.

21. Henry Steele Commager, ed., *The Blue and the Gray*, vol. 1, 578.

22. Willi Heinrich, *The Cross of Iron*, 214.

23. Galwey, *Valiant Hours*, 211–12.

24. See Keegan, *Face of Battle*, 167–72.

25. The taunting of unsuccessful warriors, or those who had not lived up to the expectations of the community, is practiced by a number of primitive groups. Veterans returning from the war in Vietnam experienced this treatment from some parts of the community.

26. Some Haida warriors were also ritual cannibals, which made even more necessary the ritual cleansing.

27. Sargon was the first great conqueror of the Middle East region. His fame and legend was such that a later Assyrian monarch would adopt the name as a sign of his power.

28. Modris Eksteins, *Rites of Spring*, chap. 9, 275–99.

29. Bruce Catton, *Glory Road*, 144. In another case, Private Wheeler mentions an instance of French and British troops picking apples from the same orchard during the Peninsular Campaign of the Napoleonic Wars. Liddell-Hart, *Private Wheeler*, 147.

30. John Ellis, *Eye Deep in Hell*, 170–73.

31. This summary is taken from Leinbaugh and Campbell, *Men*, 309–31.

5. FOXHOLES OF THE MIND

1. United States, War Department, *Soldiers Handbook: FM 21–100.*

2. W. Reibert, *Der Dienst Unterricht im Heere,* 29. This manual, apparently published privately, nevertheless follows closely the format of a service manual, giving instructions on all the minutiae of military life and the operation and care of weapons.

3. Trevor N. Dupuy, *A Genius for War.*

4. Martin van Crefeld, *Fighting Power.*

5. S. L. A. Marshall, *Men Against Fire,* pp. 55–57.

6. Frederic Smoler, "The Secret of the Soldiers Who Didn't Shoot," *American Heritage,* (March 1989): 37–43.

7. See Byron Farwell, *Queen Victoria's Little Wars,* 66, 74, 76–77, 132–33, and also his *Mr. Kipling's Army,* 105ff.

8. Russell F. Weigley, *History of the United States Army,* 438–39.

9. Charles B. MacDonald, *The Battle of the Huertgen Forest,* 86, 120, 172, 180, 196, and Richard F. Newcomb, *Iwo Jima,* 254–55.

10. James Jones, *WW II,* 54–55, 122–24, 196–201.

11. See Haley, *Rebel Yell,* entries for 3 June, 1864, 165, and 24 August, 1864, 193.

12. Stouffer, *American Soldier.*

13. Personal conversation with soldier.

14. A new and very controversial study of the treatment of German prisoners by U.S. forces at the end of the Second World War seems to indicate that these prisoners were allowed to die in great numbers. See James Bacque, *Other Losses.*

15. E. B. Sledge, *With the Old Breed,* 122–23, 155–56.

16. See the account of the actions of the Waffen-SS at Oradour-sur-Glane in James A. Huston, *Across the Face of France,* 32–49.

17. On paralysis, nostalgia, and neurasthenia, see Gabriel, *Heroes,* 45–69.

18. Newcomb, *Iwo Jima,* 261–64.

19. Hugh Coughlin, personal conversation.

20. John H. Worsham, *One of Jackson's Foot Cavalry,* 215, 217–18.

21. Gabriel, *Heroes,* 117–18.

22. Ibid., 115.

23. Leonard Cottrell, *The Anvil of Civilization,* 114

24. Even when soldiers did have shoes, a bad fit might so gall their feet that they could hardly walk. See Haley, *Rebel Yell,* 86. Private Wheeler mentions that many in his regiment went barefoot during the winter of 1812 in Spain. Liddell-Hart, *Private Wheeler,* 112.

25. John D. Billings, *Hardtack and Coffee.*

26. Lee Kennett, *GI: The American Soldier in World War II,* 99–101.

27. *Henry V,* act 4, chorus, lines 12–13.

28. There is a vast body of literature describing the living conditions in the trenches of World War One, some of it in novel form, some in memoirs, and some

in the form of analyses of the war. The following are a few of the best known: Guy Chapman, *A Passionate Prodigality*; Ernst Juenger, *In Stahlgewittern*; Frank Richards, *Old Soldiers Never Die*; Pierre Teilhard de Chardin, *The Making of a Mind: Letters from a Soldier Priest 1914–1918*; Edward Campion Vaughan, *Some Desperate Glory*; Paul Fussell, *The Great War and Modern Memory*.

29. At least this is the definition offered in the *American Heritage Dictionary*. The derivation of the word "horror" is interesting. The root refers to bristling, in this case the bristling of the hairs on the skin under conditions of apprehension or fear.

30. Jakob Walter, *The Diary of a Napoleonic Foot Soldier*, 86.

31. Facial disfiguration appears to be one of the most horrifying of insults to the human body. Certainly this is one of the standard features of horror films, from *The Phantom of the Opera* forward. In the period following World War One, photographs of men whose faces had been badly damaged became a feature of antiwar literature. See, for example, Erich Friedrich, *War against War*.

32. Robert Graves, in *Goodbye to All That*, does remark that he experienced this reaction. I have questioned a number of ex-infantrymen about this, and they have admitted to thinking in this way for quite some time after leaving the service. One, Jack Pickford, even thanked me for asking the question—"I thought that I was the only one. For a while, I thought I was going crazy." Personal conversation with Jack Pickford.

33. Ronald Blythe, *Akenfield*, 38.

34. See Gabriel, *Heroes*, 152–55, and Keegan, *Face of Battle*, 325–36.

35. The fact is, by the latter years of the war, men realized the futility of this kind of action and began to construct protective cover wherever possible. Rice C. Bull, in *Soldiering*, comments on this during the Atlanta Campaign of the American Civil War.

6. THE ACTION OF THE TIGER

1. Recent studies have shown that male lions will, on occasion, attack a pride of female lions, killing the cubs. Rats will also fight killing battles with "foreign" rats invading their areas. See Durward L. Allen, *The Wolves of Minong*, 284–85.

2. P. Leyhausen, "Remarks," *International Conference on the World's Cats*, Los Angeles, Lion Country Safari, 1971.

3. Peter Marler and William J. Hamilton, *Mechanisms of Animal Behavior*, 185–87.

4. See Robert Ardrey, *The Territorial Imperative*.

5. See Marler and Hamilton, *Animal Behavior*, chap. 5; Fritz Walther, *Gazelles and Their Relatives*, 3–6, 42–52; Eliot Howard, "Territory in Bird Life," in *Territory*, ed. Allen W. Stokes, 9–29.

6. While "territoriality," in the sense used to describe the activity of birds, is not provable in the cases of many mammals, there is evidence that many occupy certain ranges for the purpose of providing food during all or part of the year.

7. Hall, *Hidden Dimension*.

8. Such was the case in the Coconut Grove fire. Other examples can be seen in the murderous crowding which sometimes occurs at rock concerts and soccer matches. The fire at the Bradford soccer stadium comes to mind.

9. There is a good popular discussion of the Torralba site in Howell, *Early Man*, pp. 83–99.

10. See Anthony Wallace, "Psychological Preparations for War," in *War*, ed. Fried et al., 173–78.

11. Training in stalking and killing is given by the mother to her cubs among the feline species. Adolescent animals participate in the hunting activities of a number of social animal species, such as lions and wolves.

12. Benjamin Capps, *The Great Chiefs*, 18.

13. See Elman R. Service, "War and Our Contemporary Ancestors," in *War*, ed. Fried, 160–67.

14. Otterbein, *Evolution of War*, 20.

15. Mathiessen, *Mountain Wall*, and Chagnon, in *War*, ed. Fried.

16. Chagnon, in Fried, *War*, 124–41.

17. Mathiessen, *Mountain Wall*, 8–17 (battle), 44–56 (funeral), 82–83 (victory celebration).

18. Ibid., 14–15, 220.

19. Chagnon, in *War*, ed. Fried, 128–29.

20. Consider, for instance, the use of verbal threats during the Persian Gulf War, with the Iraqi leader promising that the Americans would "swim in their blood" in the "mother of all battles."

21. Artillery is the major cause of casualties on the modern battlefield, but there have been occasions when even the heaviest artillery barrages have failed to accomplish the task of killing a strongly entrenched force.

22. Keegan, *Face of Battle*, 186.

23. Quoted in Richard Holmes, *Acts of War: The Behavior of Men in Battle*, 379.

24. *Henry V*, act 3, sc. 1, lines 6–17.

25. Keegan, *Face of Battle*, 97–104.

26. Quoted in Holmes, *Acts of War*, 378.

27. Keegan, *Face of Battle*, 153–59.

28. For an example, see Charles B. MacDonald, *A Time for Trumpets*, Chaps. 18 and 19.

29. John Muirhead, *Those Who Fall*, 193–94.

30. Russell Spurr, *A Glorious Way to Die*, 276.

31. Bert Stiles, *Serenade to the Big Bird*, 10.

32. Quoted in G. J. A. O'Toole, *The Spanish War*, 274.

33. Charles Johnson Post, *The Little War of Private Post*, 119–24.

34. Thucydides, *The Peloponnesian War*, 323.

35. Huizinga, *Homo Ludens*, 97–99.

36. Harry Holbert Turney-High, *Primitive War*, 21–38.

37. Washburn and Lancaster, "The Evolution of Hunting," in *Man the Hunter*, eds. Richard B. Lee and Irven DeVore, 299.

38. Otterbein, *Evolution of War*, 20.

39. Ibid., 143–49.

40. Ardrey, *African Genesis*, 186ff.

41. Michael H. Day, *Guide to Fossil Man*, 88.

7. THE COORDINATES OF CHAOS

1. From a CNN report, 22 Jan., 1991.

2. This carried a step further that century's fascination with the idea that a perfectly conceived strategy would make unnecessary the fighting of battles.

3. Holmes, *Acts of War*, 293.

4. Arther Ferrill, *The Origins of War*, 105.

5. David Chandler, *The Campaigns of Napoleon*, 339–40.

6. English, *On Infantry*, chap. 1.

7. *Judges* 20:15–17.

8. Joseph Birdsell, "Some Predictions for the Pleistocene Based on Equilibrium Systems Among Recent Hunter-Gatherers," in *Man*, eds. Lee and DeVore, 229–40.

9. Ibid., "Comments," 247. Washburn and others in the comment group tended to corroborate these figures with evidence furnished from other sites, ranging from India to England to the Great Basin of North America. See also 245–49.

10. Samuel Noah Kramer, *From the Tablets of Sumer*, 38–39. The military significance of body counts is perhaps best illustrated by Gen. Norman Schwarzkopf's comment, "I am anti–body count," Briefing, 30 Jan., 1991.

11. Weigley, *United States Army* 440.

12. Stouffer, *American Soldier*, 284–89.

13. By the fall of 1944, the European Theater had a shortfall of 1,500 junior infantry officers, with only half that number of replacements available from officer training centers in the United States. Roland G. Ruppenthal, *Logistical Support for the Armies*, Vol. 2, 330–31.

14. At Antietam, the Union losses were 12,401, and the Confederates lost 10,318; at Borodino, the Russians lost about 44,000 men; at the Battle of Leipzig, in four days' fighting, the Allies lost 54,000 killed and wounded, while the French lost 38,000 and had another 30,000 taken prisoner.

15. This drop in morale is reflected in the diary entries for this period by such soldiers as Haley, *Rebel Yell*, 141–68.

16. One exception would be the *Ministeriales* of the Holy Roman Empire, who were technically serfs.

17. Frank B. Livingstone, "The Effects of Warfare on the Biology of the Human Species," in *War*, ed. Fried, 3–15.

18. ". . . soldiers on the whole are given medals for killing and officers for doing other things. . . . 'Officers do not kill.' . . . 'Killing is not gentlemanly.'" Keegan, *Face of Battle*, 315–16." Admittedly, this practice is far from universal.

19. George Orwell, "Politics and the English Language," in *A Collection of Essays*, 162–77.

8. THE LONG MARCH: CONSERVATION AND CHANGE

1. Bruce Bower, "A World That Never Existed," *Science News*, Apr. 28, 1989, 264–66.

2. G. Philip Rightmire, *The Evolution of Homo erectus.*

3. Richard E. Leakey, *The Making of Mankind,* 138–39.

4. Reinhart Kraatz, "A Review of Recent Research of Heidelberg Man, *Homo erectus heidelbergensis,*" in *Ancestors: The Hard Evidence,* ed. Eric Delson, 268.; Rightmire, *Evolution,* 228.

5. At the Terra Amata site in southern France, Henri de Lumley excavated a seasonal camping site used by *Homo erectus,* at which there existed clear evidence of shelter building. Leakey, *Making,* 123–24; Patricia Philips, *The Prehistory of Europe,* 43–45.

6. Fire may have been used intermittently as early as the period of *Homo habilis* and was certainly used very early by *Homo erectus.* See "Ancient Humans Get All Fired Up," *Science News,* Dec. 10, 1988, 372.

7. A popular account of the Torralba and Ambrona sites in Spain is given by their excavator in Howell, *Early Man,* 84–99.

8. Brian Fagan, *The Journey from Eden,* 117–20.

9. Richard Potts, "Hominid Hunters? Problems of Identifying the Earliest Hunter/Gatherers," in *Evolution and Community Ecology,* ed. Robert Foley, 129–66; and Delta Willis, *The Hominid Gang,* 242.

10. Delta Willis, *The Hominid Gang,* 239–40.

11. Rightmire, *Evolution,* 45.

12. Ibid., 50.

13. Karl Dietrich Adam, "The Chronological and Systematic Position of the Steinheim Skull," in Eric Delson, *Ancestors: The Hard Evidence,* 275.

14. Michael H. Day, *Guide,* 102.

15. See Jakov Radovcic, "Neanderthals and their Contemporaries," in Ibid., 310–18.

16. Richard G. Klein, *The Human Career,* 333–34.

17. "European Cave Carnage," *Science News,* Apr. 20, 1991, 254.

18. Paola Villa, et al., "Cannibalism in the Neolithic," *Science,* July 28, 1986, pp. 431–36.

19. Phillips, *Prehistory,* 122–24, 132–35.

20. Neil Roberts, "Pleistocene Environments in Time and Space," in *Hominid Evolution and Community Ecology,* ed. Robert Foley, 25–53.

21. Howell, *Early Man,* 84–99.

22. See R. A. Foley and P. C. Lee, "Finite Social Space, Evolutionary Pathways, and Reconstructing Hominid Behavior," *Science,* Feb. 17, 1989, 901–906. See also Tanner, *On Becoming Human,* for the importance of females in developing band structure.

23. Joseph Birdsell, "Some Predictions for the Pleistocene Based in Equilibrium Systems Among Recent Hunter-Gatherers," 229–40.

24. General Patton raised this point in an address to the troops at the time of the Normandy campaign.

25. Milford H. Wolpoff, "Multiregional Evolution: The Fossil Alternative to Eden," in *The Human Revolution,* eds. Paul Mellars and Chris Stringer, 87.

26. Ibid., 88–91.

27. Theodosius Dobzhansky, *Genetics of the Evolutionary Process,* 240–47.

28. Phillips, *Prehistory*, 135.

29. A recent popular discussion of the "out of Africa" hypothesis and its opposing theories is given in Fagan, *Journey*.

30. The evidence for this common ancestor is based on analyses, by Rebecca Cann, of mitochondrial DNA (transmitted only by the female). Cavalli-Sforza used other methods based on gene frequencies to construct a "tree of 42 world populations," Ibid., 27–32. See also Mark Stoneking and Rebecca L. Cann, "African Origin of Human Mitochondrial DNA," in Mellars and Stringer, *Human Revolution*, 17–30. Recently these findings have been seriously challenged. Questions concerning the sampling technique, the number of trials run on the statistical data, and the conclusions drawn have opened up the whole matter of the African origin of *Homo sapiens* and the recent date assigned to that origin. See Marcia Barinaga, "African Eve Backers Beat a Retreat," *Science*, Feb. 26, 1993, 1249–50.

31. Jeffrey T. Laitman, "Later Middle Pleistocene Hominids," in Delson, *Ancestors*, 265–67.

32. Leakey, *Making*, 157–59; Howell, *Early Man*, 123–43.

Bibliography

BOOKS

Allen, Durward L. *The Wolves of Minong.* Boston: Houghton Mifflin Co., 1979.

Allon, Yigal. *The Making of Israel's Army.* New York: Bantam Books, 1974.

Ammianius Marcellinus. Translated by John C. Rolfe. 3 vols. Cambridge, Mass.: Harvard University Press, 1935.

Ardrey, Robert. *African Genesis.* New York: Delta Books, 1963.

———. *The Territorial Imperative.* New York: Atheneum, 1966.

Bacque, James. *Other Losses.* Toronto: Stoddart Publishing Co., 1989.

Bessie, Alvah. *Men in Battle.* New York: Pinnacle Books, 1977.

Billings, John D. *Hardtack and Coffee.* Boston: George M. Smith & Co., 1887. Reprinted. New York: Time-Life Books, 1982.

Blunden, Edmund. *Undertones of War.* Harmondsworth, Middlesex: Penguin Books, 1982.

Blythe, Ronald. *Akenfield.* New York: Pantheon Books, 1969.

Borchert, Wolfgang. *Draussen vor der Tuer und Ausgewaehlte Erzaelungen.* Hamburg: Rowohlt, 1956.

Brittain, Vera. *England's Hour.* New York: Macmillan Co., 1941.

Broyles, William, Jr. *Brothers in Arms.* New York: Alfred Knopf, 1986.

Bull, Rice C. *Soldiering.* San Rafael, Calif.: Presidio Press, 1977.

Campbell, Joseph. *The Masks of God.* 4 vols. New York: Viking Penguin, 1976.

Capps, Benjamin. *The Great Chiefs.* New York: Time-Life Books, 1975.

Caputo, Philip. *A Rumor of War.* New York: Holt, Rinehart & Winston, 1977.

Catton, Bruce. *Glory Road.* New York: Doubleday, 1952.

Cederberg, Fred. *The Long Road Home.* Toronto: Stoddart, 1985.

Chandler, David C. *The Campaigns of Napoleon.* New York: Macmillan, 1966.

Chapman, Guy. *A Passionate Prodigality.* Greenwich, Conn.: Fawcett Crest, 1967.

Churchill, Winston S. *Memoirs of the Second World War.* Abridged. Boston: Houghton Mifflin, 1991.

Clammer, David. *The Zulu War.* London: David and Charles, 1988.

Collier, Basil. *The Defense of the United Kingdom.* London: Her Majesty's Stationery Office, 1957.

Commager, Henry Steele. *The Blue and the Gray.* Vol. 1. Indianapolis: Bobbs-Merrill, 1950.

Cottrell, Leonard. *The Anvil of Civilization.* New York: Mentor, 1957.

Craig, William. *Enemy at the Gates: the Battle for Stalingrad.* New York: Bantam Books, 1982.

Crawford, M. H., and P. L. Workman, eds. *Methods and Theories of Antropological Genetics.* Albuquerque: University of New Mexico Press, 1973.

Crefeld, Martin van. *Fighting Power.* Westport, Conn.: Greenwood Press, 1982.

Day, Michael H. *Guide to Fossil Man.* 4th ed. Chicago: University of Chicago Press, 1986.

Delson, Eric. *Ancestors: The Hard Evidence.* New York: Alan R. Liss, 1985.

Dobzhansky, Theodosius. *Genetics of the Evolutionary Process.* New York: Columbia University Press, 1970.

Dunn, J. C. *The War the Infantry Knew.* London: Cardinal, 1989.

Dunnigan, James. *How to Make War.* New York: William Morrow, 1982.

Dupuy, Trevor N. *A Genius for War.* Fairfax, Va.: Hero Books, 1984.

Dyer, Gwynne. *War.* New York: Crown Publishers, 1985.

Eggers, Bruce E., and Otts Lee McMillan. *G Company's War.* Edited by Paul Roley. Tuscaloosa: The University of Alabama Press, 1992.

Eksteins, Modris. *Rites of Spring.* Boston: Houghton Mifflin, 1989.

Eliade, Mircea. *The Sacred and the Profane.* New York: Harvest Books, 1959.

Ellis, John. *Eye Deep in Hell.* Baltimore: Johns Hopkins University Press, 1989.

English, John A. *On Infantry.* New York: Praeger, 1984.

Fagan, Brian. *The Journey from Eden.* London: Thames and Hudson, 1990.

Farwell, Byron. *Mr. Kipling's Army.* New York: W. W. Norton, 1981.

———. *Queen Victoria's Little Wars.* New York: W. W. Norton, 1972.

Ferrill, Arther. *The Origins of War.* London: Thames and Hudson, 1985.

Fitzgibbons, Constantine. *The Winter of the Bombs.* New York: W. W. Norton, 1979.

Fleming, Peter. *Operation Sea Lion.* New York: Simon and Schuster, 1957.

Foley, Robert. *Another Unique Species.* New York: John Wiley and Sons, 1989.

———, ed. *Hominid Evolution and Community Ecology.* Orlando, Fla.: Academic Press, 1984.

Fried, Morton, Marvin Harris, and Robert Murphy. *War: The Anthropology of Armed Conflict and Aggression.* Garden City, New York: The Natural History Press, 1968.

Friedrich, Ernst. *War against War.* 1924. Reprinted. Seattle: The Real Comet Press, 1987.

Fussell, Paul. *The Great War and Modern Memory.* New York: Oxford, 1977.

Gabriel, Richard A. *No More Heroes: Madness and Psychiatry in War.* New York: Hill and Wang, 1987.

Galland, Adolf. *Die Ersten und die Letzten.* Darmstadt: Franz Schneekluth, 1953.

Galwey, Thomas F. *The Valiant Hours.* Harrisburg, Penn.: Stackpole, 1961.

Graves, Robert. *Goodbye to All That.* 2nd ed. Garden City, New York: Doubleday Anchor, 1957.

Great Britain, Ministry of Information. *The Battle of Britain.* New York: Doubleday, 1941.

——. *Frontline.* New York: Macmillan Co., 1943.

Gur, Mordechai. *The Battle for Jerusalem.* New York: Popular Library, 1974.

Gutman, Myron P. *War and Rural Life.* Princeton, N.J.: Princeton University Press, 1980.

Hackworth, David, and Julie Sherman. *About Face.* New York: Simon and Schuster, 1989.

Hadas Moses, ed. *The Greek Poets.* New York: Modern Library, 1953.

Haley, John W. *The Rebel Yell and the Yankee Hurrah.* Cambden, Maine: Down East Press, 1985.

Hall, Edward T. *The Hidden Dimension.* Garden City, New York: Doubleday, 1966.

Heinrich, Willi. *The Cross of Iron.* Indianapolis: Bobbs-Merrill, 1956.

Herodotus. *The Persian Wars.* Translated by George Rawlinson. New York: Modern Library, 1942.

Hillary, Richard. *Falling through Space.* New York: Dell Publishing Co., 1958.

Hitchcock, Frederick L. *War From the Inside.* Philadelphia: Lippencott Co., 1904. Reprinted. New York: Time-Life, 1985.

Holmes, Richard. *Acts of War: The Behavior of Men in Battle.* New York: The Free Press, 1985.

Homer. *The Iliad.* Translated by Robert Fitzgerald. Garden City, N.Y.: Doubleday Anchor, 1974.

Hough, Richard and Denis Richards. *The Battle of Britain.* New York: W. W. Norton, 1989.

Howard, Michael. *The Franco Prussian War.* New York: Macmillan, 1962.

Howell, F. Clark. *Early man.* New York: Time-Life Books, 1970.

Huizinga, Johan. *Homo Ludens.* Boston: The Beacon Press, 1955.

Huston, James A. *Across the Face of France.* Lafayette, Ind.: Purdue University Studies, 1963.

Johnson, J. E. *Wing Leader.* New York: Ballantine Books, 1957.

Jones, James. *WW II.* New York: Ballantine Books, 1975.

Juenger, Ernst. *In Stahlgewittern.* 4th ed. Berlin: E. S. Mittler und Sohn, 1922.

Keefer, Louis E. *Scholars in Foxholes.* Jefferson, N.C.: McFarland and Co., 1988.

Keegan, John. *The Face of Battle.* New York: Viking, 1976.

Keen, Maurice. *English Society in the Later Middle Ages.* London: Penguin Books, 1990.

Kennedy, Margaret. *Where Stands a Winged Sentry.* New Haven: Yale University Press, 1941.

Kennett, Lee. *GI: The American Soldier in World War II.* New York: Scribners, 1987.

Klein, Richard D. *The Human Career.* Chicago: University of Chicago Press, 1989.

Koenigsson, Lars Koenig, ed. *Current Argument on Early Man*. Oxford: Pergamon Press, 1980.

Kramer, Samuel Noah. *From the Tablets of Sumer*. Indian Hills, Colo.: Falcon Wing Press, 1956.

Lack, D. *The Life of the Robin*. London: H. F. and G. Witherby, 1943.

Leakey, Richard. *The Making of Mankind*. New York: E. P. Dutton, 1981.

Lee, Richard B. and Irven DeVore, eds. *Man the Hunter*. New York: Aldine De Gruyter, 1968.

Leed, Eric J. *No Man's Land*. London: Cambridge University Press, 1979.

Leinbaugh, Harold P., and John D. Campbell. *The Men of Company K*. New York: Bantam, 1986.

Liddell-Hart, B. H., ed. *The Letters of Private Wheeler*. Boston: Houghton Mifflin, 1951.

Lorenz, Konrad. *On Aggression*. New York: Harcourt, Brace & World, 1963.

Low, David. *Low on the War*. New York: Simon and Schuster, 1940.

McCarthy, Carlton. *Detailed Minutiae of Soldier Life in the Army of Northern Virginia*. Richmond: X. McCarthy & Co, 1882. Reprint. New York: Time-Life Books, 1982.

MacDonald, Charles B. *The Battle of the Huertgen Forest*. New York: Jove Books, 1983.

———. *A Time for Trumpets*, New York: William Morrow & Co., 1985.

MacDonald, Lyn. *They Called it Passchendaele*. London: Michael Joseph, 1978.

Manchester, William. *Goodbye Darkness*. New York: Dell, 1982.

Manning, Frederick. *Her Privates We*. New York: Berkley Books, 1964.

Mansfield, Sue. *The Gestalts of War*. New York: Dial Press, 1982.

Marler, Peter, and William J. Hamilton. *Mechanisms of Animal Behavior*. New York: John Wiley & Sons, 1966.

Marshall, S. L. A. *Men Against Fire*. New York: William Morrow & Co., 1947.

Maschie-Taylor, C. G. N., and G. W. Lasker, eds. *Biological Aspects of Human Migration*. Cambridge New York: Cambridge University Press, 1988.

Mathiessen, Peter. *Under the Mountain Wall*. New York: Ballantine Books, 1969.

Mattingly, Garrett. *The Armada*. Boston: Houghton Mifflin Co., 1959.

Mauldin, Bill. *Up Front*. New York: Henry Holt and Co, 1945.

Meinecke, Friedrich. *The German Catastrophe*. Cambridge, Mass: Harvard University Press, 1950.

Mellars, Paul and Chris Stringer, eds. *The Human Revolution*. Princeton, N.J.: The Princeton University Press, 1989.

Morris, Eric. *Salerno*. New York: Stein and Day, 1983.

Mowat, Farley. *And No Birds Sang*. Toronto: Seal Books, 1981.

Muirhead, John. *Those Who Fall*. New York: Random House, 1986.

Murrow, Edward R. *This Is London*. New York: Simon and Schuster, 1941.

Newcomb, Richard F. *Iwo Jima*. New York: Bantam Books, 1982.

Orwell, George. *A Collection of Essays*. Garden City, New York: Doubleday Anchor, 1954.

————. *Homage to Catalonia.* Boston: The Beacon Press, 1952.

————. *The Orwell Reader.* New York: Harcourt, Brace and Co., 1956.

Otterbein, Keith F. *The Evolution of War.* HRAF Press, 1970.

O'Toole, G. J. A. *The Spanish War.* New York: W. W. Norton, 1984.

Paret, Peter. *Yorck and the Era of Prussian Reform.* Princeton, N.J.: Princeton University Press, 1966.

Parsons, I. M., ed. *Men Who March Away.* New York: Viking, 1965.

Phillips, Patricia. *The Prehistory of Europe.* London: Allen Lane, 1980.

Plato. *The Great Dialogues.* Translated by W. H D. Rowse. New York: Mentor, 1956.

Post, Charles Johnson. *The Little War of Private Post.* New York: Signet, 1961.

Reibert, W. *Der Dienst Unterricht im Heere.* Berlin: E. S. Mittler und Sohn, 1941.

Remarque, Erich Maria. *All Quiet on the Western Front.* New York: Little, Brown & Co., 1929. Reprinted. New York: Lion, 1956.

Richards, Frank. *Old Soldiers Never Die.* New York: Berkley, 1966.

Richardson, Maurice L. *London's Burning.* London: Robert Hale Ltd., 1941.

Rightmire, G. Philip. *The Evolution of Homo erectus.* Cambridge New York: Cambridge University Press, 1990.

Rindos, David. *The Origins of Agriculture.* San Diego: Academic Press, 1984.

Rodenhauser, Reiner. *Breaking Down the Barriers.* Durham, N.C.: Seeman Printery, 1961.

Ruppenthal, Roland G. *Logistical Support for the Armies.* 2 vols. Washington, D.C.: Office of the Chief of Military History, United States Army, 1959.

Sajer, Guy. *The Forgotten Soldier.* New York: Harper & Row, 1971.

Schroetter, Heinz. *Stalingrad.* New York: Ballantine Books, N.D.

Scott, John Paul. *Animal Behavior.* Garden City, New York: Doubleday Anchor, 1963.

Sears, Stephen W. *Landscape Turned Red.* New York: Popular Library, 1983.

Singer, J. David, and Melvin Small. *The Wages of War.* New York: John Wiley & Sons, 1972.

Sledge, E. B. *With the Old Breed.* New York: Bantam Books, 1983.

Solleder, Fridolin. *Vier Jahre Westfront.* Munich: Verlag Max Schick, 1932.

Spurr, Russell. *A Glorious Way to Die.* New York: Newmarket Press, 1981.

Stiles, Bert. *Serenade to the Big Bird.* New York: Ballantine Books, 1952.

Stillwell, Leander. *The Story of a Common Soldier.* Franklin Hudson, 1920. Reprint. New York: Time-Life Books, 1983.

Stouffer, Samuel A., et al. *The American Soldier: Combat and its Aftermath.* 4 vols. Princeton, N.J.: Princeton University Press, 1949.

Strachey, John. *Digging for Mrs. Miller.* New York: Random House, 1941.

Tanner, Nancy M. *On Becoming Human.* Cambridge, New York: Cambridge University Press, 1981.

Teilhard de Chardin, Pierre. *The Making of a Mind: Letters From a Soldier Priest 1914–1919.* New York: Harper & Row, 1961.

Thucydides. *The Peloponnesian War.* New York: Modern Library, 1954.

Turney-High, Harry Holbert. *Primitive War.* Columbia: University of South Carolina Press, 1971.

United States. War Department. *Soldiers Handbook, FM 21–100,* 1941.

Vaughan, Edward Campion. *Some Desperate Glory.* New York: Simon and Schuster, 1988.

Von Clausewitz, Carl. *On War.* Harmsworth, Middlesex: Penguin, 1968.

Wallace, Graham. *R.A.F. Biggin Hill.* London: Four Square Books, 1958.

Walter, Jakob. *The Diary of a Napoleonic Foot Soldier.* New York: Doubleday, 1991.

Walther, Fritz; Elizabeth Cary Mungall; Gerald A. Grau. *Gazelles and Their Relatives: A Study in Territorial Behavior.* Park Ridge, N.J.: Noyes Publications, 1983.

Weigley, Russell F. *History of the United States Army.* Bloomington: Indiana University Press, 1984.

Wiley, Bell Irvin. *The Life of Billy Yank.* Indianapolis: Bobbs-Merrill, 1952.

———. *The Life of Johnny Reb.* Indianapolis: Bobbs-Merrill, 1943.

Willis, Delta. *The Hominid Gang.* New York: Viking, 1989.

Wolff, Leon. *In Flanders Fields.* New York: Viking, 1958.

Worsham, John H. *One of Jackson's Foot Cavalry.* New York: Neale Publication Co., 1912. Reprint. New York: Time-Life Books, 1982.

Young, Michael and Peter Willmott. *Family and Kinship in East London.* Baltimore: Penguin Books, 1957.

Ziesser, Benno. *The Road to Stalingrad.* New York: Ballantine Books, 1956.

Zimen, Erik. *The Wolf: A Species in Danger.* New York: Delacorte Press, 1981.

ARTICLES

"Ancient Humans Get All Fired Up," *Science News.* Dec. 10, 1988, 372.

Bower, Bruce. "Gauging the Winds of War". *Science News.* Feb. 9, 1991, 88–91.

———. "A World That Never Existed." *Science News,* Apr. 28, 1989, 264–66.

Culetta, Elizabeth. "Pulling Neandertal back into the family tree." *Science.* Apr. 19, 1991, 376.

"European Cave Carnage." *Science News,* Apr. 20, 1991, 254.

Foley, R. A. and P. C. Lee. "Finite Social Space, Evolutionary Pathways, and Reconstructing Hominid Behavior." *Science,* Feb. 17, 1989, 901–906.

Ross, Philip E. "Mutt and Jeff" *Scientific American,* Sept. 1991, 40–48.

Smoley, Frederic. "The Secret of the Soldiers Who Didn't Shoot." *American Heritage,* March, 1989, 37–43.

Villa, Paola, et al. "Cannibalism in the Neolithic." *Science,* July 28, 1986, 431–36.

Zvelebil, Marek. "Postglacial Foraging in the Forests of Europe" *Scientific American.* May, 1986, 104–115.

Index

The Antique Drums of War was composed into type using Magna software and output on an Agfa Selectset 5000 in ten point Trump with three points of spacing between the lines. Raleigh was selected for display. The book was designed by Pat Crowder, typeset by Connell-Zeko Type and Graphics, printed offset by Thomson-Shore, Inc., and bound by John H. Dekker & Sons, Inc. The paper on which this book is printed carries acid-free characteristics for an effective life of at least three hundred years.

TEXAS A&M UNIVERSITY PRESS : COLLEGE STATION